C. S. Lewis's List

C. S. Lewis's List

The Ten Books That Influenced Him Most

Edited by
David Werther and Susan Werther

With a Foreword by
David C. Downing

Bloomsbury Academic
An imprint of Bloomsbury Publishing Inc

B L O O M S B U R Y
NEW YORK · LONDON · OXFORD · NEW DELHI · SYDNEY

Bloomsbury Academic
An imprint of Bloomsbury Publishing Inc

1385 Broadway	29 Earlsfort	50 Bedford Square
New York	Terrace,	London
NY 10018	Dublin 2,	WC1B 3DP
USA	Ireland	UK

www.bloomsbury.com

BLOOMSBURY and the Diana logo are trademarks of Bloomsbury Publishing Plc

First published 2015
Reprinted by Bloomsbury Academic 2015

© David Werther, Susan Werther, and Contributors, 2015

All rights reserved. No part of this publication may be reproduced or transmitted in any form or by any means, electronic or mechanical, including photocopying, recording, or any information storage or retrieval system, without prior permission in writing from the publishers.

No responsibility for loss caused to any individual or organization acting on or refraining from action as a result of the material in this publication can be accepted by Bloomsbury or the author.

Library of Congress Cataloging-in-Publication Data
ISBN 978-1-62892-414-5 (hardback) – ISBN 978-1-62892-413-8 (pb)
1. Lewis, C. S. (Clive Staples), 1898–1963–Books and reading. I. Werther, David, editor. II. Werther, Susan, editor.
PR6023.E926Z5996   2015
823'.912–dc23
2014041012

ISBN: HB: 9781628924145
PB: 9781628924138
ePDF: 9781628924169
ePub: 9781628924152

Typeset by Newgen Knowledge Works (P) Ltd., Chennai, India

*To James Knight
In friendship
And
In gratitude
For
His* windblown *vision and generosity*

Now the earth was formless and void, and darkness was over the surface of the deep, and the Spirit of God was hovering over the waters.
Genesis 1:2

The wind blows wherever it pleases. You hear its sound, but you cannot tell where it comes from or where it is going. So it is with everyone born of the Spirit.
John 3:8

Contents

Contributors		viii
Foreword		xi
Acknowledgments		xiv
Introduction		1
1	George MacDonald, *Phantastes* David L. Neuhouser	9
2	G. K. Chesterton, *The Everlasting Man* Donald T. Williams	31
3	Virgil, *The Aeneid* Louis Markos	49
4	George Herbert, *The Temple* Don W. King	67
5	William Wordsworth, *The Prelude* Mary Ritter	93
6	Rudolf Otto, *The Idea of the Holy* Adam Barkman	113
7	Boethius, *The Consolation of Philosophy* Chris Armstrong	135
8	James Boswell, *The Life of Samuel Johnson* Paul Tankard	157
9	Charles Williams, *Descent into Hell* Holly Ordway	181
10	Arthur James Balfour, *Theism and Humanism* Charles Taliaferro	201
Index		219

Contributors

Chris R. Armstrong is a church historian. He directs Opus: The Art of Work, an institute dedicated to understanding God's call for our work in the world, housed at Wheaton College. He also serves on Wheaton's biblical and theological studies faculty. Chris has written two books: *Patron Saints for Postmoderns*, on Gregory the Great, Dante Alighieri, Margery Kempe, Dorothy L. Sayers, and six other Christian culture-changers, and *Medieval Wisdom: An Exploration with C. S. Lewis* (forthcoming). He is senior editor of *Christian History* magazine and founding senior editor of the Patheos Faith and Work channel (www.patheos.com/Faith-and-Work.html). He blogs at gratefultothedead.wordpress.com.

Adam Barkman is Associate Professor and Chair of the Philosophy Department at Redeemer University College, Ancaster, Ontario. He received his PhD from the Free University of Amsterdam. He is the author of *C. S. Lewis and Philosophy as a Way of Life*; *Through Common Things*; and *Above All Things*; *Imitating the Saints*; and *Making Sense of Islamic Art & Architecture* (forthcoming). He is also the coeditor of *Manga and Philosophy* and *The Philosophy of Ang Lee*.

David C. Downing is the R. W. Schlosser Professor of English at Elizabethtown College, in Elizabethtown, Pennsylvania. Downing has written five scholarly books on C. S. Lewis, including *Planets in Peril* (1992), on the Ransom trilogy; *The Most Reluctant Convert* (2002); and *Into the Region of Awe: Mysticism in C. S. Lewis* (2005), a study of Lewis's interest in Christian mysticism. Downing is a consulting reader for the Publications of the Modern Languages Association (PMLA), Cambridge University Press, and a number of other scholarly journals and university presses. He supplied the introduction and notes for the Wade Annotated Edition of *The Pilgrim's Regress*, 2014.

Don W. King is Professor of English at Montreat College, Montreat, North Carolina, and he serves as Editor of the Christian Scholar's Review (www.csreview.org/). He is author of *C. S. Lewis Poet: The Legacy of His Poetic Impulse*; *Hunting the Unicorn*; *Plain to the Inward Eye: Selected Essays on C. S. Lewis*; and *The Collected Poems of C. S. Lewis: A Critical Edition*. His forthcoming books include *A Naked Tree: Joy Davidman's Love Sonnets to C. S. Lewis and Other Poems* and *Yet One More Spring: A Critical Study of Joy Davidman*.

Louis Markos is Professor of English, and Scholar in Residence at Houston Baptist University, Houston, Texas, and holds the Robert H. Ray Chair in Humanities. His books include *From Achilles to Christ: Why Christians Should Read the Pagan Classics*; *Lewis Agonistes*; and *Restoring Beauty: The Good, the True, and The Beautiful in the Writings of C. S. Lewis* (www.Loumarkos.com).

David L. Neuhouser is Scholar-in-Residence at Center for the Study of C. S. Lewis & Friends, and Professor Emeritus of Mathematics at Taylor University, Upland, Indiana. Dr Neuhouser compiled the anthologies, *George MacDonald: Selections from His Greatest Works* and *A Novel Pulpit: Sermons from George MacDonald's Fiction*. He is the author of *Open to Reason* and *George MacDonald on Mathematics and Science*.

Holly Ordway is Professor of English and Director of the MA in Cultural Apologetics at Houston Baptist University. She is the author of *Not God's Type: An Atheist Academic Lays Down Her Arms* (Ignatius Press, 2014). She holds a PhD in English literature from the University of Massachusetts Amherst; her academic work focuses on imagination in apologetics, with special attention to the writings of C. S. Lewis, J. R. R. Tolkien, and Charles Williams.

Mary Ritter is a Language Lecturer at The American Language Institute at New York University, where she teaches English and Intercultural Communication. Her research interests include teaching with technology, cultural styles of discourse, and improv theater. She is the author of "Lewis, Wordsworth, and the Education of the Soul" (www. discovery.org).

Charles Taliaferro, Professor of Philosophy, St. Olaf College, Northfield, Minnesota, is the author or editor of 18 books, including *The History of the Soul*, coauthored with Stewart Goetz, and *The Image in Mind*, coauthored with Jil Evans. He has written on C. S. Lewis in *The Scottish Journal of Theology*, in *Narnia and Philosophy: The Lion, the Witch, and the Worldview*, and in a devotional work, *Praying with C. S. Lewis*. His speaking engagements include Oxford, Cambridge, and Yale University.

Paul Tankard lived in Melbourne, Australia until a midlife career change took him back to university and the writing of two dissertations about Samuel Johnson. He is now Senior Lecturer in English at the world's southernmost university, the University of Otago in Dunedin, New Zealand. He has published dozens of essays about C. S. Lewis and the Inklings, and Johnson and his biographer, James Boswell. He is Publications Editor for the Johnson Society of Australia, and his selected edition of Boswell's journalism—the first ever edition of this material—was published in 2014 as *Facts and Inventions* by Yale University Press.

Donald T. Williams, PhD, is R. A. Forrest Scholar and Professor of English at Toccoa Falls College in the hills of NE Georgia. An ordained minister with many years of pastoral experience, he has spent several summers training local pastors in East Africa and India for Church Planting International. His most recent books include *Mere Humanity: Chesterton, Lewis, and Tolkien on the Human Condition* (Broadman, 2006); *Stars Through the Clouds: The Collected Poetry of Donald T. Williams* (Lantern Hollow Press, 2011); *Reflections from Plato's Cave: Essays in Evangelical Philosophy* (Lantern Hollow, 2012); *Inklings of Reality: Essays Toward a Christian Philosophy of Letters* (Lantern Hollow, 2012); and (with Jim Prothero) *Gaining a Face: C. S. Lewis's Romanticism* (Cambridge Scholars' Press, 2014). He blogs at www.lanternhollowpress.com.

Foreword

David C. Downing

Robert E. Havard once wrote, "Lewis, who had read everything and who seemed to remember everything he had read, supported his thesis with inexhaustible quotations."[1] Yet as a former teacher of mine liked to say, "It's not how many books you get through; it's how many books get through you." So when *The Christian Century* asked C. S. Lewis late in his life which books did most to shape his vocational attitude and his philosophy of life, he submitted a list of the ten books that had most defined who he was and how he viewed the world.[2]

Lewis didn't offer any rationale for his choices. But the ten distinguished scholars who contributed to this volume provide ample explanation, offering fresh insights about these seminal texts and also about Lewis, his worldview, and his sense of self.

The list contains a number of surprises. The first surprise might be that Lewis even tried to answer this question. Most of us might try to evade such a query, saying that our lives, our sense of calling, and our worldview have been shaped by so many writers (and other influences) that it would be arbitrary to limit these to a brief list. Or we might argue that our answers might change from year to year, and we don't want to be limited by our choices while in one particular mood or one season of life. But Lewis was usually obliging about such questions, and he considered it a part of his vocation to answer his correspondents, especially when their queries focused on faith or philosophy. And so he submitted the list.

As noted in the essays that follow, there are surprises both about the books included and those left out. Most readers probably never heard of Arthur J. Balfour's *Theism and Humanism* until they discovered this title on Lewis's list. Others will know that Lewis took delight in the poetry of George Herbert, but they will be surprised to find *The Temple* included when the best-known works of Dante, Spenser, and Milton do not appear. One wonders if Lewis might have made different choices on a different

---

[1] Robert E. Havard, "Philia: Jack at Ease," in *C. S. Lewis at the Breakfast Table*, ed. James T. Como (New York: Harcourt Brace, 1992), 219. On Lewis's memory see also page 173 in Paul Tankard's chapter on Boswell's *Life of Johnson*.
[2] C. S. Lewis, "Ex Libris," *The Christian Century*, 79 (June 6, 1962): 719.

day. Or perhaps the particular wording of the question, the phrases about "vocational attitude" and "philosophy of life," caused Lewis to select certain titles and to pass over others.

Yet the essays in this collection make a compelling case that each of these choices is well-justified. All ten books left their mark on Lewis and his thought, some pervasively so, such as George MacDonald, others more subtly, such as Boethius. Though all ten books are by "dead white males," Lewis mentioned Dorothy Sayers in another list of specifically Christian writers who most influenced him. And he often recommended Sayers' *The Man Born to Be King* to readers who asked about books to nourish them in their Christian faith.

The titles on Lewis's list would make an excellent starting point for a Great Books curriculum. They include a classical epic; an influential medieval treatise on philosophy; the best-known work by a major Metaphysical poet; the definitive Neoclassical biography; the magnum opus of a leading Romantic poet; a specimen of Victorian fantasy; works by three twentieth-century theologians and culture critics; and a "spiritual thriller" by one of Lewis's own friends.

Yet Lewis's choices are also very much a mirror of his own mind. All ten books are by Christians or by writers whose work could easily be "Lewisified," adapted and assimilated into his Christian worldview. Many are by authors who blended intellect and imagination, who distinguished themselves in several fields, not in just one genre of literature. All concerned themselves with foundational questions of life's purpose and meaning, not confining themselves to the ephemeral questions of their generation.

It has been argued that Lewis, more than any other single author, reveals for contemporary readers the intellectual richness and imaginative vitality of the Christian faith and worldview. If Lewis were to echo Isaac Newton and say he stood upon the shoulders of giants, these books were produced by the giants who provided Lewis with such a lofty footing. (But Lewis would probably not have chosen such a metaphor, given his ambiguous feelings about giants!) The essays collected here provide admirable commentary upon these monumental works, not only as influences upon Lewis but as cultural landmarks in and of themselves.

Lewis once observed that "humanity does not pass through phases as a train passes through stations: being alive, it has the privilege of always moving yet never leaving anything behind. Whatever we have been, in some sort we are still."[3] One might add that whatever books we have read—read deeply and sympathetically—also become a part of who we are. As the

---

[3] C. S. Lewis, *The Allegory of Love* (Cambridge, Cambridge University Press, 2013), 2.

essays that follow ably demonstrate, Lewis's list serves as a kind of double lens, helping us see classic books in new ways, even while these books help us see Lewis's life and thought in surprising new ways. For attentive readers, the process will come full circle, and they will find new ways to think about their own sense of calling, their own understanding of the universe and their place in it.

Acknowledgments

This volume is the fruit of a conference on "The Ten Books That Most Influenced C. S. Lewis," held in 2012 in Madison, Wisconsin, generously funded and sponsored by the Bradshaw-Knight Foundation, with cosponsorship by the C. S. Lewis Society of Madison and the Tolkien and Fantasy Society at the University of Wisconsin-Madison.

Many thanks to the conference committee: James Knight, President of the Bradshaw-Knight Foundation, and the C. S. Lewis Society of Madison; Richard West, Academic Staff Advisor to the Tolkien and Fantasy Society at the University of Wisconsin-Madison; David Werther, cofounder of the C. S. Lewis Society of Madison; and Sharon Redinger, Director of Lamppost Players Children's Theater, and conference organizer extraordinaire.

Thanks as well to Devin Brown, Bruce L. Edwards, Mark Linville, Wayne Martindale, Angus Menuge, Terry Morrison, David J. Theroux, and Michael Ward for their endorsements of this volume, and to Haaris Naqvi and Mary Al-Sayed of Bloomsbury Press for all of their support and assistance.

We gratefully acknowledge The Discovery Institute for permission to incorporate previously published material (www.discovery.org/a/515) by Mary Ritter in Chapter 5; Zossima Press for permission to incorporate material previously published in *C. S. Lewis & Philosophy as a Way of Life* (Allentown, PA: Zossima, 2009) by Adam Barkman in Chapter 6; and William Wain for permission to use extended quotations from *Sprightly Running: Part of an Autobiography* (London: Macmillan, 1962) by John Wain in Chapter 8.

Introduction

David Werther

Most of us know what we should expect to find in a dragon's lair, but . . . as I said before, Eustace had read only the wrong books. They had a lot to say about exports and imports and governments and drains, but they were weak on dragons.

C. S. Lewis, *The Voyage of the "Dawn Treader"*

In the early 1960s, the editors of the Chicago-based magazine *The Christian Century* asked 108 theologians, authors, editors, and other culturally influential individuals for "top-of-the-mind rather than pondered-upon" responses to the question "What books did most to shape your vocational attitude and your philosophy of life?"[1] *The Century*, a self-described progressive and ecumenical weekly, hoped to uncover the intellectual roots of a generation and published the results in a new feature, "Ex Libris," which ran from May 2, 1962 through May 22, 1963, appearing each issue with lists from two respondents.

The largest group of contributors was theologians and religious leaders, among them Karl Barth, Emil Brunner, Rudolf Bultmann, Martin Luther King Jr, Reinhold and Richard Niebuhr, Helmut Thielicke, and Paul Tillich. Writers who offered their list of life-shaping books included: John Dos Passos, Flannery O'Connor, Norman Mailer, Eudora Welty, and John Updike. Other public figures tapped by *The Century* were cartoonists, Al Capp and Charles Schultz, scientist Robert Oppenheimer, film director Federico Fellini, and jazz musician Dave Brubeck.

The June 6, 1962 issue of *The Christian Century* coupled the lists of advice columnist Ann Landers and "novelist, essayist, theologian" C. S. Lewis.[2] No one would have been surprised if the lists of Landers and Lewis had not overlapped; they didn't. But the Oxbridge scholar who recommended the

---

[1] "Books That Have Influenced: *A Preface to a New* Christian Century *Feature*," *The Christian Century* (May 2, 1962): 575–6. Note that respondents could provide up to ten titles, other than the Bible, "on the assumption that it would appear on almost all the lists, at least those of Westerners."

[2] C. S. Lewis, "Ex Libris," *The Christian Century*, 79 (June 6, 1962): 719.

reading of old books would have been delighted to see works by Sophocles, Plato, Shakespeare, Montaigne, and Swift in Landers' top ten.

Before looking at the books Lewis listed, a word or two about his "vocational attitude" and "philosophy of life" is in order. Characterizing Lewis's callings as novelist, essayist, and theologian is helpful but hardly exhaustive. The subtitles in volumes from Bruce Edwards' *C. S. Lewis: Life, Works, and Legacy* give a much fuller account: fantasist, mythmaker, poet, apologist, philosopher, theologian, scholar, teacher, public intellectual.[3] And for a proper appreciation of Lewis's philosophy of life, we need to know not just where he arrived but how he got there. In his first book, the autobiographical allegory *The Pilgrim's Regress*, Lewis offers this thumbnail sketch of his intellectual development: "On the intellectual side my own progress had been from 'popular realism' to Philosophical Idealism; from Idealism to Pantheism; from Pantheism to Theism; and from Theism to Christianity."[4]

In answer to *The Christian Century*'s question "What books did most to shape your vocational attitude and your philosophy of life?" Lewis provided the following titles:

Phantastes, by George MacDonald
The Everlasting Man, by G. K. Chesterton
The Aeneid, by Virgil
The Temple, by George Herbert
The Prelude, by William Wordsworth
The Idea of the Holy, by Rudolf Otto
The Consolation of Philosophy, by Boethius
The Life of Samuel Johnson, by James Boswell
Descent into Hell, by Charles Williams
Theism and Humanism, by Arthur James Balfour

The editors of *The Christian Century* did not ask Lewis "How and why did these particular works shape your calling and philosophy of life?": crucial questions to reflect upon, both for a deeper understanding of Lewis himself and for a critical consideration of one's own calling and philosophy of life. To answer these more complex questions, the C. S. Lewis Society of Madison, Wisconsin, with funding from the Bradshaw-Knight Foundation

---

[3] Bruce L. Edwards, ed., *C. S. Lewis: Life, Works, and Legacy*, 4 vols (Westport, CT: Praeger, 2007).
[4] C. S. Lewis, *The Pilgrim's Regress: An Allegorical Apology for Christianity, Reason, and Romanticism* (Grand Rapids, MI: Eerdmans, 1974), 5.

and the assistance of the Tolkien and Fantasy Society at the University of Wisconsin-Madison, invited ten Lewis scholars—each with particular expertise in one of the titles on Lewis's list—to come together and share their insights. The chapters in this volume began as presentations at that conference, "The Ten Books That Most Influenced C. S. Lewis" (October 2012).

In his autobiography, *Surprised by Joy*, Lewis notes that the impact of some of the books that were most significant came unbidden:

> In reading Chesterton, as in reading MacDonald, I did not know what I was letting myself in for. A young man who wishes to remain a sound Atheist cannot be too careful of his reading. There are traps everywhere—"Bibles laid open, millions of surprises," as Herbert says, "fine nets and stratagems."[5]

He found the first book on his list, *Phantastes*, in a bookstall at a railway station. In discussing the impact of this work of fantasy by George MacDonald, David Neuhouser argues that its significance went beyond stepping into the bright shadow of holiness, and claims that a key characteristic of Lewis's writing (its unified vision of reality), and a key character trait (humility—the virtue that enabled Lewis the author to "get out of the way"), had their roots in MacDonald.

Lewis initially encountered G. K. Chesterton's writings during World War I, while in hospital recovering from trench fever. At that time, he enjoyed Chesterton's work, but did not share his worldview. Later, Lewis would come to regard Chesterton's *The Everlasting Man*, a response to H. G. Well's *The Outline of History*, as the best overall apologetic. However, as important as the apologetic thrust of *The Everlasting Man* would be for Lewis, Don Williams points out that what initially struck and captivated Lewis was Chesterton's goodness. Williams also notes the importance of the metaphor of home for both Chesterton and Lewis.

Like Chesterton's account in *The Everlasting Man*, Virgil's *Aeneid*, provides a teleological view of history, one in which the fall of Troy can be seen as a *felix culpa* leading to the foundation of the Roman Empire. Not only do countries, states, and governments rise and fall and perhaps rise again, so do individuals. In this regard, Louis Markos compares Aeneas's losses, sacrifices, and gains with those of Lewis. Similarly, he compares

---

[5] C. S. Lewis, *Surprised by Joy: The Shape of My Early Life* (New York: Harcourt Brace & World, 1955), 191. The George Herbert quote is from "Sinne (I)," *The Temple: Sacred Poems and Private Ejaculations* (T. Buck & R. Daniel, 1638), 38–9.

Lewis's goal of communicating to his modern audience an earlier vision of the world, by affirming the goodness of hierarchy and the reality of the supernatural, with Virgil accepting Caesar Augustus's empire while, at the same time, praising the virtues of the old republic.

Virgil was a poet *par excellence* and the young Lewis aspired to be such, initially publishing two volumes of poetry: *Spirits in Bondage* and *Dymer*. Though prose would become Lewis's primary mode of expression, not least for communicating Christian truths to nonacademics and counseling hundreds of correspondents, Lewis continued to write verse. Don King shows how Lewis's religious verse, as well as his pastoral correspondence and autobiographical *A Grief Observed*, are informed by pastor-poet George Herbert's *The Temple*.

Lewis's debt to another poet, William Wordsworth, is evident in his other autobiographical writings, *The Pilgrim's Regress* and *Surprised by Joy*. Lewis took the title of the latter from Wordsworth's sonnet "Surprised by Joy."[6] Mary Ritter traces Lewis's notion of "Joy" to Wordsworth and argues that Lewis modeled *The Pilgrim's Regress* on Wordsworth's great autobiographical poem, *The Prelude*.

Rudolf Otto's *The Idea of the Holy* focuses on a particular sort of religious experience: *numinous* experience. Adam Barkman places this experience in context, looking at it in the light of other sorts of spiritual longing in Lewis's writings: Platonic *eros*; *Sehnsucht*; Joy; and Romanticism. Barkman conjectures that Lewis may have included *The Idea of the Holy* on his *Christian Century* list, not because it shaped Lewis's understanding of religious experience, but because it provided an excellent theoretical account of spiritual longing, a life-shaping phenomenon.

In *The Consolation of Philosophy*, the early medieval philosopher Boethius held that the closer we are to God, the more we become our true selves, and the more we experience real happiness. Chris Armstrong finds this Boethian account of happiness in Lewis's incomparable sermon, "The Weight of Glory" and Boethius's notion that all fortune is good in Lewis's pastoral counseling. Beyond that, noting that in *The Allegory of Love*, Lewis refers to Boethius as a "divine popularizer," Armstrong argues that Boethius himself—as a public intellectual, popularizer, and translator of ideas—exemplified what would become, centuries later, some of Lewis's own vocations.

Boethius was not the only public intellectual on Lewis's reading list. Paul Tankard points out that the eighteenth-century critic and moralist Samuel Johnson, the subject of James Boswell's famous biography, wrote for "the

---

[6] William Wordsworth, "Surprised by Joy," in *Poems* (1815).

common reader," and indeed coined that phrase. To reach a large audience Johnson employed a wide range of literary genres, making use of satire for the difficult task of moral instruction. Lewis, too, wrote in many genres and engaged in moral teaching in his satirical *The Screwtape Letters*. Indeed, Johnson modeled for Lewis the life of a public intellectual and writer. And, while others might not have recognized Johnson's sanctity, Lewis saw him as a shining example of holiness.[7]

The contrast between holiness and damnation is vividly depicted in Charles Williams' supernatural thriller, *Descent into Hell*. Holly Ordway describes how this influenced Lewis's fictional depiction of the day-to-day reality of salvation and damnation in *That Hideous Strength*, as well as the use of Williams' doctrine of substituted love in *Till We Have Faces*, the novel Lewis regarded as his best. In keeping with Williams' portrayal of the salvific significance of daily choices, Ordway notes that Williams' influence was much more than literary; there is good reason to suppose that Lewis attributed his wife Joy's remission from cancer to his own bone loss, as she was in need of calcium, and saw it as an instance of substituted love.

In *Theism and Humanism*, Arthur J. Balfour argues that moral values, and indeed reason itself, have no place in a purely physical world. Charles Taliaferro explicates Balfour's arguments for theism, placing them in the context of both nineteenth-century and contemporary philosophical debate, thereby providing an ideal framework for understanding Lewis's argument from reason in *Miracles*. Lewis employed this line of argument elsewhere, perhaps most succinctly in his 1944 sermon, "Transposition."

> We can be certain that, in this life at any rate, thought is intimately connected to the brain. The theory that thought therefore is merely a movement of the brain is, in my opinion, nonsense, for if so, the theory itself would merely be a movement, an event among atoms, which may have speed and direction, but of which it would be meaningless to use the words "true" and "false."[8]

While C. S. Lewis appropriated Arthur Balfour's argument from reason and G. K. Chesterton's trilemma, we need to remember that Lewis denied that there is anything like a mathematical proof for his philosophy of life, the Christian worldview: "I do not think there is a *demonstrative* proof (like

---

[7] C. S. Lewis to Arthur Greeves, Dec. 11, 1944, in *The Collected Letters of C. S. Lewis, Vol. III: Narnia, Cambridge, and Joy 1950–1963*, ed. Walter Hooper (London: HarperCollins, 2006), 1555.

[8] C. S. Lewis, "The Weight of Glory," in *The Weight of Glory and Other Addresses*, rev. and exp. (New York: MacMillan, 1980), 63.

Euclid) of Christianity, nor of the existence of matter, nor of the good will & honesty of my best & oldest friends."[9] However, from the absence of proof from self-evident axioms, fideism need not follow. Lewis's acceptance of Christianity is grounded in its explanatory power: "I believe in Christianity as I believe that the Sun has risen, not only because I see it, but because by it I see everything else."[10]

Part of the "everything else" Lewis saw in the light of the Christian worldview is vocation. Indeed, as Charles Taliaferro points out, in contrast to a view like that of Ronald Dworkin, that individual accomplishments can be significant and satisfying even if the grand story of the universe is tragic, Lewis and Balfour thought that if the universe ends in obliteration—as in atheistic naturalism—that finality eclipses all human achievements. But, on the other hand, insofar as we have reason to think our values and visions are significant, we have some grounds for supposing that death does not have the last word.

Crucial to Lewis's Christian conception of calling is the distinction between "membership" and "mass," a powerful awareness of which, as David Neuhouser points out, Lewis shared with "his master," George MacDonald. From the Christian perspective there can be no "massing of men" for God creates each person to be a distinct member of a spiritual body with a unique role to play. In *The Problem of Pain* Lewis conjectured that each "soul has a curious shape because it is a hollow made to fit a particular swelling in the infinite contours of the Divine substance, or a key to unlock one of the doors in the house with many mansions."[11]

Several corollaries follow. First, there can be no monotony among saints.[12] Dr Johnson, St Francis, George Herbert, John Bunyan, and George MacDonald are all shining examples of holiness but each one, not least the burly and indecorous Dr Johnson, sparkles differently. Second—in keeping with Holly Ordway's discussion of Charles Williams' *Descent into Hell*—our daily decisions, taking us closer to or farther away from our unique membership, are momentous. Third, as Boethius argues, satisfaction and fulfillment are a function of the degree to which we choose to exemplify God's idea for each of us.

Don King notes that one of the roles Lewis played—one of his callings—was that of spiritual counselor. Chris Armstrong points out that in encouraging his student Mary Neylan, Lewis drew on the Boethian insight that no fortune is bad for even the worst can be put to good use. From this it

---

[9] C. S. Lewis to Sheldon Vanauken, Dec. 23, 1950, *Collected Letters III*, 75.
[10] Lewis, "The Weight of Glory," 92.
[11] C. S. Lewis, *The Problem of Pain* (New York: HarperCollins, 2001), 152.
[12] See Lewis, "Membership," in *Weight of Glory*, 166–7, and David Neuhouser, in Chapter 1 of this volume, 21–2.

follows that when times are bad it does not mean "the game is up" but that "this is precisely the game you have been set"—a nugget of wisdom for those seeking their calling, or trying to live it out.

Mary Ritter reminds us that Lewis believed nature dies for those who live for the love of nature (e.g. Wordsworth and Coleridge). In fact, this death is just one illustration of a more general truth, the doctrine of first and second things: "every preference of a small good to a great, or a partial good to a total good, involves the loss of the small or partial good for which the sacrifice was made . . . You can't get second things by putting them first; you can get second things only by putting first things first."[13]

Paradoxically, one finds what one was made for, only by looking outside of oneself.

> At the beginning I said there were Personalities in God. I will go further now. There are no real personalities anywhere else. Until you have given up your self to Him you will not have a real self . . . The very first step is to try to forget about the self altogether. Your real, new self . . . will not come as long as you are looking for it. It will come when you are looking for Him . . . The principle runs through all life from top to bottom. Give up yourself, and you will find your real self. Lose your life and you will save it. Submit to death, death of your ambitions and favourite wishes . . . and you will find eternal life. Keep nothing back. Nothing that you have not given away will be really yours. Nothing in you that has not died will ever be raised from the dead. Look for yourself, and you will find in the long run only hatred, loneliness, despair, rage, ruin, and decay. But look for Christ and you will find Him, and with Him everything else thrown in.[14]

The necessity of giving oneself up also applies to reading, "The first demand any work of art makes upon us is surrender. Look. Listen. Receive. Get yourself out of the way."[15] If we read the books on Lewis's list in this way, we will find our view of the world expanded and our lives enriched. The editors of *The Christian Century* began their series with the hope that it would contribute to "a recovery of serious reading."[16] This volume is offered with the same hope.

---

[13] C. S. Lewis, "First and Second Things," in *God in the Dock: Essays on Theology and Ethics*, ed. Walter Hooper (Grand Rapids, MI: Eerdmans, 1970), 280.
[14] C. S. Lewis, *Mere Christianity* (New York: HarperCollins, 2001), 226–7.
[15] C. S. Lewis, *An Experiment in Criticism* (Cambridge: Cambridge University Press, 1961), 19.
[16] "Books That Have Influenced: *A Preface to a New Christian Century Feature*," *The Christian Century* (May 2, 1962): 576.

1

George Macdonald, *Phantastes*

David L. Neuhouser

C. S. Lewis called George MacDonald his "master" and claimed that by reading *Phantastes* he had "crossed a great frontier."[1] Not only was the reading of *Phantastes* an important step that led to his becoming a Christian, but it also brought Lewis to the study and enjoyment of the rest of MacDonald's writings which in turn helped him in his spiritual journey even after he became a Christian. Reading *Phantastes*, in fact reading all of MacDonald, helped Lewis acquire the virtue of humility, which, as we will see, was a significant factor in his success as an author. MacDonald believed that faith in God led to seeing all of life as related, and to a greater love of the entire world. This integrated view of God, nature, and culture helped Lewis to produce better works of literature and scholarship, and indeed Lewis became much more successful as a writer after becoming a Christian. *Phantastes*, and many of MacDonald's other books, influenced both the style and substance of Lewis's work; MacDonald's skill in making goodness and even holiness attractive (especially in his books of fantasy) was very appealing to Lewis and inspired him to do the same in his own works. Finally, the sheer number of similar ideas in the stories of Lewis and MacDonald testify to the great influence MacDonald had on Lewis.

Similarities

Despite the abundance of shared ideas in the works of these two writers, it is difficult to prove that whenever Lewis's thought or style resembles MacDonald's that MacDonald was the original source. One could just as easily argue that they had each received their inspiration from someone

---

[1] C. S. Lewis, ed., *George MacDonald: An Anthology* (New York: HarperCollins, 2001), xxxvii.

else or had arrived independently at the same thought. In a letter to Arthur Greeves, Lewis comments on an idea that both he and Greeves had written about. "Perhaps, as you say, we both took it unconsciously from 'Phantastes,' who in turn borrowed it from the dryads, etc. of classical mythology . . . so we needn't be ashamed of borrowing our trees, since they are really common property."[2]

In another letter to Greeves, Lewis wrote that MacDonald "seems to know everything and I find my own experience in it constantly,"[3] and Frank Riga suggests that this shared experience, "as much as any explicit literary influence, accounts for the similarity of their work."[4] Even if this were the whole story, the fact that Lewis found in MacDonald his own experience is an indication of how important it was for him to find a kindred spirit in MacDonald. What Lewis said about Charles Williams is likely true about MacDonald also. Lewis told Walter Hooper, "I have never been *consciously* influenced by Williams, never believed that I was in any way imitating him. On the other hand, there may have been a great deal of *unconscious* influence going on."[5] Roger Lancelyn Green and Walter Hooper comment that "Lewis could take all myth and ransack it for his *dramatis personae*, taking what he needed wherever he found it throughout literature, but making it so much his own that whatever 'original' researchers may find, there is no thought of anything like plagiarism."[6]

Although it may be impossible to prove a direct correlation between ideas found in MacDonald's work that appear in Lewis's writings, we know that Lewis was familiar with these ideas, and that they certainly influenced both the style and content of his own work.[7] As Lewis himself wrote in his diary on May 9, 1926, "One never re-reads an old favorite without finding that it has contributed more than one suspected to one's habitual stock in trade."[8] Now "stock in trade" means the materials necessary to, or used in, a trade or business. So Lewis acknowledges that all that he has read is being used in his works.

---

[2] C. S. Lewis to Arthur Greeves, July 4, 1916, in *The Collected Letters of C. S. Lewis, Volume I: Family Letters, 1905–1931*, ed. Walter Hooper (London: HarperCollins, 2004), 206.
[3] Ibid., Oct. 10, 1929, 834.
[4] Roderick McGillis, ed., *For the Childlike* (Metuchen, NJ; London: Children's Literature Association & Scarecrow Press, 1992), 111.
[5] Roger Lancelyn Green and Walter Hooper, *C. S. Lewis: A Biography* (New York and London: Harcourt Brace Jovanovich, 1974), 184.
[6] Ibid., 241.
[7] For more examples see Appendix A.
[8] C. S. Lewis, *All My Road Before Me: The Diary of C. S. Lewis, 1922–1927*, ed. Walter Hooper (San Diego, CA: Harcourt Brace Jovanovich, 1992), 390.

MacDonald's spiritual influence on Lewis

Although MacDonald clearly influenced Lewis's literary work, I believe that his impact on Lewis's spiritual life was far greater, and that this religious impact then further influenced Lewis's writing. So, before looking more specifically into MacDonald's influence on the writing of Lewis, I would like to show the profound influence on Lewis's Christian faith.

Phantastes was the first book of MacDonald's that Lewis read and in the preface to *George MacDonald: An Anthology* Lewis wrote, "What it actually did to me was to convert, even to baptize (that was where death came in) my imagination."[9] To "convert" means to change, but to baptize in a Christian sense means to kill something of the self, and Lewis's mention of death shows that death is what he meant. Now Lewis could not have meant that he no longer had any imagination, but that his imagination, as it was then, was killed. Earlier in the preface he wrote,

> A few hours later while reading *Phantastes* I knew that I had crossed a great frontier. I had already been waist-deep in Romanticism; and likely enough, at any moment to flounder into its darker and more evil forms, slithering down the steep descent that leads from the love of strangeness to that of eccentricity and thence to that of perversity.[10]

Phantastes was similar to the kind of romanticism that Lewis loved but there was a difference, a difference that Lewis much later realized was holiness. In *Surprised by Joy*, Lewis wrote,

> The woodland journeying in [*Phantastes*], the ghostly enemies, the ladies both good and evil, were close enough to my habitual imagery to lure me on without the perception of a change. It is as if I were carried sleeping across the frontier, or as if I had died in the old country and could never remember how I came alive in the new. For in one sense the new country was exactly like the old. . . . But in another sense all was changed. I did not yet know (and I was long in learning) the name of the new quality, the bright shadow, that rested on the travels of Anodos. I do now. It was Holiness.[11]

---

[9] Ibid., xxxviii.
[10] Ibid., xxxvii.
[11] C. S. Lewis, *Surprised by Joy* (New York: Harcourt Brace & World, 1955), 179.

In a letter to Arthur Greeves, Lewis commented on this quality in a passage of *Love Is Enough* by William Morris, that clarifies what he thought holiness does: "the light of holiness shines through Morris's romanticism, not destroying but perfecting it."[12]

Romanticism, though, was not the only thing that attracted Lewis. In *Surprised by Joy* he wrote, "The two hemispheres of my mind were in the sharpest contrast. On the one side a many-islanded sea of poetry and myth; on the other a glib and shallow 'rationalism.'"[13] He went on to say that materialism was also enormously attractive to him.[14] *Phantastes* helped him in this area as well: the hero of that story, Anodos, is cursed for a time by his own shadow. "The shadow is Anodos's alter ego, which is at first his skeptical self, characterized by rationalist attitudes that prevent any perception of the spiritual import of things."[15] Also, Anodos visits a family in which the mother is in touch with fairyland while her husband is a complete materialist. MacDonald's handling of these two incidents clearly favors the antimaterialist view.

In a sense, the reading of *Phantastes* was the first step in a long process that led to Lewis's conversion to Christianity. In 1923, long before Lewis became a Christian or even a theist, he wrote in his diary, "After this I read MacDonald's *Phantastes* over my tea, which I have read many times and which I really believe fills for me the place of a devotional book. It tuned me up to a higher pitch and delighted me."[16] Lewis later wrote about the long-term impact of *Phantastes*: "But when the process was complete—by which, of course, I mean 'when it had *really* begun'—I found that I was still with MacDonald and that he had accompanied me all the way and that I was now at last ready to hear from him much that he could not have told me at that first meeting."[17] In answer to a request for advice on books Lewis underscored the importance of MacDonald: "My own greatest debt is to George MacDonald, specially the 3 vols of *Unspoken Sermons*."[18]

---

[12] C. S. Lewis to Arthur Greeves, June 31, [July 1] 1930, *Collected Letters I*, 911.
[13] Lewis, *Surprised by Joy*, 170. On the importance and right relation between Reason and Imagination, see pages 94, 97, 104, 108–9 in Mary Ritter's essay on William Wordsworth's *The Prelude*.
[14] For a critical discussion of materialism, see chapter 10, *Theism and Humanism*, by Charles Taliaffero.
[15] Rolland Hein, *Christian Mythmakers* (Chicago: Cornerstone Press Chicago, 1998), 66.
[16] C. S. Lewis, *All My Road Before Me*, 177.
[17] Lewis, *George MacDonald*, xxxviii.
[18] C. S. Lewis to Mr. H. Morland, Aug. 19, 1942, in *The Collected Letters of C. S. Lewis, Vol. II: Books, Broadcasts, and the War 1931-1949*, ed. Walter Hooper (London: HarperCollins, 2004), 529.

Sehnsucht

Another nugget Lewis gleaned from *Phantastes* and other MacDonald books was the description of longing as a spiritual experience. He referred to *Sehnsucht* as a longing or a memory of a memory, a characterization reminiscent of MacDonald's "It was not a memory that came, but a memory of a memory—the shadow of a memory gone, but trying to come out from behind a veil."[19] In *Phantastes* itself, MacDonald wrote of "a kind of trance of speechless delight, which, passing as suddenly, left me faint and longing for more."[20]

In fact this longing is referred to many times in the book.[21] At one point Anodos is moved to poetry.

> But words are vain; reject them all—
>   They utter but a feeble part:
> Hear thou the depths from which they call,
>   The voiceless longing of my heart.[22]

These longings indicate a need that can't be satisfied by anything on this earth and therefore point to God. Of course, this idea was expressed earlier by St Augustine who wrote in *The Confessions*, "thou hast made us for thyself and our hearts are restless until they rest in thee."[23] But perhaps no one, not even Lewis, described the experience of *Sehnsucht* as well as MacDonald did in his novel, *Robert Falconer*.

> He lay gazing up into the depth of the sky, rendered deeper and bluer by the masses of white cloud that hung almost motionless below it, until he felt a kind of bodily fear lest he should fall off the face of the round earth into the abyss. A gentle wind, laden with pine odours from the sun-heated trees behind him, flapped its light wing in his face: the humanity of the world smote his heart; the

---

[19] George MacDonald, *A Rough Shaking* (London: Blackie & Son, 1900), 260. For an extended discussion of *Sehnsucht* and other forms of spiritual longing in the works of C. S. Lewis, see Adam Barkman's essay on Rudolf Otto's *The Idea of the Holy*.
[20] MacDonald, *Phantastes* (London: Arthur C. Fifield, 1905), 189.
[21] Ibid., "They filled me with an unknown longing," 19; "The sign or cause of coming death is an indescribable longing for something, they know not what, which seizes them, and drives them into solitude, consuming them within, till the body fails," 149; "[A] gush of wonderment and longing flowed over my soul like the tide of a great sea," 99.
[22] Ibid., 71.
[23] St. Augustine, *The Confessions*, Book 1, chapter 1.

great sky towered up over him, and its divinity entered his soul; a strange longing after something "he knew not nor could name" awoke within him, followed by the pang of a sudden fear that there was no such thing as that which he sought, that it was all a fancy of his own spirit... But once aroused, the feeling was never stilled; the desire never left him; sometimes growing even to a passion that was relieved only by a flood of tears. Strange as it may sound to those who have never thought of such things save in connection with Sundays and Bibles and churches and sermons, that which was now working in Falconer's mind was the first dull and faint movement of the greatest need that the human heart possesses—the need of the God-Man. There must be truth in the scent of that pine-wood: someone must mean it. There must be a glory in those heavens that depends not upon our imagination: some power greater than they must dwell in them. Some spirit must move in that wind that haunts us with a kind of human sorrow; some soul must look up to us from the eye of that starry flower.[24]

Phantastes, as well as the rest of MacDonald's writings, helped Lewis understand the meaning of his experiences of Joy. He refers to this in his autobiography, *Surprised by Joy*:

For I now perceived that while the air of the new region made all my erotic and magical perversions of Joy look like sordid trumpery, it had no such disenchanting power over the bread upon the table or the coals in the grate. Up till now each visitation of Joy had left the common world momentarily a desert... But now I saw the bright shadow coming out of the book into the real world and resting there, transforming all common things and yet itself unchanged... I had not the faintest notion what I had let myself in for by buying *Phantastes*.[25]

---

[24] George MacDonald, *Robert Falconer* (London: Hurst & Blackett, 1880), 122–3. Also, in the fairy tale, "The Golden Key," Mossy and Tangle look down on a sea of beautiful shadows. "Sometimes a profile of unspeakable beauty or grandeur would appear for a moment and vanish... some of the things which pleased them most they never knew how to describe.... After sitting for a while, each, looking up, saw the other in tears: they were each longing after the country whence the shadows fell." George MacDonald, "The Golden Key" in *The Light Princess and Other Fairy Tales* (New York: G. P. Putnam's Sons, 1893), 194–5.

[25] Lewis, *Surprised by Joy*, 181.

Humility

Rolland Hein has said, "In *Phantastes*, the main theme appears to address the problem of man's search for satisfactions for his personal desires and longings. The Christian concern arises because the natural process of seeking satisfactions for human desires is self-centered, and self-centeredness is spiritually destructive."[26] In *Phantastes* MacDonald wrote, "for in proportion as selfishness intrudes, the love ceases," and "it is better, a thousand-fold, for a proud man to fall and be humbled, than to hold up his head in his pride and fancied innocence."[27]

In a letter to Arthur Greeves, Lewis—touching on the topic of literary pride—wrote that he deplored his earlier intense desire to be a successful writer and noted how dangerous that would have been for his own character. He now thought that one must forget about personal success and concentrate on saying whatever one has to say in the clearest way possible with no thought of "originality." And, to reach that point, Lewis referred Greeves to MacDonald: "I think the only thing for you to do is absolutely to *kill* the part of you that wants success. It's like in Phantastes where the voice said 'Ride at him or be a slave *forever*.'"[28]

This newfound humility freed Lewis to become a great writer.

Reality

In addition to helping Lewis grow in humility, reading MacDonald gave him a more unified and accurate view of reality. In the essay "A Sketch of Individual Development," MacDonald wrote,

> To the man who believes in the Son of God, poetry returns in a mighty wave; history unrolls itself in harmony; science shows crowned with its own aureole of holiness. There is no enlivener of the imagination, no enabler of the judgment, no strengthener of the intellect, to compare with the belief in a live Ideal, at the heart of all personality, as of every law.[29]

---

[26] Rolland Hein, *The Harmony Within: The Spiritual Vision of George MacDonald* (Grand Rapids, MI: Eerdmans, 1982), 55.
[27] MacDonald, *Phantastes*, 313–14, 286.
[28] C. S. Lewis to Arthur Greeves, Aug. 18, 1930, *Collected Letters I*, 927.
[29] George MacDonald, "A Sketch of Individual Development" in *Dish of Orts* (London: Sampson Low, Marston, 1895), 75.

And in *Phantastes*, "The community of the centre of all creation suggests an interradiating connection and dependence of the parts."[30] Lewis put the same idea in these words, "I believe in Christianity as I believe that the sun is risen, not only because I see it, but because by it I see everything else."[31] It was this unified view of reality that was necessary for Lewis to become a successful writer.

Imaginative writing

Roland Hein's assessment of MacDonald is that "Few people in the history of man have had a larger vision of the beauty of holiness and goodness than he, and few have succeeded as he did in communicating the attraction to goodness that good men feel."[32] Reading MacDonald, and especially *Phantastes*, gave Lewis a vision of what imaginative writing could do in the support of Christianity. In a letter to a friend Lewis wrote,

> Isn't *Phantastes* good? It did a lot for me years before I became a Christian, when I had no idea what was behind it. This has always made it easier for me to understand how the better elements in mythology can be a real *praeparatio evangelica* for people who do not yet know whither they are being led.[33]

And from the pulpit of the University Church of St Mary the Virgin he asked,

> Do you think I am trying to weave a spell? Perhaps I am; but remember your fairy tales. Spells are used for breaking enchantment as well as for inducing them. And you and I have need for the strongest spell that can be found to wake us from the evil enchantment of worldliness which has been laid upon us for nearly a hundred years.[34]

Certainly, Lewis's fantasy does help to break the evil enchantment due to our culture. Lucy, Reepicheep, and many other characters created by Lewis have made goodness attractive.

---

[30] MacDonald, *Phantastes*, 142.
[31] C. S. Lewis, "Is Theology Poetry?" in *The Weight of Glory and Other Addresses* (New York: HarperCollins, 2001), 140.
[32] Ibid., x.
[33] C. S. Lewis to Sister Penelope, Nov. 4, 1940, *Collected Letters II*, 453.
[34] Lewis, "Weight of Glory," in *Weight of Glory* (New York: HarperCollins, 2001), 31.

In addition to showing Lewis what fantasy or myth could do in the aid of the Christian faith, reading MacDonald helped him to write mythic works. MacDonald was perhaps the greatest nineteenth-century writer of fairy tales. A comment by one critic, Michael Patrick Hearn, is typical of many literary critics' evaluation of his fairy tales. "Unquestionably, the master of the Victorian fairy tale was George MacDonald. His stories ... were moral yet more symbolic than didactic or allegorical, as were many of his contemporaries' efforts."[35] Lewis said that what MacDonald did best was "fantasy that hovers between the allegorical and the mythopoeic."[36] Lewis often refers to events and descriptions from *Phantastes* showing that these things were part of his "stock in trade." One example is a comment he made to his friend Arthur Greeves: "There was one evening of mist about three feet deep lying on the fields under the moon—like the mist in the first chapter of Phantastes."[37] And in another letter to Greeves, he said that the best parts of *Phantastes* were "the forest scene and the faery palace."[38]

In *Dish of Orts*, MacDonald wrote:

> Goethe has told us that the way to develop the aesthetic faculty is to have constantly before our eyes, that is, in the room we most frequent, some work of the best attainable art. This will teach us to refuse the evil and choose the good. It will plant itself in our minds and become our counsellor. Involuntarily, unconsciously, we shall compare with its perfection everything that comes before us for judgment ... But in the culture of the imagination, books, although not the only, are the readiest means of supplying the food convenient for it.[39]

I believe that *Phantastes* and MacDonald's other fantasy stories served this purpose for Lewis.

In conclusion, the reading of *Phantastes* baptized Lewis's imagination. This helped rescue Lewis from "slithering down the steep descent that leads from the love of strangeness to that of eccentricity and thence to that of perversity."[40] The descriptions of joy and longing in *Phantastes* helped Lewis recognize and understand his experiences of what he called "Joy" or

---

[35] Michael Patrick Hearn, *The Victorian Fairy Tale Book* (New York: Pantheon Books, 1988), xxiv–xxv.
[36] Lewis, *George MacDonald*, xxix.
[37] C. S. Lewis to Arthur Greeves, Dec. 6, 1931, *Collected Letters II*, 22.
[38] Ibid., March 21, 1916, *Collected Letters I*, 175.
[39] MacDonald, "The Imagination: Its Functions and Its Culture," *Dish of Orts*, 36–7.
[40] Lewis, *George MacDonald*, xxxvii.

Sehnsucht, the experiences which played such a great part in his Christian conversion. The reading of *Phantastes* led to his reading most of MacDonald's works, some of them many times. Although the influence of MacDonald, and *Phantastes* in particular, was significant on Lewis's writing, I believe that the spiritual influence was greater. In turn, becoming a Christian helped Lewis to become a better writer in two ways—it changed him by helping him become more humble. Thus he could forget about being original or creative and concentrate on saying what he wanted to say in the clearest and most concise way. Second, it helped him to see reality more clearly. Thus, he was able to write more realistically, even in his fantasy. MacDonald gave Lewis a vision of what writing could do in the support of Christianity. Lewis's way of promoting Christianity, even in, or perhaps especially in, his fiction, was a major factor in the popularity of his books. MacDonald showed Lewis what myth could do and how it could be done. The many examples of similarities in their ideas indicate the extent of MacDonald's influence. It is interesting to consider what Lewis would have been if he had never heard of MacDonald. He might have become a Christian anyway, as there were many other factors in his conversion. He certainly would have been a writer under almost any conditions. But it is hard to believe that his writing would have been quite the same without MacDonald.

Appendix A

Ideas from MacDonald Found in Lewis

Following are some specific examples of ideas from MacDonald that find expression in Lewis's writing.

Examples from *Phantastes*

The insignificance of size

"Form is much, but size is nothing. It is a mere matter of relation. I suppose your six-foot lordship does not feel altogether insignificant, though to others you do look small beside your old Uncle Ralph, who rises above you a great half-foot at least."[41] Lewis makes the same point about size and even uses the same illustration in *Miracles*. "There is no doubt that we all *feel* the incongruity of supposing, say, that the planet Earth might be more important than the Great Nebula in Andromeda. On the other hand, we are all equally certain that only a lunatic would think a man six feet high necessarily more important than a man five feet high."[42] The comparison of the height of two men to make the point seems too much alike to be a coincidence. Lewis must have had in his mind, perhaps unconsciously, the passage from *Phantastes*.

Becoming part of the story

In *Phantastes*, Anodos lived in a fairy palace for a while and when reading books in the library, he became the hero of the story. "[I]f the book was one of travels, I found myself the traveller. . . . Was it a history? I was the chief actor therein . . . With a fiction it was the same. Mine was the whole story."[43] Lewis used this idea in *Voyage of the "Dawn Treader."* Lucy found that when she read a story in the magic book "She was living in the story as if it were real, and all the pictures were real too."[44]

---

[41] MacDonald, *Phantastes*, 17.
[42] Lewis, *Miracles*, 83.
[43] MacDonald, *Phantastes*, 140.
[44] C. S. Lewis, *The Voyage of the "Dawn Treader"* (New York: HarperCollins, 1980), 167.

Examples from *George MacDonald: An anthology*

The next examples are taken from the MacDonald anthology that Lewis edited. Remember that one of the important results of reading *Phantastes* was that Lewis then went on to read virtually all of MacDonald. The fact that he chose these quotations shows that they were important to him and with his great memory they would have had an effect on his writing and on his life. The anthology has 365 quotations, one for each day of the year: 275 quotations from the 3 volumes of *Unspoken Sermons*; 84 from the novels; and the remaining 6 from fantasy and poems. There are actually only two from *Phantastes*. In the following examples the MacDonald quote is identified by giving the day on which it appears in the anthology.

Hatred compared to murder

MacDonald gave his opinion about the seriousness of hatred and compares it to murder.

> It may be an infinitely less evil to murder a man than to refuse to forgive him. The former may be the act of a moment of passion: the latter is the heart's choice. It is spiritual murder, the worst, to hate, to brood over the feeling that excludes, that, in our microcosm kills the image, the idea of the hated.[45]

Lewis expressed this same thought in *The Great Divorce,* "Murdering old Jack wasn't the worst thing I did. That was the work of a moment and I was half mad when I did it. But I murdered you in my heart, deliberately, for years. I used to lie awake at nights thinking what I'd do to you if ever I got the chance."[46]

Excuses

Lewis has an interesting essay "On Forgiveness" in the collection *The Weight of Glory and other Addresses* in which he says that we should not try to make excuses about our sins:

> One is to remember that God knows all the real excuses very much better than we do. If there are real "extenuating circumstances" there

---

[45] Lewis, *George MacDonald*, day 12.
[46] C. S. Lewis, *The Great Divorce* (New York: Macmillan Paperbacks, 1963), 85.

is no fear that He will overlook them. Often He must know many excuses that we have never thought of, and therefore humble souls will, after death, have the delightful surprise of discovering that on certain occasions they sinned much less than they had thought. All the real excusing He will do. What we have got to take to Him is the inexcusable bit, the sin.[47]

MacDonald had written, "'You have had great provocation and are justified in your hate?' No doubt God takes what wrong there is, and what provocation there is, into the account: but the more provocation, the more excuse that can be urged for the hate, the more reason, if possible, that the hater should be delivered from the hell of his hate."[48] And on day 310:

Think not about thy sin so as to make it either less or greater in thine own eyes. Bring it to Jesus and let Him show thee how vile a thing it is. And leave it to Him to judge thee, sure that He will judge thee justly; extenuating nothing, for He hath to cleanse thee utterly; and yet forgetting no smallest excuse that may cover the amazement of thy guilt or witness for thee that not with open eyes didst thou do the deed ... But again, I say, let it be Christ that excuseth thee. He will do it to more purpose than thou, and will not wrong thy soul by excusing thee a hair too much.[49]

A spiritual body

The quotation for day 19 in the anthology is, "There is no massing of men with God. When he speaks of gathered men, it is as a spiritual *body* not as a *mass*."[50] In the sermons from which this quote comes, MacDonald expands on the idea, "For in a body every smallest portion is individual, and therefore capable of forming a part of the body ... each has within him a secret of the Divinity; each is growing towards the revelation of the secret to himself, and so to the full reception, according to his measure of the divine."[51] Lewis expressed the same idea in an address titled "Membership," and published in *The Weight of Glory*:

---

[47] Lewis, "On Forgiveness," in *Weight of Glory*, 180.
[48] Lewis, *George MacDonald*, day 13.
[49] Ibid., day 310.
[50] Ibid., day 19.
[51] George MacDonald, *Unspoken Sermons: Series I, II, and III*. London: Series I published by Alexander Strahan, Series II and III by Longmans, Green, and Co., Series I, 1867; Series II, 1886; Series III, 1889, 75.

The society into which the Christian is called at baptism is not a collective but a Body ... If anyone comes to it with the misconception that membership of the church was membership in a debased modern sense—a massing together of persons as if they were pennies or counters—he would be corrected at the threshold ... Those who are members of one another become as diverse as the hand and the ear. That is why the worldlings are so monotonously alike compared with the almost fantastic variety of the saints.[52]

In *Mere Christianity*, Lewis talks about theology as a science in which the scientific instrument is the body of believers because each Christian has some knowledge of God that the others do not have and so must help each other to know God better.[53] The MacDonald quote for day 255 is, "Every one of us is something that the other is not, and therefore knows something—it may be without knowing that he knows it—which no one else knows: and ... it is everyone's business as one of the kingdom of light and inheritor in it all, to give his portion to the rest."[54]

Hell

In contrast to Sartre's idea in "No Exit" that hell is other people, Lewis and MacDonald both thought that hell was to be totally alone. MacDonald said, "The one principle of hell is—'I am on my own!'"[55] In His fairy tale *The Wise Woman*, a girl who is self-centered is put in a cage where she is alone with herself. In this way she is able to experience the hell it is to be in that condition. In *The Great Divorce*, Lewis puts into the mouth of his fictional MacDonald the words, "There are only two kinds of people in the end: those who say to God, 'Thy will be done,' and those to whom God says, in the end, '*Thy will be done*.'"[56] In the gray city in that book, no one can bear to live with others and so they keep moving farther and farther apart.

Prayer

Lewis once said that he was able to pray best when walking in his garden. In *Letters to Malcolm: Chiefly on Prayer*, he commented that one can pray on

---

[52] Lewis, "Membership," in *Weight of Glory*, 166–7.
[53] Lewis, *Mere Christianity*, chapter 2 of Book IV.
[54] Lewis, *George MacDonald*, day 255.
[55] Ibid., day 203.
[56] Lewis, *Great Divorce*, 72.

"a back street where one can pace up and down."[57] MacDonald had written, "Never wait for fitter time or place to talk to Him. To wait till thou go to church or to thy closet is to make Him wait. He will listen as thou walkest."[58]

More important than where we pray, is "Whose prayer does God hear?" MacDonald believed that we did not have to have our theology exactly correct for God to hear us. "If our prayers were heard only in accordance with the idea of God to which we seem to ourselves to pray, how miserable would our infinite wants be met! But every honest cry, even if sent into the deaf ear of an idol, passes on to the ears of the unknown God, the heart of the unknown Father."[59] In a letter, Lewis affirmed and expanded on that thought, "I think that every prayer which is sincerely made even to a false god or to a v. imperfectly conceived true god, is accepted by the true God and that Christ saves many who do not think they know Him."[60]

Knowledge of good and evil

Lewis believed goodness understands evil but evil does not understand goodness. In *Mere Christianity* he wrote, "Good people know about both good and evil: bad people do not know about either."[61] MacDonald had written, "The darkness knows neither the light nor itself; only the light knows itself and the darkness also. None but God hates evil and understands it."[62] Lewis illustrated this idea in his fiction. For example, in *The Magician's Nephew*, Jadis attempts to get Digory to disobey Aslan but fails when she suggests that he has no responsibility for the welfare of Polly. The good boy recognizes that this suggestion is evil while the evil Jadis has no idea that goodness would not be tempted by it.[63]

Examples from George MacDonald's novels

Animals and the afterlife

There are many more examples of MacDonald's ideas in Lewis's writings. In fact, in reading either author one is constantly finding echoes of the

---

[57] C. S. Lewis, *Letters to Malcolm Chiefly on Prayer* (New York: Harcourt Brace & World, 1963), 17.
[58] Lewis, *George MacDonald*, day 237.
[59] Ibid., day 322.
[60] C. S. Lewis to Mrs Johnson, Nov. 8, 1952, *Collected Letters III*, 245.
[61] C. S. Lewis, *Mere Christianity* (New York: HarperCollins, 2001), 93.
[62] Lewis, *George MacDonald*, 364.
[63] C. S. Lewis, *The Magician's Nephew* (New York: HarperCollins, 2000), 177.

other. I will give just a few more examples. In his only pastorate, at Arundel, MacDonald got into trouble with some of his parishioners by preaching a sermon on the possibility of animals having an afterlife. In *There and Back*, he wrote, "she had a strong feeling . . . that animals went on living after death."[64] "She heartily believed the animals were partakers in the redemption of Jesus Christ."[65] In *The Problem of Pain*, Lewis also discusses the possibility that some animals may experience life after death. He whimsically suggests that a heaven for mosquitoes could be combined with a hell for humans. In the same chapter, Lewis suggests that some animals may not experience pain in the same way that we do. "Their nervous system delivers all the letters A, P, N, I, but since they cannot read they never build it up into the word PAIN. And all animals *may* be in that condition."[66] The March 28 entry of *Diary of an Old Soul* reads, "As our dear animals do suffer less / Because their pain spreads neither right nor left, / Lost in oblivion and foresightlessness."[67]

The effects of wickedness

In *Alec Forbes of Howglen*, MacDonald wrote, "all wickedness tends to destroy individuality."[68] In *Mere Christianity*, Lewis wrote, "How monotonously alike all the great tyrants and conquerors have been: how gloriously different are the saints."[69] In *Till We Have Faces*, Orual is not able to see Psyche's palace because of her spiritual blindness.[70] Lewis uses the same device with the dwarfs in *The Last Battle*.[71] The idea that one's spiritual condition could determine what one could see was also used by MacDonald in *The Princess and the Goblin*. When Irene took Curdie to see her grandmother, Curdie's spiritual condition kept him from seeing her.[72]

[64] George MacDonald, *There and Back* (London: Kegan Paul, Trench, Trubner, 1900–10), 143.
[65] Ibid., 347.
[66] Lewis, *The Problem of Pain* (New York: Macmillan, 19731), 26.
[67] George MacDonald, *The Diary of an Old Soul* (Minneapolis, MN: Augsburg, 1994), March 28.
[68] George MacDonald, *Alec Forbes of Howglen* (London: Hurst & Blackett, 1900), 315.
[69] Lewis, *Mere Christianity*, 226.
[70] Lewis, *Till We Have Faces*, chapter 10.
[71] Lewis, *The Last Battle* (New York: HarperCollins, 2000), 165.
[72] George MacDonald, "The Old Lady and Curdie," in *The Princess and the Goblin* (Elgin, IL: Chariot, 1979), 148–55.

Knowledge of God

Both men had something to say about understanding the nature of God even though He is so much beyond us. In one of Lewis's favorite MacDonald novels, *Wilfred Cumbermede,* is this conversation:

> "I am only insisting on the perfection of God—as far as I can understand perfection," I answered.
>
> "But may not the perfection of God be something very different from anything we can understand?"
>
> "I will go further," I returned. "It must be something that we cannot understand—but different from what we can understand by being greater, not by being less."
>
> "Mayn't it be such that we can't understand it at all?" she insisted.
>
> "Then how should we ever worship him ... Surely it is because you see God to be good—. ... However goodness may change its forms," I went on, "it must still be goodness; only if we are to adore it we must see something of what it is—of itself. And the goodness we cannot see, the eternal goodness, high above us as the heavens are above the Earth, must still be a goodness that includes, absorbs, elevates, purifies all our goodness not tramples upon it and calls it wickedness. For if not such, then we have nothing in common with God, and what we call goodness is not of God."[73]

In *The Problem of Pain*, Lewis wrote:

> On the one hand, if God is wiser than we His judgement must differ from ours on many things, and not least of all on good and evil ... On the other hand, if God's moral judgement differs from ours so that our "black" may be his "white," we can mean nothing by calling him good; for to say "God is good," while asserting that His goodness is wholly other than ours, is really only to say "God is we know not what." And an utterly unknown quality in God cannot give us moral grounds for loving or obeying Him ... The Divine "goodness" differs from ours, but is not sheerly different: it differs from ours, not as white from black but as a perfect circle from a child's first attempt to draw a wheel. But when the child has learned to draw, it will know that the circle it then makes is what it was trying to make from the very beginning.[74]

---

[73] George MacDonald, *Wilfred Cumbermede* (London: Strahan, 1873), 353–5.
[74] Lewis, *Problem of Pain*, 25–7.

Many more similarities between Lewis's and MacDonald's work could be given. However, as Rolland Hein has noted, "The largest single influence on [Lewis] was that of George MacDonald, whom he hailed as the 'greatest genius' in mythmaking that he knew. . . . His greatest fascination with MacDonald, however, was not directed towards the plots to his stories, but towards the 'souls' for his fantasies, that 'something inexpressible' which he identified as myth."[75]

Lewis gave MacDonald credit for one more change in his life. In *Surprised by Joy*, he says that in his younger days he was often told "take that look off your face." But he wrote that in his late teens, he was no longer told that. "I am inclined to think that my face had been altered. That 'look' which I had so often been told to 'take off it' had apparently taken itself off—perhaps when I read *Phantastes*."[76]

---

[75] Hein, *Christian Mythmakers*, 204.
[76] Lewis, *Surprised by Joy*, 188.

Appendix B

MacDonald books read by Lewis

Following is a list of 41 of MacDonald's books.

T   indicates that we have Lewis's testimony—in his diary, letters, or books—that he read them, or we know that he read them because they appear in his MacDonald anthology.

G   indicates works that were in Arthur Greeves' personal library, and therefore it is probable that Lewis read them.

L   indicates books that were in Lewis's personal library. He may well have read others besides those in this list. If I found evidence of when he first read them, I have included the date.

T, L	*Adela Cathcart*—1930
T	*Alec Forbes of Howglen*
T, L G	*Annals of a Quiet Neighborhood*
G	*Castle Warlock*
L	*David Elginbrod*
T, L	*Diary of an Old Soul*—1929
T	*The Disciple and Other Poems*
L	*Dish of Orts*
L	*Donal Grant*
L	*England's Antiphon*
G	*The Flight of the Shadow*
T	*The Giants Heart*—1930 or earlier
T	*The Golden Key*—1916
T	The preface to *Letters from Hell* by Thistead—1916
T, L	*The Light Princess*—1947 or earlier
T, L	*Lilith*—1926
L	*The Lost Princess*
T, L, G	*Malcolm*
L, G	*The Marquis of Lossie*
L	*Miracles of Our Lord*
L	*Parables and Ballads and Scotch Songs*
T, G	*Paul Faber, Surgeon*
T, L	*Phantastes*—1916
L	*Poetical Works*, Vols I & II
L	*The Portent and Other Stories*
T	*The Princess and Curdie*—1930 or earlier

T, L	*The Princess and the Goblin—1918*
L, G	*Robert Falconer*
G	*Salted With Fire*
T, L	*The Seaboard Parish—1930*
T	*The Shadows*
T, L	*Sir Gibbie—1930*
G	*St. George and St. Michael*
T, G, L	*Thomas Wingfold, Curate*
T, L	*Unspoken Sermons: Series I, II, and III*
T, L	*What's Mine's Mine—1930*
T, L	*Wilfred Cumbermede—1930*
T	*The Wise Woman*

Bibliography

Dearborn, Kerry. *Baptized Imagination: The Theology of George MacDonald.* Aldershot, England: Ashgate, 2006.

Downing, David C. *Into the Wardrobe.* San Francisco, CA: Jossey-Bass, 2005.

Green and Hooper. *C. S. Lewis: A Biography.* New York: Harcourt Brace Jovanovich, 1974.

Hearn, Michael Patrick. *The Victorian Fairy Tale Book.* New York: Pantheon Books, 1988.

Hein, Rolland. *Christian Mythmakers.* Chicago: Cornerstone Press Chicago, 1998.

—. *The Harmony Within: The Spiritual Vision of George MacDonald.* Grand Rapids, MI: Eerdmans, 1982.

Lewis, C. S. *All My Road Before Me.* New York: Harcourt Brace Jovanivich, 1991.

—. *The Collected Letters of C. S. Lewis: Volume I, Family Letters 1905–1931*, edited by Walter Hooper. New York: HarperCollins, 2004.

—. *The Collected Letters of C. S. Lewis: Volume II, Books Broadcasts, and the War 1931–1949*, edited by Walter Hooper: HarperCollins, 2004.

—. *The Collected Letters of C. S. Lewis, Volume III: Narnia, Cambridge, and Joy 1950–1963*, edited by Walter Hooper: HarperCollins, 2007.

—. *George MacDonald: An Anthology.* San Francisco: HarperCollins, 2001.

—. *The Great Divorce.* New York: Macmillan Paperbacks, 1963.

—. "Is Theology Poetry?" In *The Weight of Glory and Other Addresses*, with an introduction by Walter Hooper, 116–40. San Francisco: HarperCollins, 2001.

—. *Letters to Malcolm Chiefly on Prayer.* New York: Harvest Book Harcourt, 1992.

—. *The Magician's Nephew*, 191–5. New York: HarperCollins, 1992.

—. "Membership." In *The Weight of Glory and Other Addresses*, with an introduction by Walter Hooper, 158–76. San Francisco: HarperCollins, 2001.
—. *Mere Christianity*. San Francisco: HarperCollins, 2001.
—. *Miracles*. San Francisco: HarperCollins, 2001.
—. "On Forgiveness." In *The Weight of Glory and Other Addresses*, with an introduction by Walter Hooper, 177–83. San Francisco: HarperCollins, 2001.
—. *The Pilgrim's Regress*. London: Geoffrey Bles, 1943.
—. *The Problem of Pain*. New York: Macmillan, 1973.
—. *Surprised by Joy: The Shape of My Early Life*. New York: Harcourt Brace & World, 1955.
—. *Till We Have Faces*. New York: Harcourt Brace, 1984.
—. *The Voyage of the "Dawn Treader."* New York: HarperCollins, 1980.
—. "The Weight of Glory." In *The Weight of Glory and Other Addresses*, with an introduction by Walter Hooper, 25–46. San Francisco: HarperCollins, 2001.
MacDonald, George. *The Diary of an Old Soul*. Minneapolis, MN: Augsburg, 1994.
—. *The Princess and the Goblin*. Elgin, IL: Chariot, 1979.

The following books are by George and Grenville MacDonald and are from the editions used in the Johannesen reprints [Johannesen, P.O. Box 24, Whitethorn, CA 95589]
MacDonald, George. *Alec Forbes*. London: Hurst & Blackett, 1900.
—. "The Golden Key." In *The Light Princess and Other Fairy Tales*, 172–215. New York: G. P. Putnam's Sons. 1893.
—. *Phantastes*. London: Arthur C. Fifield, 1905.
—. *Robert Falconer*. London: Hurst & Blackett, 1880.
—. *A Rough Shaking*. London: Blackie & Son, 1900.
—. "A Sketch of Individual Development." In *Dish of Orts*, 43–76. London: Sampson Low, Marston, 1895.
—. *There and Back*. London: Kegan Paul, Trench, Trübner, 1890–1910.
—. *Unspoken Sermons: Series I, II, and III*. London: Alexander Strahan, 1867.
—. *Unspoken Sermons: Series II*. London: Longmans, Green, 1886.
—. *Unspoken Sermons: Series III*. London: Longmans, Green, 1889.
—. *Wilford Cumbermede*. London: Strahan, 1873.
MacDonald, Greville. *George MacDonald and His Wife*. London: George Allen & Unwin, 1924.
Riga, Frank. "The Platonic Image of George MacDonald on C. S. Lewis." In *For the Childlike*, edited by Roderick McGillis, 111–32. London: Scarecrow Press, 1992.

Suggestions for further reading

Bruce, Sylvia. "Entering the Vision: A Novelist's View of *Phantastes*." *VII: An Anglo-American Literary Review* 9 (1988): 19–28.
  Sylvia Bruce gives a novelist's insights.

Lewis, C. S. *All My Road Before Me: The Diaries of C. S. Lewis*, edited by Walter Hooper. New York: Harcourt Brace Jovanovich, 1991.
   This diary written between 1922 and 1927 gives Lewis's views about *Phantastes* before he became a Christian.

—. *The Collected Letters of C. S. Lewis, Vol. I: Family Letters 1905–1931*, edited by Walter Hooper. New York: HarperCollins, 2004.

—. Ibid. *Vol. II: Books, Broadcasts, and the War 1931–1949*. 2004.

—. Ibid. *Vol. III: Narnia, Cambridge, and Joy 1950–1963*. 2007.
   There are many references to *Phantastes* and MacDonald in these letters. The index enables one to find them readily.

—. *Surprised by Joy: The Shape of My Early Life*. New York: Harcourt, Brace & World, 1955.
   This spiritual autobiography gives Lewis's testimony to the importance of its influence on his life and work in the context of other influences.

MacDonald, George. *George MacDonald: An Anthology.*
   Edited with a preface by C. S. Lewis. New York: Macmillan, 1947. In the preface, Lewis describes how MacDonald influenced him.

—. *Phantastes*. Grand Rapids, MI: Eerdmans, 1986.
   This edition of *Phantastes* has an introduction by C. S. Lewis.

Manlove, Colin. "Parent or Associate? George MacDonald and the Inklings." In *George MacDonald: Literary Heritage and Heirs,* edited by Roderick McGillis, 227–38. Wayne, PA: Zossima, 2008.
   Manlove gives a different perspective on the influence of *Phantastes* on Lewis and argues that *Phantastes* had a greater literary effect on Tolkien than on Lewis.

Suton, Max Keith. "The Psychology of the Self in MacDonald's *Phantastes.*" *VII: An Anglo-American Literary Review* 5 (1984): 9–25.
   Sutton gives a critique of the Wolff book listed below.

Tixier, Elaine. "Imagination Baptized, or 'Holiness' in the Chronicles of Narnia." In *The Longing for a Form: Essays on the Fiction of C. S. Lewis,* edited by Peter J. Schakel, 136–58. Grand Rapids, MI: Baker Book House, 1977.
   Tixier analyzes the influence of the holiness and longing in *Phantastes* on the *Chronicles of Narnia*.

Wolff, Robert Lee. *The Golden Key: A Study of the Fiction of George MacDonald*. New Haven, CN: Yale University Press, 1961.
   There is a lengthy chapter on *Phantastes*. Lewis referred to this book as "a ghastly psychological study."

2

G. K. Chesterton, *The Everlasting Man*

Donald T. Williams

> *I find it fairly easy to bracket these two men* [Chesterton and Lewis] *together . . . as massively wise people with various touches of lunacy.*[1]
>
> *What drew their audiences was the way they saluted something in the nature of things.*[2]
>
> *"Strange, gentlemen," he said as they hurried out into the garden, "that I should have hunted mysteries all over the earth, and now comes one and settles in my own back yard."*[3]
>
> *A window in Merton's mind let in that strange light of surprise in which we see for the first time things we have known all along.*[4]

Clearly no writer had a bigger impact on C. S. Lewis than George MacDonald; Lewis refers to him often simply as "my master,"[5] and the role he plays in a book like *The Great Divorce* should be alone sufficient to justify that title. It would, however, be hard to find a single book that had a more significant influence on Lewis's life and thought than G. K. Chesterton's *The Everlasting Man*. Lewis would come to own in his personal library more books by Chesterton than any other writer except MacDonald;[6] and MacDonald and Chesterton are listed first and second in Lewis's list for *The Christian Century* of ten influential books that had most influenced

---

[1] Christopher Derrick, "Some Personal Angles on Lewis and Chesterton," in *The Riddle of Joy: G. K. Chesterton and C. S. Lewis*, ed. Michael H. MacDonald and Andrew A. Tadie (Grand Rapids, MI: Eerdmans, 1989), 11.
[2] Janet Lumberg Knedlik, in the Foreword to *The Riddle of Joy: G. K. Chesterton and C. S. Lewis*, ed. Michael H. MacDonald and Andrew A. Tadie (Grand Rapids, MI: Eerdmans, 1989), xiii.
[3] G. K. Chesterton, *The Father Brown Omnibus* (New York: Dodd, Mead, 1982), 29.
[4] Ibid., 215.
[5] C. S. Lewis, ed., *George MacDonald: An Anthology* (New York: HarperCollins, 2001), xxxvii.
[6] Iain Benson, "G. K. Chesterton (1874–1936)," in *The C. S. Lewis Readers' Encyclopedia*, ed. Jeffrey D. Schultz and John G. West Jr (Grand Rapids, MI: Zondervan, 1998), 113.

his vocational attitude and philosophy of life.[7] They are clearly not in chronological order; order of importance, perhaps? It would make sense if it were so.[8] When asked in the last year of his life for the *Christian* writers who had helped him most, Lewis named four: Chesterton, Edwyn Bevan, Rudolf Otto, and Dorothy L. Sayers[9] (Curiously, Chesterton made the list while MacDonald did not.) Furthermore, Chesterton, like Lewis, was profoundly influenced by MacDonald, and in similar ways. Chesterton wrote of reading *The Princess and the Goblin* as a boy that it made "a difference to my whole existence, which helped me to see things in a certain way from the start." He continued, "Since I first read that story some five alternative philosophies of the universe have come to our colleges out of Germany, blowing through the world like the east wind. But for me that castle is still standing in the mountains; its light is not put out."[10]

Lewis wrote to Charles Williams on March 11, 1936, that "A book sometimes crosses one's path which is so like the sound of one's native language in a strange country that it feels almost uncivil not to wave some kind of flag in answer."[11] Lewis had written to tell Williams that his *The Place of the Lion* was such a book. He compares finding it to his discovery of MacDonald, Chesterton, or Morris.[12] The comparison tells us two things: that Chesterton was important enough to be mentioned in the same breath with MacDonald, and that Lewis found in him a kindred spirit. They were so kindred in fact that Humphrey Carpenter could easily refer to "the breezy outdoor Chestertonian Christianity of Lewis"[13] and use Chesterton eponymously as one of his "four aspects of [Lewis's] mind and work": "the 'Chestertonian,' the 'boyish,' the 'debater,' and the 'poet.'"[14]

---

[7] C. S. Lewis, "Ex Libris," *The Christian Century* 79 (June 6, 1962): 719.
[8] Colin Duriez, "In the Library: Composition and Context," in *Reading the Classics with C. S. Lewis*, ed. Thomas L. Martin (Grand Rapids, MI: Baker, 2000), 356f.
[9] Diana Pavlac Glyer, *The Company They Keep: C. S. Lewis and J. R. R. Tolkien as Writers in Community* (Kent, OH: Kent State University Press, 2007), 23, n. 21.
[10] Qtd. in Michael Coren, *Gilbert: The Man Who Was G. K. Chesterton* (New York: Paragon House, 1990), 20.
[11] C. S. Lewis to Charles Williams, March 11, 1936, in *The Collected Letters of C. S. Lewis, Vol. II: Books, Broadcasts, and the War 1931–1949*, ed. Walter Hooper (New York: HarperCollins 2004), 1936. Lewis wrote "ones" in the original.
[12] Ibid., 183; cf. 703.
[13] Humphrey Carpenter, *The Inklings: C. S. Lewis, J. R. R. Tolkien, Charles Williams, and their friends* (Boston, MA: Houghton Mifflin, 1979), 155.
[14] Ibid., 217.

Lewis and Chesterton: Discovery

Lewis first read Chesterton's essays when he was in hospital recovering from trench fever in World War I. This was at the height of his atheist period, when he cared only for the gods and heroes and believed in "nothing but atoms and evolution and military service."[15] Atoms ... military service: one notes the cynicism as well as the skepticism of that pairing, and thinks that no mentality could have been less open to Chesterton's way of seeing the world. Indeed, "It might have been expected," Lewis explains in his autobiography, "that my pessimism, my atheism, and my hatred of sentiment would have made [Chesterton] to me the least congenial of all authors." From this perspective it would be hard indeed to imagine anything the two men could have had in common. Yet, Lewis goes on, "It would almost seem that Providence ... quite overrules our previous tastes when it decides to bring two minds together."[16]

In hindsight, it is not hard to see Providence at work. It would take a lot of reading, thinking, and interaction with Christian friends to bring Lewis to full conversion to Christ a decade and a half later. Reading was an important factor in the process. Lewis explains, "In reading Chesterton, as in reading MacDonald [There's that pairing again!], I did not know what I was letting myself in for. A young man who wishes to remain a sound Atheist cannot be too careful of his reading."[17] The dangerous element in Chesterton that undermined Lewis's unbelief was not, initially, Chesterton's wit or his arguments (though they would eventually have their effect), but something even more profoundly subversive: "I liked him for his goodness."[18] Despite his own cynicism at the time, something in Lewis could appreciate goodness, even if he was not (yet) personally in pursuit of it.[19] Chesterton and MacDonald are associated once again, and not by accident. The quality that had attracted Lewis to MacDonald was, as he would realize later, holiness.[20] Goodness; holiness: when sound arguments have qualities like that as their heralds, they may indeed find the kind of welcome that Lewis would eventually give them.

---

[15] C. S. Lewis, *Surprised by Joy: The Shape of My Early Life* (New York: Harcourt, Brace & World, 1955), 174.
[16] Ibid., 190.
[17] Ibid., 191.
[18] Ibid.
[19] For a full discussion of Lewis's philosophy of goodness, related to beauty and truth, see Williams, *Reflections*, 131–50.
[20] Lewis, *Surprised by Joy*, 179.

There followed a period in which the wit, the arguments, and the goodness had to coexist uneasily with Lewis's prejudices against orthodox Christianity.[21] Once again Chesterton is linked with MacDonald as Lewis describes his mindset during those years. "George MacDonald had done more to me than any other writer; of course it was a pity he had that bee in his bonnet about Christianity.... Chesterton had more sense than all the other moderns put together; bating, of course, his Christianity."[22] The first mention of *The Everlasting Man* in Lewis's autobiography gives it a significant role in preparing the young atheist for that fateful evening on Addison's Walk with J. R. R. Tolkien and Hugo Dyson in 1931, which would lead to Lewis's conversion:

> Then I read Chesterton's *Everlasting Man* and for the first time saw the whole Christian outline of history set out in a form that seemed to me to make sense. Somehow I contrived not to be too badly shaken. You will remember that I already thought Chesterton the most sensible man alive "apart from his Christianity." [23]

Impact

How did *The Everlasting Man* prepare Lewis for the conversation with Tolkien and Dyson on Addison's Walk? The skeptical Lewis had that evening foolishly described myth and fairy tale as "lies breathed through silver,"[24] provoking from Tolkien the response that was later summarized in poetic form in the piece that became part of the essay "On Fairie Stories."

> *"Dear Sir,"* I said—*"Although now long estranged*
> *Man is not wholly lost nor wholly changed.*
> *Dis-graced he may be, yet is not dethroned,*
> *and keeps the rags of lordship once he owned:*
> *Man, Sub-creator, the refracted Light*
> *through whom is splintered from a single White*

---

[21] For a good summary of the process that led to Lewis's conversion and Chesterton's role in it, see Kilby, *The Christian World of C. S. Lewis*, 17–20.
[22] Lewis, *Surprised by Joy*, 213, "bating" that is, excepting.
[23] Lewis, *Surprised by Joy*, 223.
[24] J. R. R. Tolkien, "On Fairie Stories," in *The Tolkien Reader: Stories, Poems and Commentary by the Author of "The Hobbit" and "The Lord of the Rings"* (New York: Ballantine, 1966), 54. See also Humphrey Carpenter, *The Authorized Biography of Tolkien: The Creator of The Hobbit, The Lord of the Rings and the Silmarillion* (Boston, MA: Houghton Mifflin, 1977), 163.

> *to many hues, and endlessly combined*
> *in living shapes that move from mind to mind.*
> *Though all the crannies of the world we filled*
> *with Elves and Goblins, though we dared to build*
> *Gods and their houses out of dark and light,*
> *and sowed the seed of dragons—'twas our right*
> *(used or misused). That right has not decayed:*
> *we make still by the law in which we're made.*"[25]

Tolkien's full response elaborated what he would later in that essay call the doctrine of sub-creation: Human beings are creative because we are created in the image of the Creator; we make (stories, among other things) because we are made in the image of the Maker whose creation is the Story we call the history of the universe. In other words, myth and its power can only be fully understood in the light of the Christian doctrine of the *imago Dei*, which explains what myth is, why it is, and why describing it simply as lies is just too simple: "(used or misused). That right has not decayed: / we make still by the law in which we're made."

Well, Lewis had already encountered in Chesterton the idea that Christianity is "that pure and original truth that was behind all mythologies like the sky behind the clouds."[26] In addition there was Chesterton's connection of "the philosophy of stories" with man's uniqueness: He is "a creator as well as a creature."[27] Thus, "Man is not merely an evolution but a revolution."[28] And this, as Chesterton explained, is why human stories, as reflections of The Human Story, are so unlike the apocryphal "history of cows in twelve volumes" which "would not be very lively reading."[29]

So then, Tolkien and Dyson did not have to start from scratch. They were watering a seed that Chesterton had already planted when they told Lewis that, as he summarized the conversation to his friend Arthur Greeves, "The story of Christ is simply a true myth: a myth working on us in the same way as the others, but with this tremendous difference that *it really happened.*" That explained why Lewis loved the great myths and fairy stories even without believing in them and why he loved the idea of sacrifice, especially a god sacrificing himself to himself, when he met it in other myths: they were adumbrations of the truth, "God expressing Himself through the

---

[25] Ibid.
[26] G. K. Chesterton, *The Everlasting Man* (New York: Ballantine, 1977), 258.
[27] Ibid., 18.
[28] Ibid., 8.
[29] Ibid., 158.

minds of the poets, using such images as He found there, while Christianity is God expressing Himself through what we call 'real things'."[30] And they were watering another Chestertonian seed when they told Lewis that the significance of myth flows from human nature as made in the image of the Maker. Both ideas were already there in *The Everlasting Man*, which had already shown Lewis the Christian outline of history in a way that made sense. And the connections between the two ideas were there too, waiting for Tolkien and Dyson at the right moment to pull them together.

The truth that lies behind all the great myths like the sky behind the clouds; the true myth that works on us like all the others but unlike them really happened: these ideas came together on Addison's Walk on September 19, 1931, and, as a result, on September 28 Lewis realized that he had finally come to believe that Christ was the Son of God while riding in Warnie's side-car on the way to the Whipsnade Zoo. It is easy to see then why in the reading that led to Lewis's conversion Chesterton ranks second only to MacDonald and no book ranks higher than *The Everlasting Man*. It had "illuminated what Lewis already knew to be true and pulled all the previously disjointed pieces into a harmonious vision of reality."[31] It had prepared him to be able to understand and accept from Tolkien and Dyson the argument that was the tipping point in his journey to theism and Christian faith, and became central to his thinking from then on.[32] For the rest of his life Lewis would recommend *The Everlasting Man* to anyone asking him for books along the same lines as his own popular expositions of and apologies for Christian faith.

Recommendation

A survey of those recommendations in Lewis's letters is instructive. Explaining his own experience in reading the Gospels, he wrote to Mary Neylan on March 26, 1940, "The first real work of the Gospels on a fresh

---

[30] C. S. Lewis to Arthur Greeves, Oct. 18, 1931, in *The Collected Letters of C. S. Lewis, Vol. I: Family Letters 1905–1931*, ed. Walter Hooper (New York: HarperCollins 2004), 977; cf. George Sayer, *Jack: A Life of C. S. Lewis* (Wheaton, IL: Crossway, 1994), 225–7; Walter Lancelyn Green and Walter Hooper, *C. S. Lewis: A Biography* (New York: Harcourt Brace Jovanovich, 1974), 116–18.

[31] Scott R. Burson and Jerry L. Walls, *C. S. Lewis and Francis Schaeffer: Lessons for a New Century from the Most Influential Apologists of Our Time* (Downers Grove, IL: InterVarsity, 1998), 162.

[32] See, for example, C. S. Lewis, "Myth Became Fact," in *God in the Dock: Essays on Theology and Ethics*, ed. Walter Hooper (Grand Rapids, MI: Eerdmans, 1970), 63–7, which is Lewis's way of saying the things he learned from Chesterton and Tolkien.

reader is and ought to be, to raise v. acutely the question, 'Who—or What—is This?'" He then goes on to recommend *The Everlasting Man* as a book to read on "this whole aspect of the subject."[33] Writing to Rhona Bodle on December 31, 1947, Lewis calls *The Everlasting Man* "the v. best popular defence of the full Christian position" on Christ's divinity.[34] Two years later, he recommends the book to her again.[35] Writing to Sheldon Vanauken on December 14, 1950, Lewis calls *The Everlasting Man* "[t]he best popular apologetic I know."[36] Just a few days later he writes Vanauken again: "The case for Xtianity in general is well given by Chesterton: and I tried to do something in my *Broadcast Talks*."[37] So in Lewis's own mind, *Mere Christianity* is the fruit that grew from the seeds Chesterton had planted and Tolkien had watered.

Mary Van Deusen asked for other religious works that could supplement Lewis's. He responded on June 11, 1951, that lots of them could supplement and correct his own writings, including works by à Kempis, Bunyan, and Chesterton.[38] On October 5, 1955, Lewis wrote to Janet Wise that he had not found most modern theology helpful, but *The Everlasting Man* "did a great deal for me."[39] And finally he wrote to Margaret Gray on May 9, 1961, that "For a good popular defence of our position against modern waffle" there is "nothing better" than *The Everlasting Man*.[40]

In summary, from the time Lewis became a public figure known for his defense of the Christian faith right up to the end of his life, his consistent response to people asking for recommendations of more books of popular Christian apologetics that could help them as his own books had was to refer them to *The Everlasting Man*. He considered it the best general defense of the Christian faith on the market, especially of the deity of Christ, and he looked at his own work, particularly the Broadcast Talks that became *Mere Christianity*, as basically attempts to supplement it. We need not accept as final Lewis's self-deprecating evaluation of his own apologetic works to realize that he held Chesterton's book in great esteem. We have seen personal reasons for this evaluation in Lewis's own life. Let us see if the book itself still merits the position Lewis gave it.

---

[33] C. S. Lewis to Mary Neylan, March 26, 1940, *Collected Letters II*, 375.
[34] C. S. Lewis to Rhona Bodle, Dec. 1947, ibid., 823.
[35] April 28, 1949, ibid., 941.
[36] C. S. Lewis to Sheldon Vanauken, Dec. 14, 1950, in *The Collected Letters of C. S. Lewis, Vol. III: Narnia, Cambridge, and Joy 1950–1963*, ed. Walter Hooper (New York: HarperCollins 2004), 72.
[37] Ibid., Dec. 22, 1950, 75.
[38] C. S. Lewis to Mary Van Deusen, June 11, 1951, ibid., 126.
[39] C. S. Lewis to Janet Wise, Oct. 5, 1955, ibid., 652.
[40] C. S. Lewis to Margaret Gray, May 9, 1961, ibid., 1264.

The Everlasting Man

The Everlasting Man is a book that has transcended the original circumstances of its writing to become an unexpected classic. It was published in 1925 as an answer to the optimistic evolutionism of H. G. Wells's view of history in his *The Outline of History*, with its view of the inevitable progress of humanity from the prebiotic slime to Modern Man, who is destined to bring in the Millennium through enlightened scientific reason.[41] Chesterton's book was not well received at first. Nevertheless, the catholicity (small *c* here) of Chesterton's vision was such that one need not know anything about Wells or his book to appreciate Chesterton's response. Indeed, the influence of the former book has receded while the latter is still being read with profit and pleasure, and not just by Lewisians.

The everlasting man of the title is Christ, seen not only as the Son of God but as the template for true humanity: "I maintain that when brought out into the daylight these two things look altogether strange and unique. ... The first of these things is the creature called man and the second is the man called Christ."[42] Chesterton sees both man and Christ as astonishing anomalies when looked at through the lens of modern secular assumptions, anomalies which in fact have the effect of shattering those modern assumptions when they are brought into contact with the iconoclastic reality of Christ, and even man.

Chesterton attempts to adjust our vision, starting with man, by ironically taking the assumptions of the secular evolutionist more seriously than the evolutionist takes them himself, particularly the assumption that man is simply one among the animals, differing from the other ones only in degree, not in kind: "It is exactly when we do regard man as an animal that we know he is not an animal."[43] How does this conclusion follow? It hits us when we realize that the very analogies between human behavior and that of the other animals, often alleged as proof of their shared nature, actually bring into sharp relief the huge gap between them. Men build houses, birds build nests; but a bird that built as man builds, with infinite variety and creativity

---

[41] Alzina Stone Dale, *The Outline of Sanity: A Life of G. K. Chesterton* (Grand Rapids, MI: Eerdmans, 1982), 248f. See also Coren, *Gilbert*, 236–7.

[42] Chesterton, *Everlasting Man*, xvii. For a fuller summary and analysis see Williams, *Mere Humanity: G. K. Chesterton, C. S. Lewis, and J. R. R. Tolkien on the Human Condition* (Nashville: Broadman & Homan, 2006), 13–24. For a good summary of Chesterton's theses supplemented from his other writings, see Michael D. Aeschliman, *The Restitution of Man: C. S. Lewis and the Case Against Scientism* (Grand Rapids, MI: Eerdmans, 1998), 38–45.

[43] Chesterton, *Everlasting Man*, xxii.

going beyond anything demanded by utility or survival, would be "a fearful wildfowl indeed."[44] Between man and the other animals then there is a gap which naturalistic evolution by itself could not have bridged. "This creature was truly different from all other creatures; because he was a creator as well as a creature."[45] Only our being created in the image of the Creator can really explain who we are.

This high view of human nature, then reaches its highest perfection in Christ, who is shown to be both fully human and fully divine in an argument that foreshadows Lewis's famous "trilemma" from *Mere Christianity*.[46] Jesus could not have made the precise kinds of claims he made and be a good moral teacher unless those claims were themselves valid; we cannot think of Jesus as a madman or as evil; therefore we must accept the claims. The arguments are sound and the prose sparkles with Chesterton's characteristic wordplay, but the most valuable thing about the book may be the way in which it enables even those not yet fully convinced to look at the world with fresh eyes—an effect it certainly had on C. S. Lewis.

Influence

A number of moments in Chesterton's book resonate with themes throughout the Lewis *corpus*. It is of course impossible to establish whether they were "sources" of those places in Lewis. Lewis encountered these ideas in many forms, in many places, and at many times, and thus we cannot know in any given instance whether *The Everlasting Man* is the reason we find them in Lewis. We should heed Lewis's own warning in "Modern Theology and Biblical Criticism":

> What forearms me against all these Reconstructions is the fact that I have seen it all from the other end of the stick. I have watched

---

[44] Ibid., 22.
[45] Ibid., 18.
[46] Ibid., 55–6. See Donald T. Williams, "Identity Check, Are C. S. Lewis's Critics Right, or Is His 'Trilemma' Valid?" *Touchstone: A Journal of Mere Christianity* 23:3 (May–June 2010): 25–9; Williams, "Lacking, Ludicrous, or Logical?" *Midwestern Journal of Theology* 11:1 (Spring 2012): 91–102; and Donald T. Williams, *Reflections from Plato's Cave: Essays in Evangelical Philosophy* (Lynchburg: Lantern Hollow, 2012), 65–80, for a full evaluation of the trilemma argument; cf. also Scott R. Burson, and Jerry L. Walls, *C. S. Lewis and Francis Schaeffer: Lessons for a New Century from the Most Influential Apologists of Our Time* (Downers Grove, IL: InterVarsity, 1998), 176–8; and Douglas Groothuis, *Christian Apologetics: A Comprehensive Case for Biblical Faith* (Downers Grove, IL: InterVarsity, 2011), 490–3.

reviewers reconstructing the genesis of my own books in just this way. My impression is that in the whole of my experience not one of these guesses has on any one point been right; that the method shows a record of 100 per cent failure.[47]

If we do not wish to join this parade of critical failure, we had better not make the same kinds of assumptions. What then can we say of the relation between *The Everlasting Man* and Lewis's writings? A source, possibly; an influence, definitely, by Lewis's own testimony, is what we can with confidence conclude. For the many parallels do give testimony to a basic harmony of mind on the great Questions that reinforces our estimate of how important a general influence Chesterton was—as important as Lewis himself often testified.

Chesterton says, for example, "I do not believe in being dehumanized in order to study humanity."[48] One thinks of William Hingest (Bill the Blizzard) in *That Hideous Strength*: "I happen to believe that you can't study men; you can only get to know them."[49] Mark Studdock's soulless sociological studies of the village workers undertaken on behalf of the N.I.C.E. fulfill Hingest's prophecy and give meaning to the concept of "men without chests" from *The Abolition of Man*.[50] Chesterton and Lewis share the belief that a secularist scientism can only study humanity by removing Man himself from the equation.[51]

The dehumanizing influence of secular thought is pervasive and touches all fields, literature and religion not least. "The whole trouble," says Chesterton, "comes from a man trying to look at these stories [myths] *from the outside*, as if they were scientific objects."[52] The Lewis of "Meditation in a Toolshed" would have agreed. He wanted to look along as well as at the beam. And when Lewis made his "argument from reason" in *Miracles* and elsewhere (e.g. "*De Futilitate*") that materialism unwittingly eliminates from its view of the world the very reason that concluded that materialism was true, he might well have been echoing Chesterton's view that "There is in this materialism a mad indifference

---

[47] C. S. Lewis, "Modern Theology and Biblical Criticism," in *Christian Reflections*, ed. Walter Hooper (Grand Rapids, MI: Eerdmans, 1967), 159–60.
[48] Chesterton, *Everlasting Man*, 1.
[49] C. S. Lewis, *That Hideous Strength* (New York: Scribner, 1966), 71.
[50] C. S. Lewis, *The Abolition of Man* (New York: MacMillan, 1947), 34–5.
[51] See Aeschliman, *Restitution*, for a full treatment of this idea.
[52] Chesterton, *Everlasting Man*, 112 (emphasis added).

to real thought. By disbelieving in the soul, it comes to disbelieving in the mind."[53]

Other connections are not so direct, but do seem to be more than just mere verbal resemblances. Chesterton writes, "Despair does not lie in being weary of suffering, but in being weary of joy. It is when for some reason or other the good things in a society no long work that the society begins to decline; when its food does not feed, when its cures do not cure, when its blessings refuse to bless."[54] One thinks immediately of the title of Lewis's autobiography, then remembers that the phrase "surprised by joy" came (directly) from Wordsworth,[55] and then thinks again of the larger role that the concept of joy plays in Lewis's work and wonders if Chesterton might not be relevant after all. It was to a Greek poet, not to Chesterton, that Lewis attributes the question, "If water sticks in your throat, what will you take to wash it down?"[56] Lewis, the Greek poet, and Chesterton might all have been reading off the same page. Chesterton and Lewis both saw that, ironically, the call of "Joy" from beyond does not cheapen but rather enchants the merely earthly, so that without it food indeed ceases to feed or water to wash our meals down. For both writers, the ultimate end of secularism is despair.

Chesterton's central purpose in *The Everlasting Man* was to defend the humanity of man by defending the deity of Christ. Lewis's more famous argument for the deity of Christ, often called the "trilemma" (not Lewis's word) or "Lord/Liar/Lunatic" (not Lewis's phrase), is a succinct summary of an argument Chesterton had already made more fully. You cannot be a good man and (falsely) claim that you are God; you would have to be a liar or insane. And since Jesus was clearly neither a liar nor a lunatic, we must accept Him as the Son of God. Here is Lewis's paragraph from *Mere Christianity*:

> A man who was merely a man and said the sort of things Jesus said would not be a great moral teacher. He would either be a lunatic—on the level with the man who says he is a poached egg—or else he would be the Devil of Hell. You must make your choice. Either this man was, and is, the Son of God: or else a madman or something worse. You can shut Him up for a fool, you can spit at Him and kill

---

[53] Chesterton, *Everlasting Man*, 174. See Victor Reppert, *C. S. Lewis's Dangerous Idea: A Defense of the Argument from Reason* (Downers Grove, IL: InterVarsity), 2003 for a good evaluation of the argument from reason.
[54] Ibid., 181.
[55] Wordsworth's poem "Surprised by Joy – Impatient as the Wind."
[56] C. S. Lewis, *Miracles: A Preliminary Study* (New York: MacMillan, 1947), 65.

Him as a demon; or you can fall at His feet and call Him Lord and God. But let us not come with any patronizing nonsense about His being a great human teacher. He has not left that open to us. He did not intend to.[57]

Chesterton's fuller development actually anticipates some of the challenges that have been made to Lewis's better known version of the argument. Is it possible, for example, that Jesus's claims have been exaggerated or misinterpreted? "Mahomedans did not misunderstand Mahomet and suppose he was Allah. Jews did not misunderstand Moses and identify him with Jehovah." "Why," Chesterton asks, "was this claim alone exaggerated unless this alone was made?"[58] Given that the claim was made, Chesterton draws the same conclusion that Lewis would later: A good and sane man, one of the best and sanest, universally recognized as a Great Moral Teacher and Example, could not make such a claim unless it were true. "Normally speaking," Chesterton explains, "the greater a man is, the less likely he is to make the very greatest claim. Outside the unique case we are considering, the only kind of man who ever does make that kind of claim is a very small man: a secretive or self-centered monomaniac."[59] Every other conclusion except that of acknowledging those claims to deity to be true is really unthinkable:

> No modern critic in his five wits thinks that the preacher of the Sermon on the Mount was a horrible half-witted imbecile that might be scrawling stars on the walls of his cell. No atheist or blasphemer believes that the author of the Parable of the Prodigal Son was a monster with one mad idea like a cyclops with one eye.... Yet by all analogy we have really to put him there or else in the highest place of all.[60]

The highest place was the one that Lewis gave Jesus—as Chesterton had taught him.[61]

---

[57] C. S. Lewis, *Mere Christianity* (New York: MacMillan, 1943), 56.
[58] Chesterton, *Everlasting Man*, 246.
[59] Ibid., 247.
[60] Ibid., 248.
[61] See Donald T. Williams, "Identity Check: Are C. S. Lewis's Critics Right, or Is His 'Trilemma' Valid?" *Touchstone: A Journal of Mere Christianity* 23:3 (May–June 2010): 25–9; "Lacking, Ludicrous, or Logical? The Validity of Lewis's 'Trilemma,'" *Midwestern Journal of Theology* 11:1 (Spring 2012): 91–102; and *Reflections from Plato's Cave: Essays in Evangelical Philosophy* (Lynchburg, VA: Lantern Hollow, 2012), 65–80, for a full evaluation of the trilemma argument.

Coming home

The Everlasting Man was then possibly a source for many of Lewis's most characteristic ideas, definitely an influence on his conversion and a stimulus to his own writing, and clearly a book in which Lewis found words from a kindred mind. The place where that kinship appears most profoundly might be in Chesterton's use of the metaphor of home. Owen Barfield may have been the first to notice this connection. Lewis wrote to Arthur Greeves on October 17, 1929, that Barfield

> thought the idea of the spiritual world as *home*—the discovery of homeliness in that wh. is otherwise so remote—the feeling that you are coming *back* tho' to a place you have never yet reached—was peculiar to the British, and thought that MacDonald, Chesterton, and I had this more than anyone else.[62]

Here is Chesterton's way of using that metaphor in *The Everlasting Man*: "There are two ways of getting home; and one of them is to stay there. The other is to walk round the whole world till we come back to the same place."[63] He asks us to imagine

> some boy whose farm or cottage stood on such a slope, and who went on his travels to find something, such as the effigy and grave of some giant; and when he was far enough from home he looked back and saw that his own farm and kitchen garden, shining flat on the hill-side like the colours and quarterings of a shield, were but parts of some such gigantic figure, on which he had always lived, but which was too large and close to be seen.[64]

The same idea occurs in Chesterton's other apologetic masterpiece, *Orthodoxy*, which Lewis also loved. Chesterton asks, "How can we contrive to be at once astonished at the world and at home in it?"[65] Most of us can only do so by going around the world so that we can finally come home again.

That Lewis found this motif to be a profound way of understanding his own spiritual pilgrimage is suggested by the way in which it forms

---

[62] C. S. Lewis to Arthur Greeves, Oct. 17, 1929, *Collected Letters I, Family Letters*, 836.
[63] G. K. Chesterton, *Everlasting Man*, xi.
[64] Ibid.
[65] Chesterton, *Orthodoxy* (Garden City, NY: Doubleday, 1957), 11.

a set of bookends to his own career as a Christian writer. His earliest piece of Christian fiction, the somewhat autobiographical *The Pilgrim's Regress*, is practically a novelization of Chesterton's description. John flees the Landlord's Mountains and crosses the whole world in search of his Island, only to discover that the Mountains *are* the Island. He could never have realized that they were the object of his Desire without that journey, and now he must retrace his steps, circumnavigating the world twice, as it were, to come back to the place he had left and find it for the first time to be the home for which he had always yearned. As his Guide explains, "Who knows what you would have reached if you had crossed the brook without ever leaving home? You may be sure that the Landlord has brought you the shortest way: though I confess it would look an odd journey on a map."[66]

Then at the other end of Lewis's career we have The Chronicles of Narnia, which take Chesterton's motif and intensify it, if it were possible. Children from earth go not just around the world but to other worlds altogether, for adventures that ultimately teach them how to relate to their own world properly by finding Aslan there by his "other name."[67] And the theme comes to its climax in the very last book when we discover that Aslan's Country is the true home of us all.

> It was the Unicorn who summed up what everyone was feeling. He stamped his right fore-hoof on the ground and neighed, and then cried: "I have come home at last! This is my real country! This is the land I have been looking for all my life, though I never knew it till now. The reason that we loved the old Narnia is that it sometimes looked a little like this. Bree-hee-hee! Come further up, come further in!"[68]

Conclusion

The Everlasting Man is a great book in its own right, for many reasons that we have seen. It is a profound refutation of reductionism that gives us a rich portrait of human nature, fully realized only when we see it fulfilled in Christ. It highlights the uniqueness of human beings by taking more seriously than the reductionists themselves the premises of those who

---

[66] C. S. Lewis, *The Pilgrim's Regress: An Allegorical Apology for Christianity Reason and Romanticism* (Grand Rapids, MI: Eerdmans, 1958), 173.
[67] C. S. Lewis, *The Voyage of the "Dawn Treader"* (New York: Harper Trophy, 1994), 270.
[68] C. S. Lewis, *The Last Battle* (New York: Harper Trophy, 1994), 213.

would reduce us to an animal. In so doing it explains why man is different: He is a creator as well as a creature, and art is his signature. It situates the Christian "philosophy of stories" as the fulfillment of human mythology. In the process it gives an early version of the trilemma argument which interestingly supplements Lewis's own in *Mere Christianity*. In all these ways it helped George MacDonald and others prepare the soil of Lewis's heart and mind for the moment when, under the influence of Tolkien and Dyson, these themes would come together to form the foundation of an intelligent and well-considered faith in Christ. It can still do the same for other readers today. But perhaps finally the best compliment we can pay it after all is to say that it helped to start C. S. Lewis on the journey that led him home at last.

Bibliography

Aeschliman, Michael D. *The Restitution of Man: C. S. Lewis and the Case Against Scientism*. Grand Rapids, MI: Eerdmans, 1998.

Benson, Iain. "G. K. Chesterton (1874–1936)." In *The C. S. Lewis Readers' Encyclopedia*, edited by Jeffrey D. Schultz and John G. West, Jr, 113. Grand Rapids, MI: Zondervan, 1998.

Burson, Scott R. and Jerry L. Walls. *C. S. Lewis and Francis Schaeffer: Lessons for a New Century from the Most Influential Apologists of our Time*. Downers Grove, IL: InterVarsity, 1998.

Carpenter, Humphrey. *The Inklings: C. S. Lewis, J. R. R. Tolkien, Charles Williams, and their Friends*. Boston: Houghton Mifflin, 1979.

Chesterton, G. K. *The Everlasting Man*. New York: Dodd, Mead, 1925.

—. *The Father Brown Omnibus*. With a preface by Auberon Waugh. New York: Dodd, Mead, 1982.

—. *Orthodoxy*. Garden City, NY: Doubleday, 1957.

Coren, Michael. *Gilbert: The Man Who Was G. K. Chesterton*. New York: Paragon House, 1990.

Dale, Alzina Stone. *The Outline of Sanity: A Life of G. K. Chesterton*. Grand Rapids, MI: Eerdmans, 1982.

Derrick, Christopher. "Some Personal Angles on Lewis and Chesterton." In *The Riddle of Joy: G. K. Chesterton and C. S. Lewis*, edited by Michael H. MacDonald and Andrew A. Tadie, 3–19. Grand Rapids, MI: Eerdmans, 1989.

Duriez, Colin. "In the Library: Composition and Context." In *Reading the Classics with C. S. Lewis,* edited by Thomas L. Martin, 359–70. Grand Rapids, MI: Baker, 2000.

Glyer, Diana Pavlac. *The Company They Keep: C. S. Lewis and J. R. R. Tolkien as Writers in Community*. Kent, OH: Kent State University Press, 2007.

Green, Walter Lancelyn and Walter Hooper. *C. S. Lewis: A Biography.* New York: Harcourt Brace Jovanovich, 1974.

Groothuis, Douglas. *Christian Apologetics: A Comprehensive Case for Biblical Faith.* Downers Grove, IL: InterVarsity, 2011.

Kilby, Clyde S. *The Christian World of C. S. Lewis.* Grand Rapids, MI: Eerdmans, 1964.

Lewis, C. S. *The Abolition of Man.* New York: MacMillan, 1947.

—. *The Collected Letters of C. S. Lewis, Vol. I: Family Letters 1905–1931,* edited by Walter Hooper. New York: HarperCollins, 2004.

—. Ibid., *Vol. II: Books, Broadcasts, and the War 1931–1949,* 2004.

—. Ibid., *Vol. III: Narnia, Cambridge, and Joy 1950–1963,* 2007.

—. "De Futilitate." In *Christian Reflections,* edited by Walter Hooper, 57–71. Grand Rapids, MI: Eerdmans, 1967.

—. "Ex Libris," *The Christian Century* 79 (June 6, 1962): 719.

—. *The Great Divorce.* New York: MacMillan, 1946.

—. *The Last Battle.* New York: Harper Trophy, 1994.

—. "Meditation in a Toolshed." *The Coventry Evening Telegraph* 17 (July 1945): 4. Reprinted in Lewis, C. S. *God in the Dock,* 212–15. Grand Rapids, MI: Eerdmans, 1970.

—. *Mere Christianity.* New York: MacMillan, 1943.

—. *Miracles: A Preliminary Study.* New York: MacMillan, 1947.

—. "Modern Theology and Biblical Criticism." In *Christian Reflections,* edited by Walter Hooper. Grand Rapids, MI: Eerdmans, 1967.

—. "Myth Became Fact." In *God in the Dock: Essays on Theology and Ethics,* edited by Walter Hooper, 63–7. Grand Rapids, MI: Eerdmans, 1970.

—. *The Pilgrim's Regress: An Allegorical Apology for Christianity Reason and Romanticism.* Grand Rapids, MI: Eerdmans, 1958.

—. *Surprised by Joy: The Shape of My Early Life.* New York: Harcourt, Brace & World, 1955.

—. *That Hideous Strength.* New York: Scribner, 1966.

—. *The Voyage of the "Dawn Treader."* New York: Harper Trophy, 1994.

MacDonald, Michael H. and Andrew A. Tadie, eds. *The Riddle of Joy: G. K. Chesterton and C. S. Lewis.* Grand Rapids, MI: Eerdmans, 1989.

Reppert, Victor. *C. S. Lewis's Dangerous Idea: A Defense of the Argument from Reason.* Downers Grove, IL: InterVarsity, 2003.

Sayer, George. *Jack: A Life of C. S. Lewis.* Wheaton, IL: Crossway, 1994.

Tolkien, J. R. R. "On Fairie Stories." In *The Tolkien Reader: Stories. Poems, and an Essay by the Author of "The Hobbit" and "The Lord of the Rings,"* edited by Peter S. Beagle, 3–84. New York: Ballantine Books, 1966.

Wells, H. G. *The Outline of History, Being a Plain History of Life and Mankind.* Garden City, NY: Garden City, 1920.

Williams, Donald T. "Identity Check: Are C. S. Lewis's Critics Right, or Is His 'Trilemma' Valid?" *Touchstone: A Journal of Mere Christianity* 23, no. 3 (May–June 2010): 25–9.

—. "Lacking, Ludicrous, or Logical? The Validity of Lewis's 'Trilemma.'" *Midwestern Journal of Theology* 11, no. 1 (Spring 2012): 91–102.
—. *Mere Humanity: G. K. Chesterton, C. S. Lewis, and J. R. R. Tolkien on the Human Condition*. Nashville, TN: Broadman & Homan, 2006.
—. *Reflections from Plato's Cave: Essays in Evangelical Philosophy*. Lynchburg, VA: Lantern Hollow, 2012.

Suggestions for further reading

Chesterton, G[ilbert] K[eith]. *The Father Brown Omnibus*. With a Preface by Auberon Waugh, New York: Dodd, Mead, 1982.
Chesterton's most popular character, Father Brown, is often a mouthpiece for Chesterton's own philosophy.

—. *Orthodoxy*. Garden City, NY: Doubleday, 1957.
Chesterton's other apologetic masterpiece complements The *Everlasting Man* and also treats the theme of coming home.

Lewis, C. S. *The Collected Letters of C. S. Lewis, Vol. III: Narnia, Cambridge, and Joy 1950-1963*. New York: HarperCollins, 2007.
An indispensable source for Lewis's ongoing relationship to Chesterton's work.

—. *Miracles: A Preliminary Study*. New York: MacMillan, 1947.
If Chesterton taught Lewis how to see the world through Christian eyes, this may be the book that most profoundly shows it.

—. "Myth Became Fact." *God in the Dock: Essays on Theology and Ethics*, edited by Walter Hooper, 63-7. Grand Rapids, MI: Eerdmans, 1970.
Lewis's way of expressing the truths he learned from Chesterton that were nailed down by Tolkien on Addison's Walk.

—. *The Pilgrim's Regress: An Allegorical Apology for Christianity Reason and Romanticism*. Grand Rapids, MI: Eerdmans, 1958.
If someone expanded Chesterton's idea of going around the world to come home for the first time into a book, it might look like this.

—. *Surprised by Joy: The Shape of My Early Life*. New York: Harcourt, Brace & World, 1955.
Lewis's own take on Chesterton's influence.

Tolkien, J. R. R. "On Fairie Stories." In *The Tolkien Reader: Stories, Poems, and an Essay by the Author of "The Hobbit" and "The Lord of the Rings,"* edited by Peter S. Beagle, 3-84. New York: Ballantine Books, 1966.
The most profound exposition of Chesterton's "philosophy of stories."

Williams, Donald T. *Mere Humanity: G. K. Chesterton, C. S. Lewis, and J. R. R. Tolkien on the Human Condition.* Nashville, TN: Broadman & Homan, 2006.
   Contains an extended treatment of *The Everlasting Man* and its influence on both Lewis and Tolkien, especially in terms of their view of the human condition.

3

Virgil, *The Aeneid*

Louis Markos

Although most readers today, whether they be teachers, students, or critics, prefer Homer's *Iliad* and *Odyssey* to Virgil's *Aeneid*, for well over a thousand years, it was the Roman poet who was universally hailed as the greater of the two. Despite the fact that Dante dubs Homer the singing master of the world (*Inferno* IV), the author of the *Divine Comedy* makes it clear that the *Aeneid*, not the *Iliad*, is the supreme poem of the West. Indeed, from late antiquity through the late Renaissance, it was Virgil who defined what was meant by an epic, who set the parameters for heroic action and noble speech. Whereas our overly self-conscious age has found greater solace and enjoyment in the spontaneity and unmediated power of Homer than in the sophistication and allusiveness of Virgil, our pre-Romantic heirs found in the *Aeneid* a purpose, a pathos, and a profundity that moved and taught and challenged them.

C. S. Lewis, though he lived nearly all of his life in the twentieth century, thought of himself as a dinosaur, as an old European man who felt more at home in the medieval and renaissance worlds of Dante, Chaucer, Spenser, and Milton than in the progressive era of the automobile, the phonograph, and the cinema. He found his kinship and his citizenship in a world that had been created by a serendipitous crossing of the Judeo-Christian and the Greco-Roman, and no pre-Christian work helped effect that fusion more powerfully than the *Aeneid*. It was Virgil—not in opposition to but alongside the Bible—who taught Christian Europe the shape of history, the cost of empire, the primacy of duty, the transience of fame, the inevitability of death, the pain of letting go, and the burden of adapting new strategies. The keynote was melancholic and elegiac, of paradise lost and the surrendering of personal happiness, but it resonated with an unshakeable hope that the end would be good: that, to paraphrase Julian of Norwich, all would be well, and all would be well, and all manner of thing would be well.

Though Lewis wrote with deep insight and scholarly finesse about the epics of Dante, Spenser, and Milton, it was to the *Aeneid* that he returned again and again throughout his life. It was one of his anchors, one of his mainstays, a reality attested to by the fact that when the 63-year-old Lewis was asked by *Christian Century* to name the books that had most influenced his view of life and sense of vocation, he included the *Aeneid* on the list, but not the *Iliad, Odyssey, Beowulf, Divine Comedy, Faerie Queene,* or *Paradise Lost*. And if that were not confirmation enough of Lewis's life-long love affair with the *Aeneid*, just two years shy of the fiftieth anniversary of Lewis's death, A. T. Reyes prepared an edition (Yale, 2011) of Lewis's heretofore unpublished translation of Book I and lengthy portions of Books II and VI of the *Aeneid*. Rendered into iambic hexameter couplets that combine epic power with Roman *gravitas*, Lewis's translation bears witness to his ongoing personal and scholarly conversation with the dual journey of Aeneas and Virgil.

In what follows, I shall trace the profound impact that the *Aeneid* had on Lewis, not by highlighting specific allusions to the epic in *The Discarded Image* or The Chronicles of Narnia or *The Great Divorce*, but by identifying major Virgilian themes that find echoes throughout Lewis's life and work.

Eschatology and typology

Despite the fact that Virgil (70–19 BC) died two decades before the birth of Christ and did not have access to the Old Testament, his epic is undergirded by a complex view of history that is truly biblical in scope. Whereas the *Iliad* and *Odyssey* are set in an absolute heroic past where everything seems to be happening *now*, the *Aeneid* continually directs its gaze forward. True, Homer's readers are afforded brief glimpses of what will happen to Achilles and Odysseus in the future, but these glimpses are personal rather than historical. Virgil, in contrast, infuses his epic with a philosophical and theological sense of the greater forces that propel history to its appointed end. Seamlessly woven into his epic retelling of Aeneas's journey from Troy to Rome is a greater, thousand-year journey that stretches from Aeneas to the founding of Rome (753) to the establishment of the Republic (509) to the birth of the Roman Empire (27).

The proper word to describe both the Bible and Virgil's view of history is eschatology (Greek for "study of the end"). Those who hold an eschatological view of history perceive in the flow of time what the Greeks called a *telos*—a purposeful end. Far from being arbitrary or haphazard, history, like an Aristotelian plot, moves forward in accordance with necessity, probability, and inevitability. Where the uninitiated eye sees only a chronological link between event A and event B, Virgil and the writers of the Bible perceive causation and purpose. In an eschatological universe, things do not simply "happen"; every event in the present is linked to other events in the past and the future. Indeed, the full and final meaning of any given event cannot be known until we reach the end of the historical process and look backward. That does not mean, however, that we must spend our life in darkness, vainly hoping that we will live to see the longed-for *telos*. The eschatological universe of the *Aeneid* and the Bible is also a prophetic one, filled with signs and symbols and portents that provide clues of what is to come.

Thanks to these hopeful, if riddling prophecies, those who live their lives within an eschatological universe need not despair when met by failure, suffering, or death. Not only will their understanding of history provide them with the faith that good will eventually triumph; it will allow them to see as well how the bad event was a *necessary prerequisite* for achieving the good end. When viewed in isolation, the Fall of Man (Genesis 3) is the worst tragedy in human history; when viewed eschatologically, it is transformed into a good event—for it leads to the Incarnation of Christ. Likewise, that dreadful Friday when Christ was crucified is transformed by the power of eschatology into "good" Friday, for it makes possible the resurrection victory of Easter Sunday. When the great theologians of the Middle Ages, who knew their Virgil as thoroughly as they did their Bible, meditated on the Fall from the long perspective of eschatology, they came to think of it not as a simple tragedy but as a *felix culpa*: a "happy guilt."

In a similar manner, Virgil, in *Aeneid* II, presents the horrific Fall of Troy as a *felix culpa*, a conflagration out of which would one day rise the mighty phoenix of the Roman Empire. And he does so by making use of three devices that, though Virgil did not know it, are also used in the Bible. On the simplest level, Virgil finds numerous ways to insert prophecies into the course of his narrative. Near the end of Book II, as Aeneas scrambles to rescue his family from the flames that are consuming his city, Aeneas's wife (Creusa) disappears into the night. Desperate to save her, Aeneas rushes back into the midst of the conflict, only to be visited by Creusa's ghost. Slowly, sadly, she prophesies to her husband of the long journey he will take to the West where he will win another kingdom and another bride. Other such prophecies are carefully woven into Book I (where Jupiter lays out for Aeneas's divine mother, Venus, his plans to bring about, in the fullness of time, the glory of Rome), Book VI (where Aeneas's father, Anchises, meets his son in the Underworld and shows him the souls of those who will one day be his Roman descendants), and Book VIII (where Aeneas is given a shield upon which is engraved the key figures and battles that will culminate in the ascendancy and universal rule of Caesar Augustus).

A second, more subtle method that Virgil uses to draw an eschatological line from Aeneas to Augustus is to provide his hero with glimpses of the real forces that propel history forward. In Book II, as Troy collapses around him, Aeneas comes upon Helen of Troy. In a fit of rage, Aeneas raises his sword to strike her dead, but is prevented from doing so by Venus. In order to convince her son to spare Helen's life, Venus explains to him that it is not Helen but the gods who have ordained the fall of Troy. But this assurance is not enough for the despairing Aeneas who knows only that the city and people he loves are perishing in agony. And so it is that the pagan Aeneas is vouchsafed a vision that is usually confined to prophets like Isaiah, Ezekiel, and Daniel. In the wink of an eye, Venus rips away the mortal veil that covers Aeneas's eyes and allows him to see what I like to call the ghosts in the historical machine. Where other mortals see a troop of Greeks hurling down masonry, Aeneas is allowed, for a moment, to see that it is not the soldiers of Greece but Neptune himself who is toppling the wall with his trident. Though Aeneas does not understand what he sees—just as he does not understand the figures that are engraved on his shield—the vision comforts him and gives him faith that larger purposes are at work than he can possibly conceive of. The death around him is not random or meaningless; it is all working toward a greater *telos* that he cannot see.

A third, even subtler method that Virgil uses to drive home the purposeful nature of history draws him even closer to the heart of the Scriptures. In addition to the numerous Old Testament prophecies that find their fulfillment in the New, the two parts of the Bible are further linked by a series of symbols that Bible interpreters call (after Paul) types. A type is an image or a person or an event that appears in the Old Testament and then reappears, often in a slightly altered form, in the New. In its first appearance it is generally literal and historical; in its second (and sometimes third or fourth) appearance it is more allegorical and points in some way to Christ and the gospel. Elijah, who roams the wilderness dressed in sackcloth and challenges the political powers of his day, is a type of John the Baptist; further, just as Elijah passes down his ministry to Elisha (a prophet who focused more on outsiders and the dispossessed than his charismatic predecessor), so John prepares the way for Christ—he who proclaimed good news to the poor, the captives, and the brokenhearted. The near sacrifice of Isaac by his father Abraham is a type of God's actual sacrifice of his son at Calvary, just as the Passover meal and the blood of the innocent lamb spread on the doorpost prefigures the Last Supper and the crucified Lamb of God whose atoning blood will cover our sins on that final Judgment Day when we must all face the sword of the Angel of Death.

A master of poetic image and symbol, Virgil fashions for his epic a complex network of types that gives shape not only to the narrative but to the greater historical scheme of which the narrative is a part. In Book I, when Aeneas's ships are blown onto the shore of Carthage, the reader learns that the Carthaginians are not Africans but Phoenicians from Tyre who have been led to Carthage by a prophecy. Just as the Aztecs knew they had found their promised city when they saw the sign of an eagle with a snake in its mouth perched on a cactus, so the Phoenicians (led by Queen Dido) know they have found *their* promised city when they dig up the head of a warhorse. The astute reader of Book I of the *Aeneid* will immediately theorize that the symbol of the horse will henceforth be used by Virgil to signify the building of a city ... that is, until he reaches Book II and reads of a massive Wooden Horse which signifies and heralds the death of a city. Has Virgil lost symbolic control of his epic so early in his poetic journey? Of course not. Through the power of typology, Virgil presents us with a riddle: that the erection and destruction of a city are, when viewed eschatologically, the same event. Or, to put it another way, out of the fall of one city, a new (and greater) city is born.

   A second type, linked this time to a person rather than an image, occurs in Book II, when Aeneas tries to convince his father to leave Troy. Anchises at first refuses, until the gods send him a sign. As a comet soars across the sky, the head of Aeneas's son (who bears two names: Ascanius and Iulus) catches fire. Rather than burn him, however, the sacred flame shapes itself into a crown, a symbol of kingship that, when linked to the comet, is referred to as Iulus's star. Virgil's original readers would have known the story, not of Iulus's star, but of Julius Caesar's star, a comet that appeared in the sky when Caesar Augustus's (adopted) father was born and on the night before his assassination. As quickly becomes evident to even the casual reader of Virgil's epic, Aeneas himself is a type of Augustus—thus effecting a typological riddle in which father-son (Aeneas-Iulus) becomes son-father (Julius Caesar-Augustus). To complicate the typology further, Virgil, in Book IV, recounts the affair of Aeneas and Dido in such a way as to suggest that Aeneas is a type of Marc Antony, while Dido is a type of Cleopatra. Or does he? In the first half, when Aeneas gives in to the seductions of his rich, ostentatious Eastern lover he threatens to become Marc Antony, but when he (in good Roman manner) forsakes her to fulfill his duty, he once again becomes a type of Augustus—he who defeated Antony and Cleopatra at the naval battle of Actium (31 BC). Later, to drive home his point, Virgil has the battle of Actium engraved at the very center of Aeneas's shield, including a depiction of Augustus on the prow of the ship lighted onward by his father's (Julius Caesar's) star.

Now, at this point, it must be emphasized that there is a great difference between the prophecies and glimpses and types in the *Aeneid* and those in the Old Testament. Whereas the messianic prophecies of the Hebrew Scriptures (Gen. 3:15, Psalm 22, Isaiah 53, Zech. 9:9, Mic. 5:2, etc.) were all written many centuries before the birth of Christ, Virgil's "prophecies" were all written *after* the events predicted had taken place. That is to say, Virgil's prophecies are not products of divine inspiration but literary and rhetorical devices for presenting Rome and Caesar Augustus as the culmination of a divinely ordained historical process that began a thousand years earlier with the Fall of Troy and the journey of Aeneas. Still, though Virgil was not a prophet in the full sense of the word, his epic does, like the Bible, present its readers with an ordered vision of history, one in which good can come out of evil and seemingly random events are fraught with meaning.

Paradise lost and found

C. S. Lewis, like Virgil's hero, grew up in an idyllic setting full of joy and wonder and fantasy, only to have it ripped away at the age of 9 when his mother died of cancer and he was summarily shipped off to a series of British boarding schools that he hated. A veteran of World War I, Lewis, like Aeneas, knew first hand the horrors of war and the aching loss of friends and comrades. And he knew as well the difficulty of establishing himself in a new land to which he felt drawn: Italy in the case of Aeneas; Oxford University (and England) in the case of Lewis (who grew up in Belfast, Ireland). Indeed, just as Aeneas never gained full possession of Italy so Lewis was denied a full professorship at Oxford—remaining, in a very real sense, a stranger in a strange land. Like Virgil and Aeneas, Lewis spent most of his life wrestling with sadness and loss. Even at the end of his life, after Cambridge University came to his rescue and provided him with the professorship unfairly denied him by Oxford, Lewis had to wrestle one last time with grief. A life-long bachelor, Lewis married Joy Davidman in his fifties, only to lose her three years later to the same disease that robbed him of his mother. In response, he wrote *A Grief Observed*, a brief but profound book that plumbs the nature of despair in epic terms.

Lewis knew much sorrow in his life; nevertheless, when he looked back on his life—both in his allegorical autobiography (*The Pilgrim's Regress*, 1933) and his spiritual autobiography (*Surprised by Joy*, 1955)—he was able to discern a steady stream of purpose propelling him forward to Christ and to the God-given ministry of teaching, writing, and speaking to which he devoted the second half of his life. More than that, he was able to see how God had sustained him on his long journey to faith—Lewis did not become a believer until he was 32—by sending him glimpses of and desires for beauty (what he called "Joy"), friends to challenge and keep him on track (Arthur Greeves, Owen Barfield, J. R. R. Tolkien), and books to guide him toward the light (George MacDonald's *Phantastes*, G. K. Chesterton's *The Everlasting Man*). During World War II, Lewis, like Virgil, had to be coaxed into using his gifts to celebrate the belief system on which his civilization was based: for Virgil, that meant writing an epic that championed the Roman virtues of duty, justice, and order; for Lewis, it meant delivering a series of BBC Broadcast Talks on the Christian faith while Nazi planes threatened to blow the old faith on which Europe had been built into oblivion.

As a professor and an author, Lewis, like Virgil, extolled the past while yet accepting the future. Though Lewis never learned to drive and had little love for movies and telephones, he was by no means a Luddite or an obscurantist. He loved the medieval cosmological model, but he did not advocate that we give up modern science and return to the pre-Copernican world. When a woman's husband dies, Lewis once wrote, she does not become a virgin again.[1] Lewis knew that Europe could not simply return to medieval Christendom (or classical paganism), yet he believed strongly that by grounding ourselves in the Greco-Roman, Judeo-Christian classics, and learning from the strengths and weaknesses of the past, that we could build a firmer future. Lewis accepted the basics of democracy and the free market, not because he thought they were the proper "biblical model," but because they had been shown to work and to provide the most number of people with the most freedom and opportunity. Lewis's goal was not to abandon the modern world but to teach his students and readers that there is goodness in hierarchy, truth in the supernatural, and beauty in the old cosmological model. Just so, Virgil embraced the new empire of Caesar Augustus while yet extolling the virtues of the republic that Augustus had helped to end.

J. R. R. Tolkien, who understood well the Catholic (and Virgilian) notion of *felix culpa*, coined the word eucatastrophe (the Greek prefix "eu" means "good") to refer to tragic moments like the Fall of Man and Good Friday that give way to greater glory. Such a moment occurs in *The Lord of the Rings* when Gollum bites the ring off Frodo's finger . . . and then falls into Mount Doom, ending the reign of the One Ring and its Dark Lord. Chesterton, in *The Everlasting Man*, argues that the Church is like her Savior, continually dying, only to be reborn and renewed—a process that Chesterton locates as

---

[1] C. S. Lewis, "De Descriptione Temporum," in *Selected Literary Essays* (Cambridge: Cambridge University Press, 1969), 10.

well in the Virgilian movement from the Fall of Troy to the Glory of Rome. Lewis, who was influenced by both Tolkien and Chesterton, provides his readers with powerful eucatastrophes in the death-and-resurrection of Aslan (*The Lion, the Witch, and the Wardrobe*), the wounding of Ransom followed by his triumph over the Unman (*Perelandra*), and the dual humbling and exaltation of Psyche and Orual (*Till We Have Faces*). The one character in *The Great Divorce* who accepts the offer of grace extended to him is a timid young man controlled by a hideous lizard who whispers lewd thoughts into his ear. Unlike the other proud ghosts who only want their rights, this weak, pathetic soul, who cannot break away on his own from his unseemly addiction to pornography and masturbation, asks for help and allows the lizard to be killed. But the act proves to be a *felix culpa*, for the death of the lizard's attenuated *eros* gives way to the rebirth of an indestructible *agape*, as ghost and lizard are transformed into a god-like man atop a noble steed.

It is a glorious moment, made even more glorious by the Virgilian question Lewis—or, rather, his guide, George MacDonald—leaves us with: if lust which gives itself over to death can become such a mighty horse, what would mother love or patriotism or charitable work become if it too were subjected to death and rebirth?

Virgil as Proto-Christian

Like the twentieth-century Lewis, educated Christians of late antiquity and the Middle Ages were awed by the eschatological and typological structure of the *Aeneid*. In fact, it was partly on the basis of Virgil's unconsciously biblical vision of history that many in the early and medieval church came to look upon him as a proto-Christian whom the Triune God used to help prepare the pagan world for the coming of Christ. After all, did not Paul himself quote two pagan Greek poets when he presented the gospel to a group of skeptical Stoics and Epicureans at the Areopagus in Athens (Acts 17:28). And did he not begin his sermon with this promise: "Whom therefore ye ignorantly worship, him declare I unto you" (17:23).

If God could use the pagan Balaam to bless Israel (Numbers 23–24) and the pagan Cyrus to send the exiled Jews back to Jerusalem (Isa. 44:28) and the pagan Magi to present kingly gifts to the Jewish Messiah (Matthew 2), then surely he could use a pagan poet like Virgil to lay down a poetic and philosophical framework to facilitate the Christianizing of the Roman Empire. During the Renaissance, Michelangelo would pay homage to just such a belief by including, on the Sistine Chapel, the pagan sibyls and oracles alongside the prophets of the Old Testament as forerunners and heralds of the incarnate God who came to save the whole world—Jew and Gentile alike. Raphael would pay homage as well in the frescoes he painted for the Stanza of the Signatura, part of the Pope's apartments in the Vatican. On facing walls, Raphael offers the "Dispute on the Blessed Sacrament" (which celebrates the triumph of the Mass, the Church, and the theological truths embodied in the Creed) and "The School of Athens" (which celebrates the great pre-Christian philosophers of Greece and Rome). Connecting them on either side are frescoes of the classical and theological virtues and of the pagan and Christian poets—two bridges between the BC and AD worlds which were strongly identified with Virgil.

In the former category, Virgil was believed to embody to perfection the four classical (or cardinal) virtues of the ancient world: justice, fortitude, temperance, and prudence. These four virtues were considered by early and medieval Christians to constitute the highest man could reach apart from direct revelation and divine grace; as such, they foreshadowed, as well as prepared for, the coming of the three theological (or Christian) virtues: faith, hope, and love (or charity, from the Latin *caritas*). In the latter category, Virgil was hailed as the greatest poet of the ancient world, the one who synthesized the beauty and truth of all those who came before him to produce *the* supreme work of poetry. He it was who purified the Latin tongue and who, by identifying Roman *virtus* and *pietas* as the keys to the triumph of Rome, helped the early Church to understand why it was that the Triune God chose to incarnate himself during the reign of Caesar Augustus.

In fact, it was widely believed that Virgil himself had foretold the coming of Christ in a poem he wrote about 40 BC, the fourth in a series of ten eclogues, pastoral poems written in imitation of the Greek poet Theocritus that looked back nostalgically to the simple life of the shepherd.[2] Though the poem was likely intended to praise the young Octavian, the adopted son of Julius Caesar who helped avenge his father's assassination and who would later change his name to Caesar Augustus, it reads like a messianic prophecy. In the poem, Virgil speaks cryptically of a coming child from heaven who will bring peace and plenty and who will restore man and nature to the lost Golden Age:

Sicilian muse, I would try now a somewhat grander theme. . . .
Ours is the crowning era foretold in prophecy:
Born of Time, a great new cycle of centuries
Begins. Justice returns to earth, the Golden Age

---

[2] Virgil, *The Eclogues and Georgics*, trans. C. Day Lewis (New York: Anchor Books, 1964), 30–5.

> Returns, and its first-born comes down from heaven above. . . .
> This child shall enter into the life of the gods . . .
> And rule a world made peaceful by his father's virtuous acts. . . .
> Come soon, dear child of the gods, Jupiter's great viceroy!
> Come soon—the time is near—to begin your life illustrious!
> Look how the round and ponderous globe bows to salute you . . .
> Look how the whole creation exults in the age to come![3]

Remove a few references to Jupiter and the gods, and the poem might easily be mistaken for a chapter out of Isaiah or the Psalms. Dante, who chose Virgil as his guide through much of his Catholic universe, was so impressed by the messianic nature of the Fourth Eclogue that he introduced into his *Purgatory* a first-century pagan poet named Statius who explains that he accepted Christ after he realized that what the Christians were teaching squared with what his hero Virgil had prophesied in his Fourth Eclogue.

Still, though the Fourth Eclogue cemented Virgil's status as proto-Christian, it was the *Aeneid* that was most closely studied by Christians as a sourcebook of wisdom and virtue. In *Inferno* II, Dante, meditating on the eschatology of the *Aeneid*, goes so far as to suggest that Aeneas was a type of Peter and Paul. Just as the gods used Aeneas as their chosen instrument to lay the foundations of the Roman Empire, so God used Peter and Paul to begin the process by which the Roman Empire would, in the fullness of time, morph into the Roman Catholic Church. Certainly it was no coincidence that both Aeneas (the epic hero of the *Aeneid*) and Paul (the equally epic hero of the Book of Acts) began their journeys in Asia Minor and ended them in Rome. And certainly Aeneas's movement from East to West was not only geographical but moral and ethical as well, taking him from the tyrannical kingdoms of the East (Assyria, Babylon, Persia, Phoenicia) to the democratic republics of the West (Greece and Rome). So reasoned the many early Christians who studied closely the difficult choices that Aeneas makes over the course of the epic. Indeed, Medievals seeking direction from God would often open up the *Aeneid* at random and seek revelation in the first verse that their eyes fell upon (as many people still do today with the Bible).

The true myth

It is no exaggeration to say that Lewis's acceptance of Christianity was based in great part on his acceptance of the possibility of Virgil being a proto-

[3] Ibid.

Christian. Although most fans of Lewis are aware that he was an atheist for many years, many do not realize that Lewis did not move directly from atheism to Christianity. Yes, Lewis went from atheism to a belief in God (theism) at the age of 30, but it took him two more years before he could embrace Christ as the Son of God. For Lewis, the major stumbling block on his road from theism to Christianity was his extensive knowledge of Greek, Roman, Egyptian, and Norse mythology. As Lewis knew better than most, every ancient culture had its own version of the Corn King: the God who comes to earth and who dies and rises along with the seasonal cycle (Adonis, Bacchus, Mithras, Tammuz, Osiris, Balder, and so forth). A longtime disciple of Sir James Frazer's *The Golden Bough*, Lewis reasoned—as many still reason today—that the story of Christ was nothing more than the Hebrew version of the Corn King myth. That is, until he took a long evening stroll along Addison's Walk in Magdalen College, Oxford, with his good friends, J. R. R. Tolkien and Hugo Dyson.

As they walked, Tolkien suggested to Lewis that the reason that the gospel story sounded so much like the myths of Osiris or Balder was not that Christianity was a myth, but that it was the myth that came true. The ubiquitous nature of the Corn God myth suggested that all human beings were hardwired by their Creator with an ineradicable longing for God-come-to-earth and an unshakeable sense that sacrifice was necessary to right the scales of justice.[4] In all other cultures that inbuilt yearning found its expression in myth; only amongst the Jews, and at a specific moment in time and space, did this collective human yearning find its once-and-for-all historical enactment in the life, death, and Resurrection of Jesus Christ. If that were true, it meant not only that the God of the Bible had spoken to nations others than Israel (albeit in a shadowy, imprecise way), but that the myths Lewis so loved might have been one of the vehicles by which God communicated with the Gentile nations. Not just philosophers like Plato, Aristotle, and Cicero, but poets like Homer, Aeschylus, and Sophocles might be embraced as vessels of divine truth, even if that truth were filtered through pagan vices and errors. And since Virgil was the great inheritor of both the philosophers and the poets, might he not be, in truth, the supreme proto-Christian of the ancient world!

This wonderful possibility not only revolutionized Lewis's faith but inspired his art and criticism as well. *Mere Christianity* and *The Abolition of Man* rely heavily on Plato's understanding of virtue and Aristotle's understanding of ethics, just as *The Great Divorce* and *The Pilgrim's Regress*

---

[4] On Christianity as "myth become fact" see pages 35–6, 45 in Donald T. Williams' essay on G. K. Chesterton's *The Everlasting Man*.

follow Dante's conception of sin and choice, which itself is strongly indebted to Plato, Aristotle, and, of course, Virgil. The full Virgilian notion of proto-Christianity surfaces most powerfully in *Prince Caspian*, where Aslan (the Christ of Narnia) is assisted in his revival of Narnia by Bacchus and his maenads. It is significant that when Lucy and Susan first meet Bacchus and his wild followers, Susan comments that she would not feel safe with them if Aslan were not with them. Only in the presence of the true Corn King, of the myth made fact, does Bacchus become an agent for good. In a similar crossing between old pagan myth and its historical fulfillment and purification in Christ, *That Hideous Strength* presents us with a revived Merlin, whose dark, primitive wood lore must be channeled for good by Ransom, a Christ figure whom Lewis links to King Arthur, himself a Christ figure in the midst of a semi-pagan England.

And then there is *Till We Have Faces*, Lewis's strangest and most haunting novel, a work which pays homage to Virgil in a unique and memorable way. Whereas the *Aeneid* is a truly proto-Christian work, written by a poet who was unaware that he was being used by a God far greater than Jupiter, *Till We Have Faces* is a sort of simulated proto-Christian work that infuses its pagan, pre-Christian setting with intimations of Christ to come.[5] Lewis is not alone in attempting such a work. As Lewis explains in *The Discarded Image*, Boethius's *Consolation of Philosophy* was written by a Christian but in a pagan mode. That is to say, though the author's Christian faith can be detected in the work, Boethius consciously confines himself to the kind of general revelation that was accessible to Plato, Aristotle, Cicero, Virgil, and their fellow pagan poets and philosophers. As both Lewis and Tolkien well knew, the same was the case for *Beowulf*, which was almost certainly written by a Christian monk but in a pagan mode befitting its pre-Christian Anglo-Saxon setting. And the same holds true for Tolkien's own *Lord of the Rings*, an epic fantasy set in the days before God revealed himself to Abraham (Middle-earth, as Tolkien makes clear in his letters, *is* the earth), but infused with a rich Christian sensibility. In keeping with this austere lineage (which also includes Milton's *Samson Agonistes*), Lewis's choice to set *Till We Have Faces* in a BC world cut off from the Jewish Scriptures allowed him to explore some of the ways in which the God of the Bible left himself a witness even in the midst of the most seemingly barbaric religious rites.

As an apologist, Lewis ranks supreme in his ability to build bridges to modern people who have come to view Christianity as an outmoded religion

---

[5] On the "Williamsian" Christian theme of substitution and exchange in *Till We Have Faces*, see pages 189–99 in Holly Ordway's essay on *Descent into Hell*.

and the Bible as an outdated book. By appealing to universal experiences of morality (what he dubbed the Tao) and of the *numinous* (what he called "Joy") and by calling on us to reaccess the power of myth as a pointer to higher truths, Lewis succeeded in re-enchanting the world and tapping some of the oldest and most persistent longings of the human race. And it was Virgil and the *Aeneid* that helped lead him along that ancient, yet ever fresh and contemporary path.

Learning new strategies

A moment ago, I suggested a link between the East-to-West journeys of Aeneas and of Paul. In both cases, the chosen hero moves from the old world to the new, a movement that forces him to learn new strategies and to adopt new perspectives. In the case of Paul, his road to Damascus experience stops him dead in his tracks, converting him from a persecutor of the church to its greatest missionary. Still, despite the shift from legalistic bounty hunter to apostle of grace, Paul remains the same man he was. Rather than turn him into a different person, God takes Paul's strengths (his knowledge of and zeal for the Law; his single-minded endurance) and teaches him to use those strengths in a radically new way (to write a series of letters in which he demonstrates how the Law is fulfilled in Christ; to travel thousands of miles along the Roman roads proclaiming the gospel). Just as Peter is transformed from a fisherman to a fisher of men, so Paul is transformed from an angry defender of the Old Covenant (Law) to a joyous advocate of the New (Grace). The change is not an easy one to effect in the stubborn Paul—in Acts 26:14, God compares him to a donkey that kicks against the pricks—but the end result is a new *kind* of man. To his Jewish heritage, his Greek education, and his Roman citizenship, Paul adds a distinctly Christian perspective on God, man, and the universe, and a distinctly Christian focus on the virtues of faith, hope, and love.

In a similar way, Aeneas, while remaining the same basic person, is transformed from an old Trojan to a new Roman. But the process is a long and painful one. In Book II, when Aeneas is called by the ghost of Hector to abandon Troy and seek a new land, he makes it clear that he does not want the job that has been assigned to him by Jupiter. He would rather die defending his beloved city from the Greek invaders. Several times over the course of Book II, Aeneas throws himself into the fray, heedless of the mission to which he has been called. In the end, it takes two more ghostly visitations by his goddess mother and his wife's wraith to convince him to leave Troy and lead the survivors to Italy. But his education does not stop there. Having lost his wife, Aeneas goes on, at the end of Books III, IV, and V, to lose his father, his lover, and his friend. Again and again, Aeneas tries to find an excuse to end his journey and settle down—like Paul, the muleheaded Aeneas kicks hard against the pricks—but each time the gods propel him forward. Finally, in Book VI, the unwilling, recalcitrant hero is forced to face his own mortality by descending into the Underworld. But when he returns, in Book VII, to the land of the living, he is a new man, a proto-Roman whose far distant descendant will be Caesar Augustus.

In the place of Hector's prowess, courage, and devotion to family, Aeneas learns endurance, patience, and devotion to duty—all virtues that made Rome great. Aeneas never wanted the mighty task that was entrusted to him, but he was forced by the gods to move out of himself to embrace a higher destiny.

The reluctant apologist

Like Aeneas, Lewis did not consider his conversion a pleasant one. By his own admission, he was the most reluctant convert in all England, dragged kicking and screaming into the Kingdom of God, looking left and right for any means of escape.[6] Lewis wanted nothing more than to be left alone. He was happy to live a moderately virtuous life, as long as God would stay out of his affairs and mind his own business. But that was not to be. God had a mission for Lewis to fulfill, and, if I may so phrase it, he used guerilla tactics to seize hold of the stiff-necked, donkey-like Lewis. There was to be no escape from the hound of heaven, the divine hunter and bridegroom. In the end, he cornered Lewis and left him no way out. In *Surprised by Joy*, Lewis uses a chess metaphor for the "game" that God plays with him. The chapter in which God finally wins is titled "Checkmate."

However, as in the case of Paul and Aeneas, God's victory over Lewis was not the type that crushed its prey. Christ did not eradicate Lewis's person but transformed it.[7] Lewis would not have become the greatest apologist of the twentieth century if God had not made creative use of Lewis's pre-conversion experiences. The thousands of hours that Lewis devoted to his study of mythology—a study that originally kept him away from Christ—would eventually become one of the bridges that he built between modern

[6] C. S. Lewis, "Surprised by Joy," in *The Inspirational Writings of C. S. Lewis* (New York: Inspiration, 1991), 125.
[7] On creatures becoming "more themselves" in Christ, see pages 149–50 in Chris R. Armstong's essay on Boethius's *The Consolation of Philosophy*.

paganism and Christianity. Since his own views had evolved from a cynical belief that Jesus was only a myth, to a more mature belief that Jesus was the myth made fact, Lewis could draw others from a love of fantasy to an embrace of the One in whom all true magic finds its source.

More astonishingly, and more ironically, Lewis's gift for using reason and logic to defend, rather than deconstruct, the truth claims of Christianity can be traced to a most unlikely source. When Lewis was 15, his father finally rescued him from the boarding schools he despised and sent him to a private tutor named Kirkpatrick. Kirkpatrick, whose nickname was "the great knock," was a firm atheist in the skeptical, empiricist school of David Hume, and he helped convince Lewis that atheism (or at least agnosticism) was the most rational position for a modern, educated man. It was Kirkpatrick who taught Lewis to be ruthless in his assault on faulty assumptions and logical fallacies, and to trace every argument back to its presuppositions. Lewis was an apt pupil, and he became quite adept at tearing down all philosophical and theological pretensions. One might think that when Lewis became a Christian he would discard all that the atheist Kirkpatrick had taught him—but he did not. Rather, under God's guidance, Lewis took the logical methods he had learned and baptized them as a powerfully effective tool for defending the reasonableness of Christianity from its modern detractors.

When he wrote such apologetical works as *Mere Christianity*, *The Problem of Pain*, and *Miracles*, Lewis tried to construct arguments that he wished had been presented to him during his long years as an atheist. That is what prevents Lewis from "preaching to the choir," and makes his books so accessible to nonbelievers and seekers. When he wrote *The Screwtape Letters* and *The Great Divorce*, he analyzed his own struggles with temptation and sin, allowing both his triumphs and his defeats to inform his spiritual and psychological insights—which is why those books ring true on every count. His portrait of Digory in *The Magician's Nephew*, a boy whose mother is dying and who yearns to find a magic fruit that will heal her, is rendered intensely poignant by his own childhood memories of losing his mother; his portrait of Jane Studdock in *That Hideous Strength*, a woman who just wants to be left alone, is rendered equally poignant by Lewis's memories of his own stubborn attempts to keep God out of his private life.

Above all, Lewis learned from meditating on his past and from frequent rereadings of the *Aeneid* (and the Bible) that this world is not our home, that we are merely passing through on the way to a greater country. Such reflections make the pagan Aeneas morose and stoic, but not the Christian Lewis; for Lewis knew personally, as Aeneas could not, the living and loving God who propels and orchestrates our eschatological universe. Unlike Aeneas, therefore, Lewis knew many moments of joy and intimacy when the Good, the True, and the Beautiful drew tangibly near. Nevertheless, the lessons of Virgil remained strong in his mind. Though Lewis enjoyed those moments, he never sought to control or hoard them. Rather, with hope and thanksgiving, he took each moment as it came. For he knew that though this world is not our home, it is filled with inns and way stations for the refreshment of pilgrims who, like Virgil's great hero, must travel a long, long road before they can find their true home.

Bibliography

Lewis, C. S. "De Descriptione Temporum." In *Selected Literary Essays*. Cambridge: Cambridge University Press, 1969.
—. "Surprised by Joy." In *The Inspirational Writings of C. S. Lewis*. New York: Inspiration, 1991.
Virgil. *The Eclogues and Georgics*. Translated by C. Day Lewis. New York: Anchor Books, 1964.

Suggestions for further reading

Note: This essay should be read in conjunction with the essays on Chesterton's *The Everlasting Man* (for both Virgil and Chesterton share an eschatological view of history), Boethius's *The Consolation of Philosophy* (since the works of Virgil and Boethius played a major role in shaping the Middle Ages), and Wordsworth's *The Prelude* (which not only shares the epic scope of the *Aeneid* but shares its focus on a simultaneously external and inward journey that is reflected in Lewis's two autobiographical works: *The Pilgrim's Regress* and *Surprised by Joy*).

Lewis, C. S. *The Allegory of Love*. London: Oxford University Press, 1969.
  This, Lewis's first major academic work, demonstrates his gift for making complex aesthetic subjects accessible to nontechnical readers. In his long chapter on allegory, he has much to say about the influence of Virgil on medieval allegory.

—. "De Descriptione Temporum." In *Selected Literary Essays*. Cambridge: Cambridge University Press, 1969.
  This is the talk Lewis gave when he accepted the Chair of Medieval and Renaissance Literature at Cambridge. In it, he breaks down the artificial wall between the supposedly dark and ignorant Middle Ages and the enlightened Renaissance and shows that any major medieval or renaissance figure has more in common with Virgil than with any European writer after 1800.

—. *The Discarded Image*. Cambridge: Cambridge University Press, 1964.
In this, Lewis's last academic work, he maps out for modern readers the medieval cosmological model. Early in his study, he notes that the Bible, Virgil, and Ovid were three of the greatest influences on the Middle Ages.

—. *A Preface to Paradise Lost*. New York: Oxford University Press, 1961.
This still influential study of *Paradise Lost* begins by making an important distinction between primary epics (Homer) and secondary epics (Virgil and Milton) and then mounts a vigorous defense of the style of secondary epics.

—. *Studies in Medieval and Renaissance Literature*. Cambridge: Cambridge University Press, 1980.
This fine collection includes an essay on Dante's similes that shows the strong influence of Virgil on Dante. It also includes a wonderful meditation on the character of Statius, whom, according to Dante's *Purgatory*, came to Christ through reading Virgil's Fourth Eclogue.

Markos, Louis. *From Achilles to Christ: Why Christians Should Read the Pagan Classics*. Downers Grove, IL: Intervarsity, 2007.
This book includes a close analysis of the *Aeneid* that is guided by Lewis's belief that Christ was the myth that became fact. As such, it treats the *Aeneid* both within its own historical and literary context and as prefiguring the greater revelations of Christ and the New Testament.

Martin, Thomas L., ed. *Reading the Classics with C. S. Lewis*. Grand Rapids, MI: Baker, 2000.
This excellent collection of essays takes up Lewis's interactions with authors, literary periods, and genres. It offers a good context for the influence of the *Aeneid* on Lewis.

Reyes, A. T., ed. *C. S. Lewis's Lost* Aeneid. New Haven: Yale University Press, 2011.
Anyone interested in the influence of the *Aeneid* on Lewis must read this well-conceived and well-edited book. Reyes offers a very helpful overview of Lewis's life-long love affair with the *Aeneid*, and Lewis's translation is highly readable and trots along at a swift, infectious pace.

Ward, Michael. *Planet Narnia: The Seven Heavens in the Imagination of C. S. Lewis*. New York: Oxford University Press, 2008.
The provocative thesis of this book is that Lewis modeled his seven Chronicles of Narnia on the seven planets and their influences. Although Virgil is only referenced once, this book shares with Lewis and Virgil a cosmic, eschatological scope.

4

George Herbert, *The Temple*

Don W. King

At first glance it is surprising that C. S. Lewis lists among the ten most important books to shape his "vocational attitude" and "philosophy of life"[1] George Herbert's *The Temple: Sacred Poems and Private Ejaculations*. Lewis's references to Herbert in his published writings are infrequent and widely scattered; while he devotes an entire essay to Herbert's contemporary, John Donne,[2] Lewis never writes extensively about Herbert, even in the volume where we might most reasonably expect him to offer a concentrated discussion of Herbert, *English Literature in the Sixteenth Century*.[3] Yet a closer view reveals that Herbert influences Lewis in at least three profound ways. The first is the "poetic" voice that gives expression to Lewis's spiritual life as revealed in his religious poetry. The second is the "pastoral" voice Lewis develops as a correspondent to the many who write him letters concerning their spiritual difficulties. The third is the "pathos" of Lewis's voice in *A Grief Observed*. This essay will explore how *The Temple* serves as one of the most important "spiritual directors" in the poems, letters, and late prose of Lewis.

First a brief review of the life and work of George Herbert. Born on April 3, 1593, Herbert was the fifth of seven sons born into a family of ten children. His father, Richard, died when he was 4, and his mother, Magdalen, remained a widow 12 years, remarrying when Herbert was 16. Her remarriage was a fortunate one since her second husband was the brother and heir of Lord Danvers, Earl of Danby. In this role she became

---

[1] C. S. Lewis, "Ex Libris," *The Christian Century* 79 (June 6, 1962): 719.
[2] C. S. Lewis, "Donne and Love Poetry in the Seventeenth Century," in *Seventeenth Century Studies Presented to Sir Herbert Grierson*, ed. John Dover Wilson (Oxford: Clarendon, 1938). Reprinted in *Selected Literary Essays*, ed. Walter Hooper (Cambridge: Cambridge University Press, 1969).
[3] C. S. Lewis, *English Literature in the Sixteenth Century Excluding Drama* (Oxford: Clarendon, 1954).

a patron of the arts, later supporting, among many others, John Donne.[4] Herbert was educated at Trinity College, Cambridge, being awarded the Master of Arts in 1615. In 1619 he was appointed Orator for the University, continuing in this important role until 1627. He accounted himself so well as Orator that he drew the attention and favor of the king, James I. For a time it appeared Herbert would find an important post in the king's court; however, when the king died in 1625, so did any hopes Herbert might have had regarding a royal appointment. Accordingly, he decided to enter into sacred orders, and in 1630 he assumed pastoral duties in the small country parish of Bemerton. His only volume of poetry, *The Temple*, was published shortly after his death in 1633.[5] Herbert was not sure his poems were worth publishing, asking near his death that they be sent to his friend Nicholas Farrer:

> I pray deliver this little book to my dear brother Farrer, and tell him he shall find in it a picture of the many spiritual conflicts that have passed betwixt God and my soul, before I could subject mine to the will of Jesus my master: in whose service I have now found perfect freedom. Desire him to read it; and then, if he can think it may turn to the advantage of any dejected poor soul, let it be made public; if not, let him burn it; for I and it are less than the least of God's mercies.[6]

Isaak Walton, Herbert's first biographer, writes that "he lived, and . . . died, like a saint, unspotted of the world, full of alms-deeds, full of humility, and all the examples of a virtuous life."[7] While some might fault Walton for hagiography, Herbert's saintly reputation was widely hailed; after his death he was often referred to as "Holy Mr Herbert," and he influenced a number of other seventeenth-century poets, including Henry Vaughan and Thomas Traherne.

---

[4] See Donne's sonnet tribute to her, "To the Lady Magdalen Herbert, of St. Mary Magdalen," in *The Complete Poetry of John Donne*, ed. John T. Shawcross (Garden City, NY: Anchor, 1967), 333. In addition, Donne preached her funeral sermon in the parish church of Chelsea.

[5] In addition, his reflections on his life as a priest was posthumously published as *A Priest to the Temple* (or *The Country Parson*) in 1652. Lewis's personal library held by the Marion E. Wade Center at Wheaton College contains his copies of both *The Temple: Sacred Poems and Private Ejaculations* and *A Priest to the Temple*; both contain extensive underlining.

[6] Izaac Walton, *The Lives of Doctor John Donne, Sir Henry Wotton, Mr. Richard Hooker, Mr. George Herbert, and Doctor Robert Sanderson* (London: Methuen, 1985), 223. Walton's *Life of Herbert* originally appeared in 1670. See http://anglicanhistory.org/walton/herbert.html

[7] Ibid., 226.

Lewis's few references to *The Temple* appear both in his letters and books. In a letter to his friend Arthur Greeves,[8] Lewis shares that he is coming out of an emotional low, referencing Herbert's poem from *The Temple*, "The Flower": "I once more feel the sun and rain And relish versing."[9] On March 26, 1940, Lewis writes to Mary Neylan who had asked him to recommend helpful books of theology; as a part of his response, he tells her "you wd. also find it most illuminating to re-read now many things you once read in 'Eng. Lit' without knowing their real importance—Herbert, Traherne, *Religio Medici*."[10] Later, after Greeves embraces Unitarianism, Lewis offers a pointed critique in his letter of December 11, 1944: "Where are the shining examples of human holiness wh. ought to come from Unitarianism if it is true? Where are the Unitarian 'opposite numbers' to St Francis, George Herbert, [John] Bunyan, Geo. Macdonald, and even burly old Dr. [Samuel] Johnson?"[11] To another correspondent he writes on March 27, 1951, regarding how difficult it is to maintain the sense that God is in control of his everyday life:

> The whole difficulty with me is to keep control of the mind and I wish one's earliest education had given one more training in that. There seems to be a disproportion between the vastness of the soul in one respect (i.e. as a mass of ideas and emotions) and its smallness in another (i.e. as central, controlling ego). The whole inner weather changes so completely in less than a minute. Do you read George Herbert—
>
> *If what soul doth feel sometimes*
> *My soul might always feel—*
>
> He's a good poet and one who helped bring me back to the Faith.[12]

---

[8] C. S. Lewis to Arthur Greeves, Oct. 3, 1929, in *The Collected Letters of C. S. Lewis, Vol. I: Family Letters 1905-1931*, ed. Walter Hooper (New York: HarperCollins, 2004), 830.

[9] George Herbert, *The Poems of George Herbert*, ed. Helen Gardner (London: Oxford University Press, 1961), 156. The exact quote in Herbert's poem, "The Flower," is: "I once more smell the dew and rain / And relish versing."

[10] C. S. Lewis to Mary Neylan, March 26, 1940, in *The Collected Letters of C. S. Lewis, Vol. II: Books, Broadcasts, and the War, 1931-1949*, ed. Walter Hooper (New York: HarperCollins, 2004), 376.

[11] C. S. Lewis to Arthur Greeves, Dec. 11, 1944, in *The Collected Letters of C. S. Lewis, Vol. III, Supplement: Narnia, Cambridge, and Joy, 1950-1963*, ed. Walter Hooper (New York: HarperCollins, 2007), 1555.

[12] C. S. Lewis to Warfield M. Firor, March 27, 1951, *Collected Letters III*, 105-6. The exact quote from Herbert's poem, "The Temper (I)," is: "If what my soul doth feel sometimes, / My soul might ever feel!" (47).

When Mary Van Deusen asks Lewis how to endure a bad parish priest, Lewis replies: "The motto wd. be of course Herbert's lines about the sermon 'If all lack sense, God takes a text and preaches patience'."[13] Still later he relates that *The Temple* is among those works that "were incomparably more important [to his spiritual life] than any professed theologians."[14] On May 9, 1961, Lewis tells another correspondent that "George Herbert at his best is extremely nutritious."[15]

The most telling of these references is when Lewis writes that Herbert is "a good poet and one who helped to bring me back to the Faith." In his autobiography, *Surprised by Joy*, Lewis underscores this debt to Herbert. As Lewis's atheism comes under assault, he says: "A young man who wishes to remain a sound Atheist cannot be too careful of his reading. There are traps everywhere—'Bibles laid open, millions of surprises,' as Herbert says, 'fine nets and stratagems.' God is, if I may say it, very unscrupulous."[16] The Herbert poem Lewis has in mind is the sonnet "Sinne (I)":

> Lord, with what care hast thou begirt us round!
>   Parents first season us: then schoolmasters
>   Deliver us to laws; they send us bound
> To rules of reason, holy messengers,
>
> Pulpits and Sundayes, sorrow dogging sinne,
>   Afflictions sorted, anguish of all sizes,
>   nets and stratagems to catch us in,
> Bibles laid open, millions of surprises,
>
> Blessings beforehand, tyes of gratefulnesse,
>   The sound of glorie ringing in our eares:
>   Without, our shame; within, our consciences;
> Angels and grace, eternall hopes and fears.
>
>   Yet all these fences and their whole array
>   One cunning bosome-sinne blows quite away.[17]

---

[13] C. S. Lewis to Mary Van Deusen, Dec. 28, 1953, *Collected Letters III*, 397. The exact quote from Herbert's "The Church-Porch," *Poems*, 19, is: "The worst speak something good: if all want sense, / God takes a text, and preacheth patience."
[14] C. S. Lewis to Corbin Scott Carnell, Oct. 13, 1958, *Collected Letters III*, 978.
[15] C. S. Lewis to Margaret Gray, May 9, 1961, *Collected Letters III*, 1265.
[16] C. S. Lewis, *Surprised by Joy: The Shape of My Early Life* (New York: Harcourt, Brace & World, 1955), 191.
[17] Herbert, "Sinne (I)," *Poems*, 38–9.

A few pages later in *Surprised by Joy* Lewis singles out Herbert from a group of other writers—all who he says were inadvertently leading him out of his atheism: "But the most alarming of all was George Herbert. Here was a man who seemed to me to excel all the authors I had ever read in conveying the very quality of life as we actually live it from moment to moment; but the wretched fellow, instead of doing it all directly, insisted on mediating it through what I would still have called 'the Christian mythology.'"[18] Later he compares himself to a fox being hunted, and includes Herbert in the "pack" of writers and thinkers who he claims are chasing him.[19] And regarding how the human conscience sometimes bothers us, Lewis writes: "When our conscience won't come down to brass-tacks but will only vaguely accuse or vaguely approve, we must say to it, like Herbert, 'Peace, prattler'—and get on."[20]

I think the most important comment Lewis makes regarding his debt to Herbert is his phrase that Herbert conveys "the very quality of life as we actually live it from moment to moment"; that is, *The Temple* resonates with Lewis (and many others) because, as Herbert says, it is "a picture of the many spiritual conflicts that have passed betwixt God and my soul." As a result, the poems in *The Temple* expose a heart before God that is open, vulnerable, honest, and longing for intimacy while at the same time it is questioning, entreating, demanding, troubled, and discontent. Herbert's poems are transparent conversations: sometimes with himself, sometimes with God, and sometimes with his warring notions of himself and God. His poems probe matters of faith and unbelief, certainty and doubt, joy and despair, delight and depression, obedience and rebellion. Herbert addresses God sometimes as a loving father and other times as a distant taskmaster. As Herbert plumbs the depths of his spiritual life, we are permitted an inside view into a soul that is supremely aware of self and yet desperately longing for union with God. When we read his poems we are permitted to look upon a soul whose quality of life as "it is lived from moment to moment"

---

[18] Lewis, *Surprised by Joy*, 214.
[19] Ibid., 225. Lewis makes passing reference to Herbert in many other letters as well as *The Allegory of Love: A Study in Medieval Tradition* (Oxford: Clarendon, 1936); *English Literature in the Sixteenth Century Excluding Drama* (Oxford: Clarendon, 1954); *Studies in Words* (Cambridge: Cambridge University Press, 1960); *Studies in Medieval and Renaissance Literature,* ed. Walter Hooper (Cambridge: Cambridge University Press, 1966); *Spenser's Images of Life,* ed. Alastair Fowler (Cambridge: Cambridge University Press, 1967); and *God in the Dock: Essays on Theology and Ethics,* ed. Walter Hooper (Grand Rapids, MI: Eerdmans, 1970).
[20] C. S. Lewis, *Letters to Malcolm: Chiefly on Prayer* (London: Geoffrey Bles, 1964), 52. The exact quote from Herbert's "Conscience," *Poems,* 96, is: "Peace pratler, do not lowre: / Not a fair look, but thou dost call it foul: / Not a sweet dish, but thou dost call it sowre: / Musick to thee doth how!"

parallels our own felt-experiences; moreover, what emerges in *The Temple* is Herbert's growth as the pastor of his own soul—informed by the grace, mercy, and love of God as expressed in the person of Jesus Christ. Lewis, whose own well-documented pilgrimage to faith was not without "many spiritual conflicts that . . . passed betwixt God and [his] soul," found the poems in *The Temple* to portray with sharp, startling, and often surprising poignancy "the very quality of life as [he] actually [lived] it from moment to moment."

Herbert's poetic voice in *The Temple* has a striking influence on Lewis's poetic voice, particularly in his religious verse. Lewis began his publishing career—not as a prose writer—but as a poet. In fact, his first two published works were volumes of poetry: *Spirits in Bondage* (1919), a volume of lyrical poems, followed by *Dymer* (1926), a long narrative poem in rhyme royal (both published under the pseudonym, Clive Hamilton, using his own first name and his mother's maiden name). Moreover, throughout his life—indeed up until the last year of his life—Lewis continued to write poetry; some poems were included in prose works like *The Pilgrim's Regress*, the Chronicles of Narnia, and the Ransom Space Trilogy, and others were published independently in magazines, journals, and newspapers. Of the more than 250 poems he wrote throughout his life, over 50 (or one fifth of all his poems) may be classed as religious.[21]

A quick survey of these poems illustrates Lewis's journey of faith from atheism to Christianity. Lewis's religious verse begins with his youthful, jaundiced perception of God as found in *Spirits in Bondage* where he portrays God as cruel and malicious. Moreover, Owen Barfield says that Lewis's early poetry, *Dymer* in particular, "is practically the only place where the voice of the earlier Lewis [pre-conversion to Christ] . . . is heard speaking not through the memory of the later Lewis but one could say in his own person."[22] However, a radical shift in his understanding of God is revealed in the poetry of *The Pilgrim's Regress*—Lewis's autobiographical allegory that chronicles his movement from atheism to Christianity; this shift corresponds with Lewis's conversion to Christ in 1931 and his subsequent gradual maturation as a Christian. While my focus in this essay will be on the religious poems found in *The Pilgrim's Regress*, it is important to note here that Lewis's later religious poems offer seasoned ruminations on life as a Christian, focusing upon the character of God;

---

[21] See C. S. Lewis, *The Complete Poems of C. S. Lewis: A Critical Edition*, ed. Don W. King (Kent, OH: Kent State University Press, 2015). All quotations from Lewis's poems in this essay are from *The Collected Poems of C. S. Lewis: A Critical Edition*.

[22] Owen Barfield, "C. S. Lewis," address at Wheaton College, Wheaton, IL, Oct. 16, 1964.

biblical themes, events or motifs; and the Christian life, including prayer, the nature of love, joy in Christ, spiritual pride, the Incarnation, the Resurrection, angels, thanksgiving, grief, doubt, heaven, hell, and temptation.[23] In many of these religious poems Lewis's poetic voice reflects the influence of Herbert's poetic voice from *The Temple*. In what follows I suggest how Herbert's honest efforts to understand the mystery of the Christian life—especially the actions of God—in poems from *The Temple* find expression in some of the religious poems of *The Pilgrim's Regress*.

By the time Lewis published *The Pilgrim's Regress* in 1933, fourteen years after *Spirits in Bondage* and two years after his conversion to Christ, his view of God had undergone profound changes. He no longer viewed God as malicious, arbitrary, and cruel.[24] The 16 poems of *The Pilgrim's Regress* reflect this changed perspective, and as a group they rank among the best of Lewis's poetry, perhaps in part because they so intimately and immediately reflect aspects of Lewis's new life in Christ. Yet while in *The Pilgrim's Regress* Lewis is no longer in open conflict with God, a number of the poems illustrate his tentative understanding of what it means to live as a believer under a God he once regularly referred to as the great "Interferer." The first poem to appear in *The Pilgrim's Regress*, "He Whom I Bow To," a sonnet written in rhyming alexandrines, does not appear until three-quarters of the way through the book. This late appearance suggests that as John, the hero of *The Pilgrim's Regress*, awakens to the truth of his broken spiritual condition

---

[23] Given the popularity of *The Problem of Pain*, *Miracles*, and *Mere Christianity*, attention should be given to his religious verse since many offer commentary on his prose apologetics as well as powerful insights into his maturation in Christ.

[24] Many passages in *Surprised by Joy* chronicle this change. The culmination of Lewis's evolving view of God is revealed where he writes of his conversion from atheism to theism, perhaps the most quoted portion of *Surprised by Joy*: "You must picture me alone in that room in Magdalen, night after night, feeling, whenever my mind lifted even for a second from my work, the steady, unrelenting approach of Him whom I so earnestly desired not to meet. That which I greatly feared had at last come upon me. In the Trinity Term of 1929 I gave in, and admitted that God was God, and knelt and prayed: perhaps, that night, the most dejected and reluctant convert in all England. I did not then see what is now the most shining and obvious thing; the Divine humility which will accept a convert even on such terms. The Prodigal Son at least walked home on his own feet. But who can duly adore that Love which will open the high gates to a prodigal who is brought in kicking, struggling, resentful, and darting his eyes in every direction for a chance of escape? The words *compelle intrare*, compel them to come in, have been so abused by wicked men that we shudder at them; but, properly understood, they plumb the depth of the Divine mercy. The hardness of God is kinder than the softness of men, and His compulsion is our liberation" (228–9).

and need for God's grace, he gives evidence of this awakening through the seemingly spontaneous overflow of poetry.[25] The speaker admits that he embraces "in heart / Meanings, I know, that cannot be the thing thou art."[26] He confesses that language used to address God is so inadequate that "prayers always, taken at their word, blaspheme." In essence the poem is an open admission that because we cannot truly understand the God to whom we pray, our words in prayer are empty, impotent, null. God, then, has to translate our feeble words; otherwise "all men are idolaters, crying unheard / To senseless idols, if thou take them at their word." Indeed, God has to "protect" us from false worship by transforming "our literal sense" and "our halting metaphors" into words that genuinely communicate what we mean.

Herbert's sonnet "Prayer (I)"[27] shares a similar perspective. However, unlike Lewis's "He Whom I Bow To," which is itself a prayer to God, Herbert's poem is a series of phrases, similes, metaphors, and apostrophes that offer brief, multifaceted descriptions of prayer. For instance, prayer is "the Churches banquet," "the soul in paraphrase, heart in pilgrimage," "reversed thunder," "a kinde of tune, which all things heare and fear," and "exalted Manna." The last two lines link directly to "He Whom I Bow To": "Church-bels beyond the starres heard, the souls bloud, / The land of spices; something understood." That is, Herbert relates that prayer works in a way that we can only partially understand—it is "something understood" intuitively rather than rationally—something that hints at what we really mean. It is "Gods breath in man returning to his birth." Both poems suggest there is a divine mystery about the way in which human prayer "works," with all the credit given to God.

---

[25] I use here the word "seemingly" because versions of most of the poems in *Pilgrim's Regress* were written as early as 1930. In Walter Hooper's 1994 edition of Lewis's *Poems* (London: Fount), he writes that "fourteen of [Lewis's] religious lyrics were sent to Owen Barfield during the summer of 1930 under the general title 'Half Hours with Hamilton,' and they are some of the most beautiful poems Lewis wrote. Most of these same poems were to appear a couple of years later in his semi-autobiographical *The Pilgrim's Regress* (1933). They were always Lewis's favourites of his own poems" (xv). "Half Hours with Hamilton or Quiet Moments" in holograph is available at the Marion E. Wade Center, Wheaton College, CSL/MS-53. The manuscript bears this epigraph: "It is hoped that this little selection from my works, from which all objectionable matter has been carefully excluded, will be found specially suitable for Sunday and family reading, and also to the higher forms of secondary schools."
[26] C. S. Lewis, *The Pilgrim's Regress: An Allegorical Apology for Christianity, Reason and Romanticism* (London: Geoffrey Bles, 1933), 144–5. In Lewis, *Collected Poems*, 225.
[27] Herbert, "Prayer (I)," *Poems*, 44.

Among the most powerful poems in *The Pilgrim's Regress* is "You Rest Upon Me All My Days," recalling poems in *Spirits in Bondage* which accuse God of being cruel and malicious; the difference in this poem, however, is that Lewis comes to see that God, while demanding and jealous, loves rather than hates the speaker.[28] The speaker grapples with a fierce omnipotence, much as a dog straining at the leash of an unyielding master. He feels like a person trapped in a burning desert bathed by unrelenting, suffocating light and heat. God, like the sun, is the "inevitable Eye" that confines a desert traveler in smothering tents and "hammers the rocks with light."[29] God here is an unyielding, unrelenting, uncompromising force. In desperation the speaker longs for "one cool breath in seven / One air from northern climes / The changing and the castle-clouded heaven / Of my old Pagan times." It is difficult not to slip into the "personal heresy" and to read these lines as recalling Lewis's affection for Norse myth and literature in terms of both its religious and metaphorical influences on his youth and young adulthood. Regardless, these lines suggest a powerful longing for freedom from the "heat" of God's eye; he is ready to retreat from the demands of an unyielding God toward the comfortable fastness of his pagan days. Such an option, however, is denied him: "But you have seized all in your rage / Of Oneness. Round about, / Beating my wings, all ways, within your cage, / I flutter, but not out." Here God is pictured as possessive, jealous, and demanding, and the speaker pictures himself as a bird trapped in a cage, straining earnestly though vainly to wing his way out.

The poem leaves two distinct impressions. The first is of a "convert" who yearns for his pre-conversion days where, rightly or wrongly, he believes life held more freedom, more satisfaction. Indeed, the tone is similar to George Herbert's "The Collar"[30]—the title offers a triple pun: the white collar a priest would wear, an animal collar attached to a leash used to restrain a raging beast, and choler—an irascible spirit or disposition to irritation. In the poem Herbert fumes against his life as both a Christian and a priest;

---

[28] The poem is found in *The Pilgrim's Regress*, Book 8, chapter 6; the chapter is entitled "Caught." John, the protagonist, having thought he had escaped from the Landlord, suddenly awakened to the fact that there was nowhere to escape him: "In one night the Landlord—call him by what name you would—had come back to the world, and filled the world, quite full without a cranny. His eyes stared and His hand pointed and His voice commanded in everything that could be heard or seen . . . all things said one word: CAUGHT—Caught into slavery again, to walk warily and on sufferance all his days, never to be alone; never the master of his own soul, to have no privacy, no corner whereof you could say to the whole universe: This is my own, here I can do as I please" (147).

[29] Lewis, *Pilgrim's Regress*, 147–8.

[30] Herbert, "The Collar," *Poems*, 143–4. See also Lewis, *Collected Poems*, 225–6.

indeed, the opening line pictures Herbert kneeling, perhaps at the altar of his own church, and suddenly furiously smashing his fist down on the altar: "I struck the board, and cry'd, No more. / I will abroad. / What shall I ever pine, and sigh? . . . Shall I be still in suit? Have I no harvest but a thorn?" Then he recalls, in the manner of Lewis in "You Rest Upon Me All My Days," earlier periods in his life when all was rich, blessed, and fruitful: "Sure there was wine / Before my sighs did drie it: there was corn / Before my tears did drown it." As he rages, he tells himself to throw over his spiritual life and instead to "recover all thy sigh-blown age / On double pleasures." He mocks and belittles his impotent efforts to live a Christian life: "Leave thy cold dispute / Of what is fit and not. Forsake thy cage, / Thy ropes of sands, / Which petty thoughts have made." As in Herbert's poem, Lewis's speaker is frustrated ("beating my wings") yet thwarted ("I flutter, but not out").

The second impression of Lewis's poem is that God is an all-encompassing, smothering, demanding deity, uncompromising in His jealous possession of a follower. Such a God seizes "all in [His] rage / Of Oneness." These impressions combine to highlight the speaker in "You Rest Upon Me All My Days" as one who regards with nostalgia his pre-conversion lifestyle, yet he also has grudging appreciation for this jealous God because now he senses it is Yahweh, not Moloch that he worships. On the other hand, Herbert's "The Collar" ends with a dramatic reversal of tone. The speaker continues to fume against the sterility of his Christian life, but then unexpectedly he is brought up short: "But as I rav'd and grew more fierce and wilde / At every word, / Me thoughts I heard one calling, *Child!* / And I reply'd, *My Lord.*" His stiff-necked bucking against God—and his mistaken view of the real character of God—is instantly broken once he hears in his conscience the gentle, comforting call of a loving father to a recalcitrant, rebellious child.

Since "You Rest Upon Me All My Days" largely resolves the question of God's real character, the remainder of Lewis's religious verse in *Pilgrim's Regress* turns to consider what it means to live as a Christian. For example, "My Heart Is Empty,"[31] with its alternating alexandrines and trimeters,

---

[31] The poem is found in *The Pilgrim's Regress*, Book 8, chapter 10; the chapter is entitled "Archetype and Ectype," 162. John and the hermit (History) discuss John's fear that "the things the Landlord really intends for me may be utterly unlike the things he has taught me to desire." The hermit assures him that the Landlord is the author of desire and that only He can fulfill John's desire. Furthermore, the hermit affirms that John's loss of his initial desire is normal: "First comes delight: then pain: then fruit. And then there is joy of the fruit, but that is different again from the first delight. And mortal lovers must not try to remain at the first step: for lasting passion is the dream of a harlot and from it we wake in despair. You must not try to keep the raptures: they have done their work. Manna kept, is worms." The hermit sings the poem and is overheard by John. In Lewis, *Collected Poems*, 226.

examines the contradiction between living the expected "abundant life" and the cold reality of spiritual torpor, linking it in some ways to Herbert's "The Collar." "My Heart Is Empty" is a candid admission that the speaker's spiritual life is a dry, arid wasteland: "All the fountains that should run / With longing, are in me / Dried up. In all my countryside there is not one / That drips to find the sea." What is worse, he has no desire to experience God's love, except as it serves to lessen his own pain: "I have no care for anything thy love can grant / Except the moment's vain / And hardly noticed filling of the moment's want / And to be free from pain." Yet the speaker avoids despair by calling out to the one "who didst take / All care for Lazarus in the careless tomb." The vigor of his faith in Christ is seen in his belief that if God will intervene in his own Lazarus-like life, he may survive for later rebirth, much as a seed "which grows / Through winter ripe for birth." Just as the dormant seed avoids the chilling winter wind, so he will endure this winter of his life: "Because, while it forgets, the heaven remembering throws / Sweet influence still on earth, /—Because the heaven, moved moth-like by thy beauty, goes / Still turning round the earth."

The pleading tone of Lewis's poem is similar to Herbert's "Dullness": "Why do I languish thus, drooping and dull, / As if I were all earth? / O give me quickness, that I may with mirth / Praise thee brim-full!"[32] The reason for Lewis's dullness is never explained. Herbert's dullness, however, is directly connected with his vision of God's beauty and his inability to give expression to this in his verse. Unlike "the wanton lover" who finds beauty in "his fairest fair"—especially "her curled hair"—Herbert sources beauty in the actions of Christ, particularly his "bloudy death . . . [that] makes thee / Pure red and white." In spite of his acknowledgment of this, he is burdened with writing dull, ineffective poetry: "Where are my lines then? my approaches? views? / Where are my window-songs?" He blames his feeble flesh, certain God has imbued him with a mind for writing beautiful poetry that reflects the beauty of Christ. His final plea is a simple prayer: "Lord, cleare thy gift, that with a constant wit / I may but look towards thee: / *Look* onely; for to *love* thee, who can be, / What angel fit?"[33] In Lewis's moments of spiritual drought, Herbert's poetic musings on a similarly arid period in his life must have been a solace.

I mentioned earlier that later religious poems by Lewis may be influenced by Herbert. In his "Yes, You Are Always Everywhere" Lewis explores the mystery of the Eucharist. After admitting that he has tried to pursue God's "scent" in forests, stars, music, and poetry—all in his longing to be intimate

---

[32] Herbert, "Dullness," *Poems*, 105.
[33] Emphasis Herbert.

with Christ—he finally turns "to the appointed place where you pursue." When he does so, the elements of communion take on a mysterious beauty and resolve his search:

> Not in Nature, not even in Man, but in one
> Particular Man, with a date, so tall, weighing
> So much, talking Aramaic, having learned a trade;
> Not in all food, not in all bread and wine
> (Not, I mean, as my littleness requires)
> But this wine, this bread . . . no beauty we could desire.[34]

Herbert's "The Bunch of Grapes," also exploring the mystery of communion, may have influenced Lewis's poem. In his poem Herbert confesses he has lost his joy but finds solace in ideas he draws from Numbers 13, the biblical account where spies sent by Moses into the land of Canaan bring back a cluster of rich grapes, emblematic of the rich inheritance God wants to give the Israelites when they enter the land. However, the Israelites reject this blessing because of the fearful report the spies bring with them about the people of Canaan. Finding himself consumed by his broken, sin-filled human flesh, stricken by the Law and unable to meet its demands, Herbert wonders "where's the cluster? the taste / Of mine inheritance."[35]

What Herbert realizes, however, is that because of God's new covenant with humankind, he has access to much more than did the Israelites:

> But can he want the grape, who hath the wine?
>   I have their fruit and more.
> Blessed be God, who prosper'd *Noahs* vine,
>   And made it bring forth grapes good store.
>   But much more him I must adore,
> Who of the Laws sowre juice sweet wine did make,
> Ev'n God himself being pressed for my sake.[36]

The beautiful analogy Herbert creates—comparing Christ to a cluster of grapes and His blood to wine ("God himself being pressed for my sake")—makes articulate one of the deepest mysteries of the Eucharist. If Lewis can

---

[34] Lewis, "Yes, You Are Always Everywhere," *Collected Poems*, 422.
[35] Herbert, "The Bunch of Grapes," *Poems*, 119.
[36] Ibid.

find in holy communion a beauty not to be found anywhere else, Herbert gives voice to this beauty in an extraordinarily striking manner.

While I could offer dozens of other examples of how Herbert's poems may have influenced Lewis's poetic voice,[37] I turn now to how Herbert's sweet, tender, sympathetic, and kindly pastoral voice in *The Temple* may have influenced Lewis's own pastoral voice. Once Lewis became well known—primarily because of books such as *The Problem of Pain*, *The Screwtape Letters*, and *Mere Christianity*—he received thousands of letters from correspondents seeking spiritual counsel.[38] In his response to many of these spiritual seekers, I believe Lewis borrows Herbert's pastoral voice. There are so many rich examples of this in his letters that I will limit myself to Lewis's spiritual advice to a selected correspondent, New Zealander, Rhona Bodle. She writes Lewis first in late 1947 about her difficultly in believing that Christ was God. In his reply of December 31, 1947, Lewis replies,

> I think it possible that what is keeping you from belief in Christ's Divinity is your apparently strong desire to believe. If you don't think it true why do you *want* to believe it? If you do think it true, then you believe it already. So I wd. recommend less anxiety about the whole question. You believe in God and trust Him. Well, you can trust him about this. If you go on steadily praying and attempting to obey the best light He had given you, can you not rely on Him to guide you into any further truth He wishes you to know? Or even if He leaves you all your life in doubt, can't you believe that He sees that to be the best state for you? I *don't* mean by this that you should cease to study and make enquiries: but that you shd. make them not with frantic desire but with cheerful curiosity and a humble readiness to accept whatever conclusions God may lead you to. (But always, all depends on the steady attempt to obey God all the time. "He who *does* the will of the Father shall know of the doctrine.") ... It is only fair to tell you that my impression is that you are in fact v. much nearer to belief in Christ than you supposed.[39]

Then after suggesting some helpful books for her to read, Lewis adds: "I'm pretty sure where you'll land, myself, and you will then wonder how you

---

[37] Other notable poems for comparison include "The Temper (I)" and "Legion," "The Windows" and "The Apologist's Evening Prayer," and "Conscience" and "Out of the Wound We Pluck."
[38] Walter Hooper, Lewis's literary executor, estimates that Lewis wrote upwards of 10,000 letters in his lifetime.
[39] C. S. Lewis to Rhona Bodle, Dec. 31, 1947, *Collected Letters II*, 823; emphasis Lewis.

ever doubted it. But you needn't keep looking over your shoulder too often. Keep your eye on the Helmsman, keep your conscience bright and your brain clear and believe you are in good hands."[40]

Lewis's friendly advice to Bodle may have been informed by a sonnet such as Herbert's "The Holdfast":

> I threatened to observe the strict degree
>   Of my deare God with all my power & might.
>   But I was told by one, it could not be;
> Yet I might trust in God to be my light.
> Then will I trust, said I, in him alone.
>   Nay, ev'n to trust in him, was also his:
>   We must confesse that nothing is our own.
> Then I confesse that he my succor is:
> But to have nought is ours, not to confesse
>   That we have nought, I stood amaz'd at this,
>   Much troubled, till I heard a friend expresse,
> That all things were more ours by being his.
> What Adam had, and forfeited for all,
> Christ keepeth now, who cannot fail or fall.[41]

Perhaps just as Herbert had been to Lewis "a friend" expressing spiritual wisdom in his own struggles with faith, so Lewis through his "pastoral" correspondence was being a friend to Bodle during her pilgrimage to belief.

After Bodle reports some success in following Lewis's advice, he replies on June 22, 1948:

> Splendid! As long as you keep in your present way holding fast to God, whether the Incarnation can be accepted or not—you can't go wrong.[42] Because, you see, it is not really you who are holding fast to Him but He to you: and He will bring you to wherever He wants . . . You are wondering if the Incarnation is true. Well, if it's not true God doesn't want you to believe it.[43]

He goes on to say: "Your own argument, that you at any rate have come to know God only thro' Christ is a v. strong one: I don't mind betting you will

---

[40] Ibid., 824.
[41] Herbert, "The Holdfast," *Poems*, 133–4.
[42] Before his conversion, Lewis struggled with the doctrine of the Incarnation. See C. S. Lewis to Arthur Greeves, Oct. 18, 1931, *Collected Letters I*, 975–7.
[43] C. S. Lewis to Rhoda Bodle, June 22, 1948, *Collected Letters II*, 857. In his use of "holding fast" twice, Lewis may have been alluding to Herbert's poem.

come to the Xtian belief in the end."⁴⁴ On February 10, 1949, he sees her moving ever closer to faith in Christ:

> I doubt whether I, or anyone else, needs to interfere. The route you are following at present seems to be the right one. Adding to Pascal's "if you had not found me you wd. not seek me" (a sentence I have long loved), the very obvious further step "And if I had not drawn you, you wd. not have found me," and seeing both in the light of Our Lord's words "No man cometh to me unless the Father have drawn him"—well, it is pretty clear that you are being conducted.⁴⁵

In subsequent letters, Lewis, though no Calvinist, urges Bodle to see the work of God in her life as irresistible grace. Other letters follow in which he responds to her queries about systematic spiritual reading and the like. After she tells Lewis she has come to faith in Christ, Lewis's response is delightfully short and gracious—"Welcome home!"⁴⁶—and recalls the simple yet profoundly moving tone of Herbert's poem, "Love (III)":

> Love bade me welcome: yet my soul drew back,
>   Guiltie of dust and sinne.
> But quick-ey'd Love, observing me grow slack
>   From my first entrance in,
> Drew nearer to me, sweetly questioning,
>   If I lack'd any thing.
>
> A guest, I answer'd, worthy to be here:
>   Love said, You shall be he.
> I the unkinde, ungratefull? Ah my deare,
>   I cannot look on thee.
> Love took my hand, and smiling did reply,
>   Who made the eyes but I?
>
> Truth Lord, but I have marr'd them: let my shame
>   Go where it doth deserve.
> And know you not, sayes Love, who bore the blame?
>   My deare, then I will serve.
> You must sit down, sayes Love, and taste my meat:
>   So I did sit and eat.⁴⁷

---

44 Ibid.
45 Ibid., Feb. 10, 1949, 915.
46 Ibid., June 24, 1949, 947.
47 Herbert, "Love (III)," *Poems*, 180.

In Lewis's correspondence with Bodle we see gentleness, kindness, insight, honesty, and, above all, grace—in short a pastoral voice informed at least in part, I believe, by Herbert's pastoral voice as revealed in *The Temple*.[48] Moreover, having fully experienced God's grace himself after many years of agnosticism and atheism, Lewis was both awed and honored to be something of a spiritual midwife for Bodle . . . and countless others.

The final aspect of *The Temple*'s influence upon Lewis centers on how the pathos of Herbert's voice in many of his poems may have influenced the pathos we find in Lewis's *A Grief Observed*, perhaps his most unsettling book.[49] So disturbing is its tone of pathos that some argue it is not about Lewis's anguish over the death of his wife, Joy Davidman, but it is instead a fictional account of grief. Mary Borhek critiques the position of those who hold this view: "The only reasons I can see for believing the book to be a fictionalized account are a desire to distance oneself from the extreme discomfort of confronting naked agony and an unwillingness to grant a revered spiritual leader and teacher permission to be a authentic, fallible, intensely real human being."[50] Others object to Lewis's candid expressions of anger at God, suggesting the book demonstrates Lewis's loss of faith: "There is no case for Christianity in this book. Gone are the persuasive arguments and the witty analogies. Gone, too, are the confidence and urbanity evident in *The Problem of Pain*. . . . The fundamental crisis of the book is a crisis of *meaning*, a crisis of such paralyzing magnitude that Lewis tries to distance himself from it in every possible way."[51] An excellent study by Noelene Kidd argues the book "is not simply a record of Lewis's grief at the loss of his beloved wife . . . but a dissection of grief itself. The work is chiefly an apology concealed by art."[52] In conversations with Michael Ward, I have heard him offer a terse summary of *A Grief Observed*: it is the yelp of a

---

[48] Lewis's pastoral voice is all the more remarkable when we consider that for many his reputation is based on the rhetorical power of his lectures and apologetics, his sharp public debates at the Socratic Club, and his "no-holds-barred" arguments with other members of the Inklings.

[49] That Lewis knew this would be the case explains why it was published under the pseudonym N. W. Clerk, the N. W. (Anglo-Saxon shorthand for *nat whilk*, "I know not whom"), a return to the way he signed many of his topical poems. In fact, the book was never published under Lewis's name while he lived.

[50] "A Grief Observed: Fact or Fiction?" *Mythlore* 16 (Summer 1990): 9. See also George Musacchio, "C. S. Lewis' *A Grief Observed* as Fiction," *Mythlore* 12 (Spring 1986): 25–7.

[51] John Beversluis, *C. S. Lewis and the Search for Rational Religion* (Grand Rapids, MI: Eerdmans, 1985), 41, 161 (emphasis Beversluis). See also his "Beyond the Double Door," *Christian History* 4, iii (1985): 28–31.

[52] Noelene Kidd, "*A Grief Observed*: Art, Apology, or Autobiography?" *The Canadian C. S. Lewis Society*, no. 97 (Spring 2000): 4.

wounded animal. Still others find the book, while a deeply moving account of loss, overly introspective and emotional, verging on the maudlin. Yet Lewis avoids sinking into self-pity in part because of a clipped, prose style characterized by short, simple sentences and brief, almost snapshot-like paragraphs. In effect, he becomes a surgeon analyzing a patient's medical chart; ironically, of course, he is both surgeon and patient. I believe Lewis found in the pathos of several poems from *The Temple* a model for the pathos he gives expression to in *A Grief Observed*.

Examples of Lewis's pathos in *A Grief Observed* are ubiquitous. Early in part one he writes: "Not that I am (I think) in much danger of ceasing to believe in God. The real danger is of coming to believe such dreadful things about Him. The conclusion I dread is not 'So there's no God after all,' but 'So this is what God's really like. Deceive yourself no longer.'"[53] Later in the same section he notes: "Cancer, and cancer, and cancer. My mother, my father, my wife. I wonder who is next in the queue."[54] One poem from *The Temple* that may have influenced the pathos of these reflections is "Affliction (IV)":

> Broken in pieces all asunder
>   Lord, hunt me not,
>   A thing forgot,
> Once a poore creature, now a wonder,
>   A wonder tortur'd in the space
> Betwixt this world and that of grace.
> My thoughts are all a case of knives,
>   Wounding my heart
>   With scatter'd smart,
> As watring pots give flowers their lives.
>   Nothing their furie can controll,
>   While they do wound and prick my soul.[55]

Both writers call into question the character of God. Is He really loving, caring, and compassionate? Or is He actually cruel, callous, and capricious? Both writers bare their raw emotions, hoping perhaps that by articulating their pain and grief they may find some relief. It is worth noting, however, that Herbert's pathos is different from Lewis's. While Lewis is reacting violently to the loss of his wife, Herbert's pathos is more humble, less strident, and

---

[53] C. S. Lewis, *A Grief Observed* (London: Faber & Faber, 1961), 9–10.
[54] Ibid., 14.
[55] Herbert, "Affliction (IV)," *Poems*, 80–1.

more intercessory than is Lewis's. Lewis comes near to "cursing God and dying"; Herbert, on the other hand, is more bewildered than blaspheming. Herbert's pathos is that of a lover longing to get nearer to his beloved; Lewis's pathos is that of an injured animal struggling to get out of the jaws of a trap. To use a metaphor Lewis would approve of, Herbert never puts God in the dock; Lewis puts God in the dock, and then he becomes the prosecuting attorney, packed jury, and prejudiced judge.

In part two of *A Grief Observed* Lewis continues such questionings, commenting bitterly: "Oh God, God, why did you take such trouble to force this creature out of its shell if it is now doomed to crawl back—to be sucked back—into it?"[56] Still later in this section he says,

> "Because she is in God's hands." But if so, she was in God's hands all the time, and I have seen what they did to her here. Do they suddenly become gentler to us the moment we are out of the body? And if so, why? If God's goodness is inconsistent with hurting us, then either God is not good or there is no God: for in the only life we know He hurts us beyond our worst fears and beyond all we can imagine. If it is consistent with hurting us, then He may hurt us after death as unendurably as before it.[57]

In Herbert's "Longing" we find a similar tone:

> With sick and famisht eyes,
> With doubling knees and weary bones,
> To thee my cries,
> To thee my grones,
> To thee my sighs, my tears ascend:
> No end?
>
> My throat, my soul is hoarse;
> My heart is wither'd like a ground
> Which thou dost curse.
> My thoughts turn round,
> And make me giddie; Lord, I fall,
> Yet call.[58]

---

[56] Lewis, *A Grief Observed*, 18.
[57] Ibid., 24–5.
[58] Herbert, "Longing," *Poems*, 139.

In both cases Lewis and Herbert confess honestly their doubt, anguish, and uncertainty; neither is sure of the goodness of God.

In the third and fourth parts of *A Grief Observed* Lewis's anger begins to subside, and his pathos slowly moderates, replaced by reasoning: "Feelings, and feelings, and feelings. Let me try thinking instead. From the rational point of view, what new factor has H.'s [Joy's] death introduced into the problem of the universe? What grounds has it given me for doubting all that I believe? I knew already that these things, and worse, happened daily."[59] Earlier his most memorable simile in *A Grief Observed* posits Heaven as an uninhabited house with locked doors:

> Go to Him when your need is desperate, when all other help is vain, and what do you find? A door slammed in your face, and a sound of bolting and double bolting on the inside. After that, silence. You may as well turn away. The longer you wait, the more emphatic the silence will become. There are no lights in the windows. It might be an empty house. Was it ever inhabited?[60]

But in part three he ameliorates this view, noting, "I have gradually been coming to feel that the door is no longer shut and bolted. Was it my own frantic need that slammed it in my face? . . . Perhaps [my] own reiterated cries deafen [me] to the voice [I] hoped to hear."[61] Still later he adds "my mind no longer meets that locked door."[62] The last time he refers to the door, he seems reconciled to the lack of an answer: "[It is] a rather special sort of 'No answer.' It is not the locked door. It is more like a silent, certainly not uncompassionate, gaze. As though He shook His head not in refusal but waiving the question. Like, 'Peace, child; you don't understand.'"[63]

In *The Temple* several poems reflect a similar kind of reasoning and engagement, all efforts by Herbert to understand the workings of God in his life. In his poem "Grief," Herbert's tone touches upon the depth of the pathos he feels: "O who will give me tears? Come all ye springs, / Dwell in my head & eyes: come clouds, & rain: / My grief hath need of all the watry things, / That nature hath produc'd."[64] He looks to draw the water from rivers to supply his tears since his two eyes are "two shallow foords, two little spouts." Even poetry—Herbert's default coping response—is inadequate:

---

[59] Lewis, *Grief Observed*, 31.
[60] Ibid., 9.
[61] Ibid., 38.
[62] Ibid., 49.
[63] Ibid., 54–5.
[64] Herbert, "Grief," *The Temple*, 154.

> Verses, ye are too fine a thing, too wise
> For my rough sorrows: cease, be dumbe and mute,
> Give up your feet and running to mine eyes,
> And keep your measures for some lovers lute,
> Whose grief allows him musick and a ryme:
> For mine excludes both measure, tune, and time.
>   Alas, my God![65]

While Herbert's "The Flower," unlike "Grief," celebrates his sense of God's "return" in his felt experience, it too gives evidence of reasoning and engagement with God:

>   Who would have thought my shrivel'd heart
> Could have recover'd greenesse? It was gone
>   Quite under ground; as flowers depart
> To see their mother-root, when they have blown;
>   Where they together
>   All the hard weather,
> Dead to the world, keep house unknown.[66]

Herbert then notes his further amazement that God seems alternately to quicken and to wither him spiritually, ending the poem with an analogy Lewis would have been proud of: "These are thy wonders, Lord of love, / To make us see we are but flowers that glide: / Which when we once can finde and prove, / Thou hast a garden for us, where to bide."[67]

Happily, Lewis's dark view of God lifts a bit toward the end of *A Grief Observed* so that he is able to suggest God may be a gardener—so careful of his plants that he prunes them when necessary—or a smith—so expert with the anvil and hammer that he beats the raw metal into perfect shapes. This view is best seen when Lewis comes to see God as "the great iconoclast" since he is nothing like what metaphors intimate:

> Not my idea of God, but God. Not my idea of H., but H. Yes, and also not my idea of my neighbour, but my neighbour. For don't we often make this mistake as regards people who are still alive—who are with us in the same room? Talking and acting not to the man himself but to the picture—almost the *précis*—we've made of him in our own minds?

---

[65] Ibid., 155.
[66] Herbert, "The Flower," *Poems*, 156.
[67] Ibid., 157.

And he has to depart from it pretty widely before we even notice the fact. In real life—that's one way it differs from novels—his words and acts are, if we observe closely, hardly ever quite "in character," that is, in what we call his character. There's always a card in his hand we didn't know about.[68]

Herbert's "Discipline" captures a similar thought and could serve as an epilogue to *A Grief Observed*:

Throw away thy rod,
Throw away thy wrath:
> O my God,
Take the gentle path.

For my hearts desire
Unto thine is bent:
> I aspire
To a full consent.

Not a word or look
I affect to own
> But by book,
And thy book alone.

Though I fail, I weep:
Though I halt in pace,
> Yet I creep
To the throne of grace.

Then let wrath remove;
Love will do the deed:
> For with love
Stonie hearts will bleed.

Love is swift of foot;
Love's a man of warre,
> And can shoot,
And can hit from farre.

---

[68] Lewis, *Grief Observed*, 53.

> Who can scape his bow?
> That which wrought on thee,
>   Brought thee low,
> Needs must work on me.
>
> Throw away thy rod;
> Though man frailties hath,
>   Thou art God:
> Throw away thy wrath.[69]

I need not provide additional examples. The marked contrast between the tone of *A Grief Observed* and almost everything else Lewis wrote has proven problematic. My point is that Lewis may have been profoundly influenced to write so personally and introspectively as a result of his reading, thinking about, and meditating on poems from *The Temple*.

I have argued in this essay that George Herbert's *The Temple* serves as one of the most important "spiritual directors" in the poems, letters, and late prose of C. S. Lewis. Lewis knew Herbert's poems and prose quite well, and may have patterned his own work as a religious poet and pastoral correspondent on this seventeenth-century country priest. When Herbert was about to enter sacred orders, a friend tried to dissuade him, arguing that such a vocation was "too mean an employment, and too much below his birth and the excellent abilities and endowments of his mind." Herbert replied:

> It hath been formerly judged that the domestic servants of the King of Heaven should be of the noblest families on earth. And though the iniquity of the late times have made clergymen meanly valued, and the sacred name of priest contemptible; yet I will labour to make it honorable, by consecrating all my learning, and all my poor abilities to advance the glory of that God that gave them; knowing that I can never do too much for him, that hath done so much for me, as to make me a Christian. And I will labour to be like my Saviour, by making humility lovely in the eyes of all men, and by following the merciful and meek example of my dear Jesus.[70]

I cannot help but believe that Lewis was deeply moved by Herbert's humility, piety, and winsome voice, finding in these qualities the very things he

---

[69] Herbert, "Discipline," *Poems*, 154.
[70] Walton, *Lives*, 192–3.

needed as anodynes to his own besetting sin of pride as he suggests in his poem "The Apologist's Evening Prayer":

> From all my lame defeats and oh! much more
> From all the victories that I seemed to score;
> From cleverness shot forth on Thy behalf
> At which, while angels weep, the audience laugh;
> From all my proofs of Thy divinity,
> Thou, who wouldst give no sign, deliver me.
>
> Thoughts are but coins. Let me not trust, instead
> Of Thee, their thin-worn images of Thy head.
> From all my thoughts, even from my thoughts of Thee,
> O thou fair Silence, fall, and set me free.
> Lord of the narrow gate and the needle's eye,
> Take from me all my trumpery lest I die.[71]

Herbert was an exemplar for Lewis and central to Lewis's journey to faith in Jesus Christ. As Lewis put it, Herbert was "one who helped to bring me back to the Faith."[72] For that reason, all who love Lewis owe it to themselves to read, meditate upon, and grapple to their souls the poems found in *The Temple*. Such an activity may lead to a spiritual transaction of the most profound kind—an encounter with the holy, one leading to a deeper understanding of the compassion, grace, and mercy of God.

Bibliography

Barfield, Owen. "C. S. Lewis." Address given at Wheaton College, Wheaton, IL, Oct. 16, 1964.
Beversluis, John. "Beyond the Double Door." *Christian History* 4, iii (1985): 28–31.
—. *C. S. Lewis and the Search for Rational Religion*. Grand Rapids, MI: Eerdmans, 1985.
Borkhek, Mary. "A Grief Observed: Fact or Fiction?" *Mythlore* 16 (Summer 1990): 4–9, 26.
Donne, John. "To the Lady Magdalen Herbert, of St. Mary Magdalen." In *The Complete Poetry of John Donne*, edited by John T. Shawcross, 333. Garden City, NY: Anchor, 1967.

---

[71] Lewis, "The Apologist's Evening Prayer," *Collected Poems*, 328.
[72] C. S. Lewis to Warfield M. Firor, March 27, 1951, *Collected Letters III*, 106.

Herbert, George. "Affliction (IV)." In *The Poems of George Herbert*, edited by Helen Gardner, 80-1. London: Oxford University Press, 1961.
—. "The Bunch of Grapes." Ibid., 118-19.
—. "The Church-Porch." Ibid., 3-20.
—. "The Collar." Ibid., 143-4.
—. "Conscience." Ibid., 96-7.
—. "Discipline." Ibid., 169-70.
—. "Dullness." Ibid., 105-6.
—. "The Flower." Ibid., 156-7.
—. "Grief." Ibid., 154-5.
—. "The Holdfast." Ibid., 133-4.
—. "Longing." Ibid., 139-41.
—. "Love (III)." Ibid., 180.
—. "Prayer (I)." Ibid., 44.
—. "Sinne (I)." Ibid., 38-9.
—. "The Temper (I)." Ibid., 47-8.
—. "The Windows." Ibid., 58-9.
—. A Priest to the Temple (or The Country Parson). London: T. Maxey, 1652.
—. *The Temple: Sacred Poems and Private Ejaculations*. Cambridge: T. Buck & R. Daniel 1633.
Kidd, Noelene. "*A Grief Observed*: Art, Apology, or Autobiography?" *The Canadian C. S. Lewis Society* No. 97 (Spring 2000): 4-11.
Lewis, C. S. "The Apologist's Evening Prayer." In *The Collected Poems of C. S. Lewis: A Critical Edition*, edited by Don W. King. Kent, OH: Kent State University Press, 2015.
—. *The Collected Letters of C. S. Lewis, Vol. I: Family Letters, 1905-1931*, edited by Walter Hooper. New York: HarperCollins, 2004.
—. *The Collected Letters of C. S. Lewis, Vol. II, Books Broadcasts, and the War, 1931-1949*, edited by Walter Hooper. New York: HarperCollins, 2004.
—. *The Collected Letters of C. S. Lewis, Vol. III: Narnia, Cambridge, and Joy, 1950-1963*, edited by Walter Hooper. New York: HarperCollins, 2007.
The Collected Poems of C. S. Lewis: A Critical Edition, edited by Don W. King. Kent, OH: Kent State University Press, 2015.
—. "Donne and Love Poetry in the Seventeenth Century." In *Studies Presented to Sir Herbert Grierson*, edited by John Dover Wilson, 68-84. Oxford: Clarendon Press, 1938. Reprinted in *Selected Literary Essays*, edited by Walter Hooper, 106-25. Cambridge: Cambridge University Press, 1969.
—. *Dymer*. In *The Collected Poems of C. S. Lewis: A Critical Edition*, edited by Don W. King. Kent, OH: Kent State University Press, 2015, 144-218. First published under the pseudonym Clive Hamilton. London: J. M. Dent, 1926. Reprinted as by C. S. Lewis, London: J. M. Dent, 1950.
—. "Ex Libris," *The Christian Century* 79 (June 6, 1962): 719.
—. *A Grief Observed*. London: Faber & Faber, 1961.
—."Half Hours with Hamilton or Quiet Moments," manuscript available at the Marion E. Wade Center, Wheaton College, Wheaton, IL. CSL/ MS-53.

—. "He Whom I Bow To." In *The Pilgrim's Regress*, 144–5. London: Geoffrey Bles, 1933. In *The Collected Poems of C. S. Lewis: A Critical Edition,* edited by Don W. King. Kent, OH: Kent State University Press, 2015.
—. "Legion." In *The Collected Poems of C. S. Lewis: A Critical Edition,* edited by Don W. King. Kent, OH: Kent State University Press, 2015.
—. *Letters to Malcolm: Chiefly on Prayer*. London: Geoffrey Bles, 1964.
—. "My Heart Is Empty." In *The Pilgrim's Regress*, 162. London: Geoffrey Bles, 1933. In *The Collected Poems of C. S. Lewis: A Critical Edition*, edited by Don W. King. Kent, OH: Kent State University Press, 2015.
—. "Yes You Are Always Everywhere." In *The Collected Poems of C. S. Lewis: A Critical Edition*, edited by Don W. King. Kent, OH: Kent State University Press, 2015.
—. "Out of the Wound We Pluck." In *The Collected Poems of C. S. Lewis: A Critical Edition*, edited by Don W. King. Kent, OH: Kent State University Press, 2015.
—. *Spirits in Bondage*. In *The Collected Poems of C. S. Lewis: A Critical Edition,* edited by Don W. King. Kent, OH: Kent State University Press, 2015. Originally published under the pseudonym of Clive Hamilton. London: Heinemann, 1919.
—. *Surprised by Joy: The Shape of My Early Life*. New York: Harcourt, Brace & World, 1955.
—. "You Rest Upon Me All My Days." In *The Pilgrim's Regress*, 147–8. London: Geoffrey Bles, 1933. In *The Collected Poems of C. S. Lewis: A Critical Edition*, edited by Don W. King. Kent, OH: Kent State University Press, 2015.
Musacchio, George. "C. S. Lewis' *A Grief Observed* as Fiction," *Mythlore* 12 (Spring 1986): 24–7.
Walton, Izaac. *Life of Herbert*, 1670.

Suggestions for further reading

First and foremost, this essay should be read in conjunction with:

Herbert, George. *A Priest to the Temple* or *The Country Parson*. London: T. Maxey, 1652.
—. *The Temple: Sacred Poems and Private Ejaculations*. Cambridge: T. Buck & R. Daniel, 1633.

Lewis, C. S. *A Grief Observed*. London: Faber & Faber, 1961.
—. *The Collected Poems of C. S. Lewis: A Critical Edition*, edited by Don W. King. Kent, OH: Kent State University Press, 2015.
—. *The Pilgrim's Regress: An Allegorical Apology for Christianity, Reason and Romanticism*. London: J. M. Dent, 1933.
—. *Surprised by Joy: The Shape of My Early Life*. New York: Harcourt, Brace & World, 1955.

Walton, Izaak. *The Lives of Doctor John Donne, Sir Henry Wotton, Mr. Richard Hooker, Mr. George Herbert, and Doctor Robert Sanderson.* 1670.

Next in importance:

Lewis, C. S. *English Literature in the Sixteenth Century Excluding Drama.* The Oxford History of English Literature. Vol. 3. Oxford: Clarendon Press, 1954.
In this majestic tome running almost 700 pages, Lewis surveys the nondramatic English and Scottish literature of the sixteenth century. In one closely argued case after another, Lewis comments on the significant and not-so-significant writers of this age. One is most impressed by the sheer magnitude of Lewis's effort, not to mention his fortitude as he plows his way through writer after writer. He groups his chapters around religious controversies, "drab" verse and prose, and the "golden" period highlighted by the appearance of Sir Philip Sidney and Edmund Spenser. Lewis refers to Herbert six times.

—. *Letters to Malcolm: Chiefly on Prayer.* London: Geoffrey Bles, 1964.
In this imaginary correspondence between an older man and a younger one, much of Lewis's pastoral voice comes through, influenced in no small part by the pastoral voice Lewis may have picked up from Herbert.

—. *Selected Literary Essays,* edited by Walter Hooper. London: Cambridge University Press, 1969.
This is a rich collection of hard to find literary essays. Of special note in the collection is the essay, "Donne and Love Poetry in the Seventeenth Century." Lewis refers to Herbert's poems "Christmas" and "Discipline."

Other books where Lewis refers to Herbert include:

Lewis, C. S. *God in the Dock: Essays on Theology and Ethics,* edited by Walter Hooper. Grand Rapids, MI: Eerdmans, 1970.

—. Review of *The Oxford Book of Christian Verse,* in the *Review of English Studies* 17 (January 1941): 95–102.

—. *Spenser's Images of Life,* edited by Alastair Fowler. Cambridge: Cambridge University Press, 1967.

—. *Studies in Words.* Cambridge: Cambridge University Press, 1960.

Also important are these works by Lewis:

Lewis, C. S. *The Allegory of Love: A Study in Medieval Tradition.* Oxford: Clarendon Press, 1936.

—. *The Discarded Image: An Introduction to Medieval and Renaissance Literature.* Cambridge: Cambridge University Press, 1964.

—. *Studies in Medieval and Renaissance Literature.* Collected by Walter Hooper. Cambridge: Cambridge University Press, 1966.

5

William Wordsworth, *The Prelude*

Mary Ritter

When C. S. Lewis first read William Wordsworth as a teenager, he violently disliked him. In 1918, however, he wrote to his friend Arthur Greeves, "You remember perhaps how violent my criticisms of him once were, but I am becoming a reformed character. I feel very weak and tired these days and inclined to lose interest in anything that needs continued attention."[1] A year later (1919) at the age of 21 he read Wordsworth's *The Prelude* and he was not very impressed by it. He reported the following to Greeves:

> You will perhaps be surprised to hear that I am reading "The Prelude" by way of graduating in Wordsworth-ism. What's even funnier, I rather like it! I'm coming to the conclusion that there are two orders of poetry—real poetry and the sort you read while smoking a pipe. "The Prelude" [is] nearly always on the second level but very comfortable and interesting all the same.[2]

A month later, he adds, "I finished the Prelude and liked it. It is about as bad as a poem could be in some ways but one considers the great passages not too dearly bought at the price of the rest."[3] Clearly, he is warming to Wordsworth.

Five years later, his appreciation of the poem is even greater: "I brought Wordsworth out to the garden and there in the delicious coolness I read

---

[1] C. S. Lewis to Arthur Greeves, Aug. 7, 1918, in *The Collected Letters of C. S. Lewis, Vol. I: Family Letters 1905–1931*, ed. Walter Hooper (New York: HarperCollins, 2004), 393.
[2] Ibid., Sept. 18, 1919, 466.
[3] Ibid., Oct. 18, 1919, 468.

Book I of *The Prelude*. This poem is really beginning to replace *Paradise Lost* as my literary metropolis."[4] Many years later, in 1951, he writes,

> Dear Dom Bede—
> A succession of illnesses and a holiday in Ireland have so far kept me from tackling Lubac. The *Prelude* has accompanied me through all the stages of my pilgrimage: it and the Aeneid (which I never feel you value sufficiently) are the two long poems to wh. I most often return.[5]

About ten years after this, Lewis listed *The Prelude* as one of the ten books that most shaped his "vocational attitude and [his] philosophy of life."[6] Here, then, is a puzzle. What did Lewis discover in this poem over the years that changed his mind from violent dislike to having a place on the list of the ten most influential books? What did he find that made *The Prelude* so important to him? I would like to suggest a few answers to this question.

There are a great many superficial similarities between Wordsworth and Lewis, but I think that for Lewis to include a writer on this list, there had to be more than mere agreement or correspondence between Lewis and the writer: it had to be a case of deep admiration and a sense that he taught Lewis something important. I think Lewis learned from Wordsworth fundamental ideas about the proper status and function of Reason and Imagination. I think he learned how to appreciate and understand and describe Nature. Wordsworth also taught Lewis what it meant to be a poet. Wordsworth set a standard of poethood by which all other poets, including Lewis himself, had to be judged. Wordsworth helped Lewis see that to write was his vocation and that he, too, was fit for it. However, Lewis may have gotten these things from Coleridge or other Romantics. It is hard to separate these threads.

Where I think one sees a profounder debt is here: Lewis regarded Wordsworth's poetry as an important stepping-stone on the path that led to his conversion. He considered Wordsworth as one who came close to perceiving the deepest truths, yet fell short in the end. He felt Wordsworth led him in the right direction along the slow path of his conversion. Wordsworth, however, did not go far enough: Lewis frequently referred to

---

[4] C. S. Lewis, June 14, 1924, *All My Road Before Me: The Diary of C. S. Lewis, 1922–1927*, ed. Walter Hooper (San Diego: Harcourt Brace Jovanovich, 1992), 333.

[5] C. S. Lewis to Dom Bede, April 23, 1951, in *The Collected Letters of C. S. Lewis Vol. III: Narnia, Cambridge, and Joy 1950–1963*, ed. Walter Hooper (New York: HarperCollins, 2007), 111.

[6] C. S. Lewis, "Ex Libris," *The Christian Century* 79 (June 6, 1962): 719.

Wordsworth as a cautionary example of the loss of "Joy" that must result in treating Nature as a god.

More than this, Wordsworth's poetry furnished Lewis with the concept and language by which he understood his own conversion: Lewis's idiosyncratic understanding of "Joy," especially, was adapted from Wordsworth's use of the term. Finally, Lewis's *The Pilgrim's Regress* was not merely modeled on *The Prelude*, but was, in fact, an interpretation and revision of Wordsworth's poem. One could also say it was a story he wrote again in *Surprised by Joy*.

In order to understand what Lewis found in it, we must describe *The Prelude* in brief. It is the first epic that traces the journey of the poet's mind as it grows and apprehends its environment and the poet's place in it. It is a spiritual autobiography that follows Wordsworth's central metaphor that wisdom is gained through a kind of journey in which we end up back where we started, but wiser and higher, renovated and renewed. Wordsworth's descriptions of his encounters with Nature and how they framed his mind provide the content of much of the poem. The goal of the poem is to describe what fitted him to be a poet and in telling the story, of course, he demonstrates that fitness.[7] The poem suggests that the poet's mind develops by perceiving, understanding, and obeying the consciousness of nature.

The general procedure in *The Prelude* is to record an experience from the poet's past, usually a solitary experience in nature, for example, a recollection of the poet's taking a neighbor's boat out alone into a lake one evening, and then to examine its philosophical and psychological significance and thus show how nature fostered in him the insights of a poet. We can call these episodes moments of Joy or "spots of time," as he does.

> There are in our existence spots of time,
> That with distinct pre-eminence retain
> A renovating virtue ... [and by which] our minds
> Are nourished and invisibly repaired;[8]

The Prelude is not really a narrative, then, but rather a recording of these moments of insight into transcendent Nature that form the poet's mind and fit him to be a poet.

The books in which we most see the influence of *The Prelude* are *The Pilgrim's Regress* and *Surprised by Joy*, and these books are about how Lewis

---

[7] Monique R. Morgan, "Narrative Means to Lyric Ends in Wordsworth's *Prelude*," *Narrative* 16, no. 3 (2008): 298–330.
[8] William Wordsworth, *The Prelude* [1805] (New York: Norton, 1979), XII, 208–11.

became a Christian and the crucial role imagination played in leading him to Christianity. I would argue that Lewis's understanding of what the Imagination is and does is very indebted to Wordsworth in particular and not just to Romantics in general. It is important to note here that ultimately "Imagination" has a quite technical definition for Lewis and cannot be confused with creativity, invention, daydreaming, or other things we often call imaginative. This is what he says about imagination in *Surprised by Joy*:

> It will be clear that at this time—at the age of six, seven, and eight—I was living almost entirely in my imagination . . . But imagination is a vague word and I must make some distinctions. It may mean the world of reverie, daydream, wish-fulfilling fantasy. Of that I knew more than enough. I often pictured myself cutting a fine figure. But I must insist that this was a totally different activity from the invention of Animal-Land. Animal-Land was not (in that sense) a fantasy at all. I was not one of the characters it contained. I was its creator, not a candidate for admission to it. Invention is essentially different from reverie; if some fail to recognize the difference . . . that is because they have not themselves experienced both. Anyone who has will understand me. In my daydreams I was training myself to be a fool; in mapping and chronicling Animal-Land I was training myself to be a novelist. Note well, a novelist; not a poet. My invented world was full (for me) of interest, bustle, humor, and character; but there was no poetry, even no romance, in it. It was almost astonishingly prosaic. Thus, if we use the word imagination in a third sense, and the highest sense of all, this invented world was not imaginative. But certain other experiences were, and I will now try to record them. The thing has been much better done by Traherne and Wordsworth, but every man must tell his own tale.[9]

Then he goes on to describe a "spot of time" in which he experienced "Joy." Joy also is a very important and singular term for Lewis, but in brief here what he reports is that a memory of a memory "suddenly arose in me without warning" and filled him with a "sensation" of bliss and desire that only lasted "a moment of time." Once the "whole glimpse [was] withdrawn, the world turned commonplace again."[10] What is notable is that this is a kind of seeing rather than a making, it is a sort of inspiration that he does not seem to be in control of, it is backwards-looking and fleeting, and it seems

---

[9] C. S. Lewis, *Surprised by Joy: The Shape of My Early Life* (New York: Houghton Mifflin Harcourt, 1956), 15.
[10] Ibid., 16.

to involve an altered consciousness. The faculty that allows or perceives this kind of seeing is called Imagination.

This is what Wordsworth says of this faculty:

> Imagination—here the Power so called
> Through sad incompetence of human speech,
> That awful Power rose from the mind's abyss
> Like an unfathered vapour that enwraps,
> At once, some lonely traveller. I was lost;
> Halted without an effort to break through;
> But to my conscious soul I now can say—
> "I recognise thy glory:" in such strength
> Of usurpation, when the light of sense
> Goes out, but with a flash that has revealed
> The invisible world, doth greatness make abode,
> There harbours; whether we be young or old,
> Our destiny, our being's heart and home,
> Is with infinitude, and only there;
> With hope it is, hope that can never die,
> Effort, and expectation, and desire,
> And something evermore about to be.[11]

Wordsworth here makes some great claims for Imagination: it is the power that grants insight; it is the faculty that recognizes glory; it surpasses reason; it reveals the invisible world; and it apprehends infinitude.

Wordsworth argues elsewhere that what this faculty perceives is certainly truth, but Lewis is not so sure. Certainly before his conversion, he seems not to trust entirely the truth of what the imagination perceives; what it perceives has to be vetted by reason. This distrust is evident in a letter he writes to Owen Barfield in the late 1920s:

> So I return to my position, that even if poetic imagination has truth, it vouches only for itself. The explicit beliefs—whether dogmative or tentative—which spring up in the tracks of retreating vision must be tried on their own merits. If after reading "Huge and mighty forms that do not live Like living men, moved slowly through my thoughts By day, and were a trouble in my dreams" [quoting *The Prelude*, 398–400] I emerge saying "Why not? How likely that such things are": and if the

---

[11] Wordsworth, *Prelude*: VI: 47–63.

same day I read "When all is done, human life is . . . but like a froward child that must be played with and humoured" [quoting Temple][12] . . . and emerge from that thinking "Yes. What are all our spiritual activities but a keeping ourselves snug and warm for a few minutes in this steppe of matter,"—then clearly I cannot use imaginative assurance in deciding between these two opinions.[13]

And further, "From all this I conclude . . . that, granting the truth of poetical imagination, we can never argue from it to the truth of any judgment which springs up in the mind as it returns to normal consciousness."[14] This suggests that Lewis thinks we cannot blindly accept what is learned from the poetical imagination, but he seems otherwise to have a very similar idea to Wordsworth as to what the poetical imagination actually is and does.

In order to see just how similar, we need to look at Joy, and Lewis's use and correction of the idea of Joy. In looking at Joy, I think, we see most clearly what is definitely Wordsworth and not just Romantic in a general sense. Lewis tells the story of his conversion in *Surprised by Joy* and *The Pilgrim's Regress* in the main as his search of Joy. He describes the first step in his conversion as an experience of Joy. Joy has a singular definition for Lewis: it is the experience "of an unsatisfied desire which is itself more desirable than any other satisfaction."[15] According to Lewis, Joy is not an experience of contentment or plenitude, but a fleeting, sensuous experience of desire for an object that is wholly other and transcendent.

In *Surprised by Joy*, Lewis describes three early "spots of time" in which he experienced Joy: the first is a memory of his brother's toy garden, which is prompted by the sight of "a flowing currant bush on a summer day"; the second is a powerful vision of what he calls "the Idea of Autumn," which washes over him while reading *Squirrel Nutkin*; and the third is a powerful insight into the idea of "Northernness," which he experiences while reading *The Saga of King Olaf*.[16]

He retells his first experience of Joy again, I think, in the following passage from *The Pilgrim's Regress*:

> suddenly he looked up and saw that he was so far away from home that he was in a part of the road he had never seen before. Then came the

---

[12] Sir William Temple, "Upon Poetry," in *Miscellanea*, Part II, Section 4 (London: Simpson, 1690).
[13] C. S. Lewis to Owen Barfield, 1927, *Collected Letters III*, 1609–10.
[14] Ibid., 1608.
[15] Lewis, *Surprised by Joy*, 17–18.
[16] Ibid., 16–17.

sound of a musical instrument, from behind it seemed, very sweet and very short, as if it were one plucking of a string or one note of a bell, and after it a full, clear voice—and it sounded so high and strange that he thought it was very far away, further than a star. The voice said, Come. Then John saw that there was a stone wall beside the road in that part: but it had (what he had never seen in a garden wall before) a window.... Through it he saw a green wood full of primroses: and he remembered suddenly how he had gone into another wood to pull primroses, as a child, very long ago—so long that even in the moment of remembering the memory seemed still out of reach. While he strained to grasp it, there came to him from beyond the wood a sweetness and a pang so piercing that instantly he forgot his father's house, and his mother, and the fear of the Landlord, and the burden of the rules. All the furniture of his mind was taken away. A moment later he found that he was sobbing, and the sun had gone in: and what it was that had happened to him he could not quite remember, nor whether it had happened in this wood, or in the other wood when he was a child. It seemed to him that a mist which hung at the far end of the wood had parted for a moment, and through the rift he had seen a calm sea, and in the sea an island . . . But even while he pictured these things he knew, with one part of his mind, that they were not like the things he had seen—nay, that what had befallen him was not seeing at all. But he was too young to heed the distinction: and too empty, now that the unbounded sweetness passed away, not to seize greedily whatever it had left behind. He had no inclination yet to go into the wood: and presently he went home, with a sad excitement upon him, repeating to himself a thousand times, "I know now what I want."[17]

Although Joy was his favorite name for it, Lewis had other names for this experience, the experience he was trying to share and explain in some ways for the rest of his life. In this, too, he was like Wordsworth, who in *The Prelude*, as in many of his other poems, is trying to describe the same thing over and over again.

One name Lewis adopted was the "numinous" experience: "What is certain is that now, at any rate, the numinous experience exists and that if we start from ourselves we can trace it a long way back . . . Going back about a century we find copious examples in Wordsworth—perhaps the finest being that passage in the first book of the Prelude where he describes

---

[17] C. S. Lewis, *The Pilgrim's Regress* (Glasgow: William Collins, Sons, 1933), 8.

his experience while rowing on the lake in the stolen boat."[18] In Lewis, this feeling may be described as *awe, Joy, sweet desire, enormous bliss, longing,* or *Sehnsucht,* and the object which excites it as the *Numinous, the far-off country, a glory, a gleam, the sublime,* or the *supernatural.*[19]

I contend, then, that Lewis developed this notion of Joy from his reading of Wordsworth's poetry in general and *The Prelude* in particular. In *The Prelude*, Wordsworth's speaker describes various "spots of time" which may be understood as moments of insight into the divine spirit immanent in nature.[20] As Wordsworth explains, even as a young child "[He] felt / Gleams like the flashing of a shield;—the earth / And common face of nature spake to [him] / Remberable things."[21] These vivid sensual experiences early in life find later correspondence with his inner modes of being; they stir his creative faculties to the production of poetry in which he celebrates his experience of the Spirit.[22] As Duncan Wu explains, "the psychological hinge on which the spots of time turn [is this]: in each there is at some profound level an unsatisfied craving in the mind—a yearning for what has been taken away."[23]

Here is another experience of Joy from *The Prelude*:

> When into air had partially dissolved
> That vision, given to spirits of the night
> And three chance human wanderers, in calm thought
> Reflected, it appeared to me the type
> Of a majestic intellect, its acts
> And its possessions, what it has and craves,
> What in itself it is, and would become.
> There I beheld the emblem of a mind
> That feeds upon infinity,[24]

---

[18] C. S. Lewis, *The Problem of Pain* (New York: HarperCollins, 2001), 7. For an extended discussion of the different forms of spiritual longing found in the works of C. S. Lewis, see Adam Barkman's chapter on Rudolf Otto's *The Idea of the Holy.*

[19] For more on the nature of the numinous, see especially pages 123–32 in Adam Barkman's essay on Rudolf Otto's *The Idea of the Holy.*

[20] Wordsworth, *Prelude*, XI: 257.

[21] Wordsworth, *Prelude* I: 585–8.

[22] Daniel K. Kuhn, "The Joy of the Absolute: A Comparative Study of the Romantic Visions of William Wordsworth and C. S. Lewis," in *Imagination and the Spirit: Essays in Literature and the Christian Faith Presented to Clyde S. Kilby*, ed. Charles A. Huttar (Grand Rapids, MI: Eerdmans, 1971), 189–214.

[23] Duncan Wu, "Tautology and Imaginative Vision in Wordsworth," *Romanticism on the Net* 2 (May 1996): 6; doi:10.7202/005717ar.

[24] Wordsworth, *Prelude*, XIV, 63–71.

What we see here is something Lewis often mentioned: that in Joy there was an experience of both having and craving at the same time. Also, notably, both authors assume the naturalness, spirituality, and universality of Joy.[25] As he reveals in *Surprised by Joy*, Lewis experiences more fleeting and irregular moments of Joy than does Wordsworth, though, like Wordsworth's, his experiences are often evoked by images, real or imagined, of nature. I maintain that Lewis uses the term "Joy" deliberately and that this is a tribute to Wordsworth.

Considering the fact that for both authors, there seems to be a sense of loss in these experiences, it is interesting that Wordsworth often describes these "spots of time" as Joyful: indeed, "Joy" is one of his favorite words, used at least 45 times in *The Prelude*. For example, the poet recalls feeling a "sublimer Joy" on certain lonely nighttime walks in which he "drink[s] the visionary power."[26] Later he tells the reader to "Wonder not / If such my transports were, for in all things / I saw one life, and felt that it was Joy."[27] In another passage in which he describes what imagination perceives in nature, he says "To unorganic Natures were transferred / My own en*joy*ments; or the Power of truth, / Coming in revelation."[28] In yet another passage, he says, "O Nature! Thou hast fed / My lofty speculations; and in thee . . . I find / A never-failing principle of Joy / And purest passion."[29] For Wordsworth, Joy is what is granted when the Imagination has an insight into the infinite spirit that is in Nature:

> And even the motion of our human blood
> Almost suspended, we are laid asleep
> In body, and become a living soul:
> While with an eye made quiet by the power
> Of harmony, and the deep power of Joy,
> We see into the life of things.[30]

These quotations reveal that Joy for Wordsworth, too, has a particular meaning that is not ordinarily associated with the word.

Consider, too, that the title of Lewis's spiritual autobiography *Surprised by Joy* comes from Wordsworth's "Surprised by Joy"[31] a poem about memory

---

[25] Ibid., Book 3.
[26] Ibid., II: 321.
[27] Ibid., 428–31.
[28] Ibid., 392–3.
[29] Ibid., 447–51.
[30] *Tintern Abbey*, 45–50.
[31] The first line of this poem is "Surprised by joy—impatient as the Wind."

and intense longing for a love who is wholly other because she is dead. Thus, I maintain that Lewis was indebted to Wordsworth for both the concept and the term Joy.

This concept is certainly not important for either Wordsworth or Lewis because it is aesthetic or creative. Joy is an experience of something behind the veil, of something spiritual that is immanent. For Wordsworth, this was the pantheistic spirit that rolls through all things. For Lewis, though, the desire in Joy is ultimately the desire for God in response to God's calling; all other objects that seem to evoke the desire are "false Florimels."[32] The story of his search for the fulfillment of the desire these moments of Joy inspire in him is the story of his spiritual development into a Christian. This is the explicit story in *The Pilgrim's Regress* and *Surprised by Joy*. In *Surprised by Joy*, Lewis recognizes the similarity of his story to Wordsworth's story of his development as a poet in *The Prelude*, pointing out, as I quoted earlier, that writing this story "has been much better done by Traherne and Wordsworth."[33] His tale is different because he does not simply find pantheism, as Wordsworth does, but traces Joy beyond pantheism to Christianity.

What is really vital to Lewis, then, is the way in which Joy leads to God. In the end, Lewis can say of his own experiences of Joy, "I still cannot help thinking . . . that the experiences themselves contained, from the very first, a wholly good element. Without them my conversion would have been more difficult."[34] Although these experiences prepared the way, it was his conversion that finally mattered. Still, Pantheism, which Joy led to earlier, was an important stepping-stone along the way.

Pantheism played an important role in Lewis's conversion. In his two spiritual autobiographies, Lewis recounts the various stages of his conversion, which he once described as follows: "My own progress had been from 'popular realism' to Philosophical Idealism; from Idealism to Pantheism; from Pantheism to Theism; and from Theism to Christianity."[35] Although he does not explicitly identify his own Pantheism with Wordsworth's, Lewis clearly indicates that it inspired or at least influenced his own. This stage is the first in which Lewis really accepts the idea of an *active* divine spirit: it is therefore crucial to his conversion to Christianity. Moreover, for Lewis this stage was powerful and long lasting: according to Hooper, it lasted for most of the 1920s and therefore for most of Lewis's twenties

---

[32] Lewis, *Pilgrim's Regress*, 13.
[33] Lewis, *Surprised by Joy*, 16.
[34] C. S. Lewis, *Christian Reflections* (Cambridge: Eerdmans, 1994), 23.
[35] Lewis, *Pilgrim's Regress*, 9.

(Lewis became a theist in 1929).[36] In 1924, for example, Lewis gave a paper to the Philosophical Society on "The Hegemony of Moral Values," in which "he accepted the primacy of a spiritual reality, which was essentially one of divine immanence rather than transcendence—the spirit within man and all reality, rather than a personal Father above him."[37] This is, of course, pantheism in a nutshell and succinctly describes Wordsworth's philosophy in *The Prelude*. Wordsworth identifies this spirit as one that "rolls through all things" but is best perceived in solitude and in nature.[38]

In *The Pilgrim's Regress*, Romanticism is most clearly represented by Mr Halfways, who is identified with John Keats. As his name suggests, Mr Halfways can get John only halfway to his destination, which is, unbeknownst to him, conversion to Christianity, but pantheism, identified with Wordsworth, can get John almost all the way there. As I understand the geography of *The Pilgrim's Regress*, the land of Wisdom— which is south of the Christian road, but not too far—is informed by Wordsworth. In Book 8 (in which John accepts the grace of God), chapter 4 of *The Pilgrim's Regress*, titled "John Finds His Voice," John begins as a Wordsworthian pantheistic optimist, but ends by praying to a God who is more transcendent than immanent. In the very next chapter, John meets Christ and accepts his offering. Lewis thus suggests that pantheism is a significant stepping-stone to Christianity: it grasps God's immanence but not his transcendence.

Moreover, in the introduction to *The Pilgrim's Regress*, Lewis calls love of the higher levels of Nature "the real *praeparatio evangelica*."[39] In Book 8, the character of History confirms this suggestion by explaining to John that nature-loving Romanticism, which is explicitly identified in the introduction of the book with *The Prelude*,[40] is the most recent of the revelations sent by God to man in order to guide man to himself (though this revelation can be corrupted or obscured by Satan). At the end of *The Prelude*, Wordsworth suggests to Coleridge that they are possessed of a revelation and that their mission is to convey it to mankind. He says that they are "Prophets of Nature" who can show men through their poetry that the mind of man has the potential for divinity even greater than that of Nature.[41] In *The Pilgrim's Regress*, History also explains to John that the Romantics possessed an especially sophisticated revelation, and that their

---

[36] Walter Hooper, ed., *C. S. Lewis: A Complete Guide to His Life and Works* (New York: HarperCollins, 1998), 329.
[37] Ibid.
[38] William Wordsworth, "Tintern Abbey," 102.
[39] Lewis, *Pilgrim's Regress*, 18.
[40] Ibid., 11.
[41] Wordsworth, *Prelude* XIII, 442–52.

peculiar calling was to make men see nature differently by revealing to them images of Nature that improved on Nature or that renewed Nature in their eyes. Essentially, then, Lewis validates Wordsworth's version of his project; he accepts Wordsworth's claim to be a "Prophet of Nature."

The Pilgrim's Regress is subtitled *An Allegorical Apology for Christianity, Reason, and Romanticism,* but in his introduction, Lewis points out that he would not have used the word "Romanticism" if he had the book to re-title, for "Romanticism" has so many meanings that it is too broad for his purpose, which is to defend a certain kind of romanticism, one associated with his understanding of "Joy." I contend that Lewis was concerned about defending Wordsworth's particular brand of romanticism especially, which was being widely debunked at the time Lewis was writing *The Pilgrim's Regress.*

Lewis, then, felt a deep sympathy for and perhaps indebtedness to the Wordsworth of *The Prelude*. In the end, however, he disagreed with this Wordsworth. For *The Prelude* is, from a traditionally Christian point of view, theologically unsound. Wordsworth's theology makes no mention of the Trinity, the Fall, or salvation, and treats heaven and hell as if they were states of mind only. As one scholar puts it, Wordsworth is "apparently endeavouring in this poem to express a philosophy free from the complication of technical theology."[42]

Lewis regarded Wordsworth as one who ultimately misinterpreted and therefore missed God's calling; perhaps this increased Lewis's sympathy for him. We see this sympathy in a passage in *Surprised by Joy* in which Lewis says: "I insisted that he [God] ought to appear in the temple I had built him; not knowing that he cares only for temple building and not at all for temples built. Wordsworth, I believe, made this mistake all his life. I am sure that all that sense of the loss of vanished vision which fills *The Prelude* was itself vision of the same kind, if only he could have believed it."[43] Wordsworth was thus also important to Lewis as a cautionary model. Wordsworth represented to Lewis what he might have remained and what others might become.

Lewis's doctrine of "first and second things" was perhaps written with this in mind. In it, Lewis argues that "every preference of a small good to a great, or a partial good to a total good, involves the loss of the small or partial good for which the sacrifice was made ... You can't get second things by putting them first; you can get second things only by putting first things first."[44] According to Lewis, because Wordsworth treated nature as a god,

---

[42] Joseph Warren Beach, "Reason and Nature in Wordsworth," *Journal of the History of Ideas* 1.1/4 (1940): 348.
[43] Lewis, *Surprised by Joy*, 166–7.
[44] C. S. Lewis, *God in the Dock: Essays on Theology and Ethics*, ed. Walter Hooper (Grand Rapids, MI: Eerdmans, 1970), 280.

Wordsworth lost both God and nature. Similarly, in *The Four Loves*, Lewis warns that

> Nature "dies" on those who try to live for a love of nature. Coleridge ended by being insensible to her; Wordsworth, by lamenting that the glory had passed away. Say your prayers in a garden early, ignoring steadfastly the dew, the birds and the flowers, and you will come away overwhelmed by its freshness and *Joy*; go there in order to be overwhelmed and, after a certain age, nine times out of ten nothing will happen to you.[45]

Again, in a sermon he gave in 1941, Lewis argues that

> Wordsworth's expedient was to identify it [Joy] with certain moments in his own past. But all this is a cheat. If Wordsworth had gone back to those moments in the past, he would not have found the thing itself, but only the reminder of it; what he remembered would turn out to be itself a remembering. The books or the music in which we thought the beauty was located will betray us if we trust to them; it was not in them, it only came through them, and what came through them was longing. These things—the beauty, the memory of our own past—are good images of what we really desire; but if they are mistaken for the thing itself, they turn into dumb idols, breaking the hearts of their worshippers. For they are not the thing itself; they are only the scent of a flower we have not found, the echo of a tune we have not heard, news from a country we have never yet visited.[46]

Because Wordsworth pursued "second things," he lost both the "first" and the "second things" in the end.

Wordsworth, then, is often used as an example in Lewis's writings of one who lost the "Joy" through neglecting to discover its true source. In *The Pilgrim's Regress*, he may even be the philosopher—or one of the philosophers—pictured as the tragic figure of Wisdom. Wisdom believes that "all this show of sky and earth floats within some mighty imagination ... [or] Rather we must say that the world is not in this mind, or in that, but in Mind itself, in that impersonal principle of consciousness which flows eternally through us."[47] After his baptism, John sees Wisdom in Limbo, where

---

[45] C. S. Lewis, *The Four Loves* (New York: Harcourt Brace Jovanovich, 1960), 32.
[46] C. S. Lewis, *The Weight of Glory and Other Addresses* (New York: Macmillan, 1949), 7.
[47] Lewis, *Pilgrim's Regress*, 128.

it is Wisdom's doom "to live for ever in desire without hope."[48] Wordsworth to Lewis was a tragic figure because he powerfully represented to Lewis one who, unlike himself, remained enchanted by a "false Florimel."

Wordsworth is not just in the imagery and content of *The Pilgrim's Regress*, though; he is also in the frame of the story, for the frame is modeled on *The Prelude*. And *The Prelude* itself was no mere cautionary tale to Lewis. *The Prelude* gave Lewis a model for thinking about his own spiritual and artistic developments, which were inextricably intertwined, as they were for Wordsworth. In *Surprised by Joy* and *The Pilgrim's Regress*, Lewis follows the example of *The Prelude*, completing and correcting the story of the education of the soul that *The Prelude* begins.

Most notably, Lewis imagines his childhood in much the same way that Wordsworth does his in *The Prelude*. This way is so unique, moreover, that it cannot simply be counted a common feature of the spiritual autobiography of Christian Europe, for it is not so much a catalogue of events or actions or reasoned positions, but a narrative of "spots of time" or experiences of Joy and their effects on the development of the writer's mind. This is not to deny that both of Lewis's books are influenced by earlier spiritual autobiographies—such as Bunyan's *The Pilgrim's Progress* for example—but to suggest that there is a strong Wordsworthian influence among these other influences, as a closer comparison of *The Pilgrim's Regress* and *The Prelude* will, I hope, prove.

In both these works, the protagonist's awareness of the divine grows from intuitions or Joy experienced in early childhood. In *The Pilgrim's Regress*, as I quoted above, the child John first experiences Joy in remembering a green wood full of primroses,[49] which is soon followed by a vision of an island with smooth turf,[50] both images of nature. In *The Prelude*, most of Book 1 is devoted to Wordsworth's recollections of "spots of time" in his early childhood in which he experienced a sensuous connection to or insight into nature. Both books open with an image of the protagonist going for a walk: in *The Pilgrim's Regress*, for example, John is first introduced as he scampers out of his parents' garden across the road into the woods; *The Prelude* describes the feel of a gentle breeze on the solitary walker's face. Both books, indeed, are full of the imagery of walking, which recalls the metaphor of the spiritual journey. Both works report a curious incident involving a bird, too. In *The Prelude*, the boy Wordsworth steals or perhaps kills a bird and is effectively reprimanded by nature; in *The Pilgrim's Regress*,

---

[48] Ibid., 179.
[49] Ibid., 33.
[50] Ibid.

John tries to kill a bird, but he is promptly reprimanded by his nurse. Here we see Lewis correcting Wordsworth's account, for he does not believe that Nature is really a moral teacher. A human, the child's nurse, has to deliver the moral lesson, which she has probably learned in church, that Nature alone communicates for Wordsworth. Also, in both works, the protagonists experience powerful revelations on a mountain or cliffside; this, of course, recalls Moses's revelation on the Mount.

In both works, too, the correct relation of Reason and Imagination is of central importance. In both, the divine spirit is perceived not primarily through the faculty of "Reason" (though both authors respect "Reason" in its right place) but through experience, and experience that is filtered through the sensuous faculty which Wordsworth (and Lewis, following the Romantics) calls the "Imagination." In his intercourse with the divine spirit, Wordsworth reports: "I felt, and nothing else; I did not judge / I never thought of judging."[51] In *The Pilgrim's Regress*, the figure of Reason is somewhat helpful in John's coming to Christianity, but the imaginative John departs from her long before he crosses the canyon that divides the secular world and the religious world in the story. For both writers, "Reason" needs to be supplemented by faith in the divine, which is in turn supported by intuition of the divine, which intuition is fueled by the "Imagination." Imagination is higher than Reason, then, though for Lewis both need to be redeemed.

On this point about the right relation of Reason and Imagination, what we need to understand about Lewis is that he *believed* in Imagination but did not trust it for a long time. He, too, believed that Imagination bypassed Reason, but for many years, he believed Imagination to be subrational rather than suprational. If we understand this, we can understand how he could say that his "imagination was baptized" by his reading of *Phantastes* in 1916,[52] but it took his reason about 15 years to catch up to it. Essentially, Reason and Imagination cannot be put in proper relation in Lewis until he converts. In *The Pilgrim's Regress*, we see Lewis express this in the geography of the world John lives in. To the north, he depicts the rational element (mostly logical in nature) without imagination. To the south, we see imagination without the rational element, reaching its nadir in the occult or mysticism. All the Romantics are, in a sense, south of the road for Lewis. What we need to note, though, is that this very conception is romantic in

---

[51] Wordsworth, *Prelude*, XI: 237–8.
[52] C. S. Lewis, *All My Road Before Me: The Diary of C. S. Lewis, 1922–1927*, ed. Walter Hooper (San Diego, CA: Harcourt Brace Jovanovich, 1992), xxxviii.

nature; a non-Romantic might have depicted this geography in terms of reason versus emotion or reason versus spiritedness or mind versus body.

Moreover, the idea of the road that runs between the north and south is quite Wordsworthian. According to Joseph Pearce, "The influence of Coleridge and Wordsworth is clearly present in the placing of the *via media* of orthodoxy between the extremes of heresy or idolatry."[53] The true road, which runs between the self-defeating syllogisms of the head and the mysticism of the imagination, is one on which Reason and Imagination, both of which have been united by faith, can walk. And this, according to Christopher C. McClinch, constitutes a unique vision in Christian apologetics. "Coupled with his universalist view of salvation, and indeed leading to it in many ways," McClinch argues, "was a fairly unique vision of the roles of imagination and reason in a properly balanced spiritual and intellectual life." Shaped by his experiences of Joy, Lewis believed that the role of the imagination was to lead the reason in the right direction. "Thus," McClinch continues, "perhaps the most persistent pattern that runs throughout his [Lewis's] work—whether scholarly, apologetic, or imaginative—is an attempt to baptize the reader's imagination in hopes that the reason will follow."[54]

To return to the structural similarities between *The Pilgrim's Regress* and *The Prelude*, both texts share the same thematic structure, a recurring one in Wordsworth's poetry, in which the protagonist begins in a good position, close to divinity, and then experiences a fall, in which he is disillusioned and led away from the divine spirit, and finally, the protagonist reascends to his former good position and rises even higher above it, attaining a final position in which the protagonist is satisfied with his more profound relation to the divine spirit. Both the characters of the poet and of John, then, experience a psychological or spiritual *felix culpa*, or happy fall, like that of the nonfigurative *felix culpa* of Adam and Eve in Milton's *Paradise Lost*. Lewis explicitly reveals that John's fall is like that of Wordsworth's in *The Prelude* by quoting the following famous passage from *The Prelude*, in which Wordsworth expresses his most profound alienation from the standard of morality that Nature had formerly provided him: "Sick, wearied out with contrarieties, he yields up moral questions in despair."[55]

---

[53] Joseph Pearce, *C. S. Lewis and the Catholic Church* (San Francisco: Ignatius, 2003), 48.
[54] Christopher C. McClinch, "Reason, Imagination, and Universalism in C. S. Lewis," MA thesis, (Blacksburg, VA: Virginia Polytechnic Institute and State University, 2002), 80.
[55] Lewis, *Pilgrim's Regress*, 145; Wordsworth, *Prelude* [1805] X, 899–900. For an extended discussion of *felix culpa*, see pages 51, 55–6 in Louis Markos' essay on Virgil's *Aeneid*.

This quotation prefaces the chapter in which John and Virtue, sickened and disillusioned with all that they have found in the northland, turn to leave the northland and head south. In both works, this moment of sickening disillusionment is the lowest point of the pilgrim's progress; from this point on, the pilgrim begins his ascent toward the divine.

Moreover, as in *The Prelude*, the purpose of the journey is not fully discovered until the end, though it is hinted at before: in *The Prelude*, the purpose and culmination of the journey is reached when Wordsworth realizes that he is called by Nature to be a poet and her prophet; in *The Pilgrim's Regress*, this is reached when John walks beyond his own former home in Puritania and crosses the brook into the Landlord's world, or heaven.

Both poems also powerfully express their frustration with certain philosophies: Wordsworth rejects Burke's understanding of the French Revolution and John must ultimately leave the House of Wisdom, which is where various personified philosophies live, in order to seek what he finally perceives as the real source of all good philosophies: God.

Moreover, it is noteworthy that in both works, Virtue is represented as a passion. Once Virtue fights the Southern Dragon in *The Pilgrim's Regress*, he is enflamed and impassioned by the southern spirit, which he corrects and saves by killing its dragon. For Wordsworth, too, virtue is a passion which one feels in the limbs, and which is often renovated and re-impassioned by intercourse with that spirit which "rolls through all things."

Finally, in the ascension that both characters experience, they receive back their "Reason" and "Imagination" in new and better forms. Book 7, chapter 7 of *The Pilgrim's Regress* is subtitled "John's Imagination Re-awakes" and describes the renovation of John's imagination by the help of Contemplation, one of the daughters of wisdom. This is surely modeled on Book 11 of *The Prelude,* titled "Imagination, How Impaired and Restored," in which Wordsworth tells much the same story, describing the renewal of his relationship to Nature. In *The Pilgrim's Regress*, moreover, Reason becomes a constant companion of John once he has crossed the canyon, or converted to Christianity. This echoes the return of Wordsworth's moral reasoning powers that accompanies his restored "Imagination."

I hope, then, that I have been able to clarify the questions with which I began. What did Lewis see in Wordsworth? Why did he so admire *The Prelude*? Lewis learned from the Romantics as a whole, and Wordsworth in particular, fundamental ideas about the proper status and function of Reason and Imagination. He learned how to understand and describe Nature. Wordsworth *forced him to think very seriously about what the role of the poet should be,* and to be a poet was his ambition for many years.

Wordsworth helped him see that to teach through writing was his vocation and that he, too, was fit for it (though pride had to be avoided in doing so).

More importantly, I maintain that Lewis's understanding of "Joy" was particularly Wordsworthian; that he viewed his own pantheist stage, influenced by Wordsworth's pantheism, as an important stepping-stone to his conversion; that he valued Wordsworth also as a cautionary model of one who ultimately misunderstood the divine call; and that *The Pilgrim's Regress* is modeled on *The Prelude*. Wordsworth's poetry gave Lewis a way to understand his own history, by documenting his moments of Joy, and a language by which to express his own story. It is no wonder, then, that Lewis counted *The Prelude* among the ten works that most influenced his life and thought.

Bibliography

Beach, Joseph Warren. "Reason and Nature in Wordsworth," *Journal of the History of Ideas* 1.1/4 (1940): 348.

Hooper, Walter. *C. S. Lewis: A Complete Guide to His Life and Works*. New York: HarperCollins, 1998.

Kuhn, Daniel K. "The Joy of the Absolute: A Comparative Study of the Romantic Visions of William Wordsworth and C. S. Lewis." In *Imagination and the Spirit: Essays in Literature and the Christian Faith Presented to Clyde S. Kilby*, edited by Charles A. Huttar, 189–214. Grand Rapids, MI: Eerdmans, 1971.

Lewis, C. S. *All My Road Before Me*, edited by Walter Hooper. San Diego: Harcourt Brace Jovanovich, 1992.

—. "Christianity and Culture." In *Christian Reflections*, edited by Walter Hooper, 12–36. Grand Rapids, MI: Eerdmans, 1994.

—. *The Collected Letters of C. S. Lewis, Vol. I: Family Letters 1905–1931*, edited by Walter Hooper. New York: HarperCollins, 2004.

—. *The Collected Letters of C. S. Lewis, Vol. III: Narnia, Cambridge, and Joy, 1950–1963*, edited by Walter Hooper. New York: HarperCollins, 2007.

—. "Ex Libris," *The Christian Century* 79 (June 6, 1962): 719.

—. *The Four Loves*. New York: Harcourt Brace Jovanovich, 1960.

—. "Interview." *The Canadian C. S. Lewis Journal* 58 (1987): 27.

—. *The Pilgrim's Regress: An Allegorical Apology for Christianity Reason and Romanticism*. Glasgow: William Collins Sons, 1933.

—. *The Problem of Pain*. New York: HarperCollins, 2001.

—. *Surprised by Joy: The Shape Of My Early Life*. New York: Houghton Mifflin Harcourt, 1956.

—. *They Stand Together: The Letters of C. S. Lewis to Arthur Greeves, 1914–1963*, edited by Walter Hooper, New York: Macmillan, 1979.

—. "The Weight of Glory." In *The Weight of Glory and Other Addresses*, 1949. Rev. and exp. edition, edited with an introduction by Walter Hooper, 3–19. New York: Macmillan, 1980.

McClinch, Christopher C. "Reason, Imagination, and Universalism in C. S. Lewis." MA thesis, Virginia Polytechnic Institute and State University, 2002. http://scholar.lib.vt.edu/theses/available/etd-05292002-153921/unrestricted/etd.pdf.

Morgan, Monique R. "Narrative Means to Lyric Ends in Wordsworth's *Prelude*," *Narrative* 16, no. 3 (2008): 298–330.

Pearce, Joseph. *C. S. Lewis and the Catholic Church*. San Francisco: Ignatius, 203. Wordsworth, William. *The Prelude*. New York: Norton, 1979.

Wu, Duncan. "Tautology and Imaginative Vision in Wordsworth." *Romanticism on the Net* 2 (May 1996): n.p. Internet. May 1, 1998.

Suggestions for further reading

Note: this chapter can be usefully paired with Adam Barkman's chapter on *The Idea of the Holy* by Rudolf Otto because they both deal with Lewis's sense of Joy or the *numinous*.

Lewis, C. S. "First and Second Things." In *God in the Dock: Essays on Theology and Ethics*. Grand Rapids, MI: Eerdmans, 1970, and "The Weight of Glory." In *The Weight of Glory and Other Addresses*. Grand Rapids, MI: Eerdmans, 1949.

In these two works, Lewis elaborates his doctrine of first and second things, which is useful in understanding why he regards Wordsworth's relationship to Nature as a cautionary tale.

—. *Narrative Poems,* edited by Walter Hooper. London: Fount Paperbacks, 1969.

In reading Lewis's poetry, especially his early poems, the reader sees how indebted Lewis is to the Romantics in general and to Wordsworth in particular for his ideas about the role of poet and even about the form and language of poetry.

Lewis, C. S. *Letters of C. S. Lewis,* edited with a memoir, by W. H. Lewis. New York: Harcourt, Brace & World, 1966.

Lewis's letters are delightful to read in general, but of special interest are his letters to Dom Bede Griffiths and Owen Barfield. In these, he discusses points of philosophy and theology, offering intimate insights into the process of his conversion.

—. "Preface." In *Pilgrim's Regress*. London: J. M. Dent and Sons, 1933.

In the preface to his spiritual biography, Lewis provides a concise taxonomy of Romanticism, classifying its different branches and identifying those with which he found affinities.

—. *The Problem of Pain*. London: Centenary, 1940.
In the opening chapter of this book, Lewis again discusses the concept of Joy, which he here calls the "numinous." He argues that this sense of longing for union with a holy power is universal and contends that it is bound up with our conscience.

—. *Surprised by Joy: The Shape of My Early Life*. London: Geoffrey Bles, 1955.
Although this was written more than 20 years after *Pilgrim's Regress*, it is best read together with the earlier work, as they give both a poetic and a prosaic explanation of Joy and its ends.

—. *Till We Have Faces*. London: Geoffrey Bles, 1956.
In this retelling of the myth of Cupid and Psyche, Lewis again treats the subject of Joy and suggests that it can lead even those who most rail against God to an understanding of and forgiveness by divinity.

McClinch, Christopher C. "Reason, Imagination, and Universalism in C. S. Lewis." MA thesis, Virginia Tech University, 2002.
This is an interesting study on the relationship between the ideas of reason and imagination in Lewis's works. The author explores Lewis's understanding of his own conversion as being initiated by the imagination and considers Lewis's writing of fiction as motivated by the desire to convert others by appealing to their imaginations.

6

Rudolf Otto, *The Idea of the Holy*

Adam Barkman

Rudolf Otto was an influential German theologian who was active in the first half of the twentieth century and whose most important work, *Das Heilige* or *The Idea of the Holy*, was a significant influence not only on the field of comparative religion in general, but on C. S. Lewis the philosopher, theologian, and imaginative writer in particular. Until the day he died, Otto was a self-confessed Lutheran who tried to navigate through both secular efforts to reduce religious experience to something more primary, and existential efforts which insisted that religion is a purely subjective phenomenon.[1] In many ways Otto, who tried to defend both rational and nonrational aspects of religion, was a kindred spirit to Lewis, who himself found in Christ the unity of both romance and reason. Nevertheless, in broad strokes, Lewis, who had a philosophical training and underwent a philosophical conversion to orthodox Christianity,[2] emphasized rationality and orthodoxy more than Otto. For example, in his edition of Otto's *Religious Essays* (a supplement to *The Idea of the Holy*), Lewis underlined Otto's claim that Christianity is superior to other religions *not* "as truth is superior to falsehood but as Plato is superior to Aristotle."[3] Otto's point is that Christianity has a "highly individual and particular spirit"—a felt spiritual intensity (and perhaps also a moral edge) over other religions. But Lewis, who said he converted to Christianity because he thought it "true,"[4]

---

[1] The existentialists that Otto most strongly opposed were those associated with Rudolf Bultmann's school of thought. Philip Almond, *Rudolf Otto: An Introduction to His Philosophical Theology* (Chapel Hill, NC: The University of North Carolina Press, 1984), 5.

[2] Lewis says his conversion to Christianity was "almost purely philosophical." C. S. Lewis, "Autobiographical Note," prepared by the Macmillian [sic] Company in 1946 (The Marion E. Wade Center, Wheaton College), 1.

[3] Rudolf Otto, *Religious Essays: A Supplement to "The Idea of the Holy,"* trans. Brian Lunn (London: Oxford University Press, 1931; Marion E. Wade Center, Wheaton College), 114.

[4] C. S. Lewis, "Modern Man and His Categories of Thought," in *C. S. Lewis: Essay Collection & Other Short Pieces*, ed. Lesley Walmsley (London: HarperCollins, 2000), 619.

did not feel the same way; rather, Lewis says that there is only one right answer (just as 1 + 1 = 2), but some answers may be closer to the truth than others (just as 3 is closer than 4).

Back in 1981, the great Lewis scholar James Como complained, "there is no major treatment of [Rudolf Otto's *The Idea of the Holy*] or description of its influence in any work on C. S. Lewis."[5] Although David Downing's controversial book *Into the Region of Awe: Mysticism in C. S. Lewis* comes the closest to doing this, Como's complaint is still justified, which is to say that although *The Idea of the Holy* has been a major influence on the Oxford don, few Lewis scholars have read it—much less tried to see, in some detail, how it fits into Lewis's thought.[6] My purpose in this chapter is to go a ways toward doing this, though probably not as fully as Como would like. Nevertheless, since the most important Ottonian influence on Lewis was his robust conception of the *numinous* experience or experience of "the Holy," I think it best for me to focus on this. Moreover, since Otto's *numinous* overlaps in many important ways with other experiences Lewis encountered and spoke of over the years—Platonic *eros* in 1915, *Sehnsucht* in 1922, "Joy" in 1924, and "Romanticism" in 1932—my intention is to situate Lewis's 1936 encounter with Otto's *numinous*, chronologically and philosophically, within the Oxford don's larger theory of spiritual longing. In other words, there is a lot of ground that needs to be covered before getting to Otto and his *numinous*.

Cf. "We want the Faith wh is true not a Faith wh will historically survive. They are not *necessarily* the same ('When the Son of Man cometh, shall He find faith on the earth!')." C. S. Lewis, marginalia in his edition of *An Interpretation of Christian Ethics* by Reinhold Niebuhr (London: Student Christian Movement Press, 1937; The Rare Book Collection, The University of North Carolina at Chapel Hill), 44. Cf. "If Christianity is untrue, then no honest man will want to believe it, however helpful it might be: if it is true, every honest man will want to believe it, even if it gives him no help at all." C. S. Lewis, "Man or Rabbit?" in *Lewis: Essay Collection: Faith, Christianity and the Church* (London: HarperCollins, 2000). 352. Cf. "And what you say about [T. S.] Eliot's 'collapse into Anglo-Catholicism' instead of 'newer and stranger things' ... is profoundly disquieting. You don't seem even to consider the hypothesis that he might have embraced this belief because he thought it *true*—that he might be looking for the true, not the 'new and strange' (of course the two might turn out to coincide, but we've no right to assume that *a priori*, and the seeking of the former is a quite different activity from seeking the latter)." C. S. Lewis to Eliza Marian Butler, Sept. 12, 1940, in *The Collected Letters of C. S. Lewis, Vol. II: Books, Broadcasts, and the War 1931–1949*, ed. Walter Hooper (New York: HarperCollins, 2004), 443.

[5] James Como, *Why I Believe in Narnia: 33 Reviews and Essays on the Life & Work of C. S. Lewis* (Allentown, PA: Zossima Press, 2008), 74.

[6] David Downing, *Into the Region of Awe: Mysticism in C. S. Lewis* (Downers Grove, IL: InterVarsity, 2005).

Platonic "eros"

The first species of spiritual longing is Platonic *eros*, or, as Lewis called it, "Eros Religion"[7] or "spiritual *eros*."[8] My reason for beginning with this term is twofold. First, Plato was the first to give a *philosophical* description of spiritual longing.[9] And second, despite the fact that Lewis's first *feeling* of spiritual longing was when he was less than 10 years old (when he saw his brother's toy garden),[10] Lewis's first *intellectual* encounter with spiritual longing was in Plato's dialogues, which he started reading back in 1913 at the age of 15. Indeed, the best example of Platonic *eros* is found in Plato's *Phaedrus*, which Lewis read in 1915 and reread many times over the course

---

[7] Lewis mentioned this term in regard to Spenser's *Faerie Queene*: "Arthur is an embodiment of what Professor Nygren calls 'Eros Religion', the thirst of the soul for the Perfection beyond the created universe. . . . It is in this very nature of the Platonic quest and the Eros religion that the soul cannot know her true aim till she has achieved it. The seeker must advance, with the possibility at each step of error, beyond the false Florimells to the true, and beyond the true Florimell to the Glory. Only such an interpretation will explain the deep seriousness and the explicitly religious language of Arthur's subsequent soliloquy (55–60)." C. S. Lewis, *Poetry and Prose in the Sixteenth Century*, in The Oxford History of English Literature, vol. 4 (Oxford: Clarendon Press, 1997), 383.

[8] Lewis used this term when he again spoke about *The Faerie Queene*: "This leads us on to the Platonic aspect of the poem. Platonically considered, Arthur is the purged philosophical soul, smitten with a spiritual *eros* for the One, the First Fair, and trying like Plotinus to make the flight alone into the alone. When at III, iv, 54, he wishes that Florimell were his Faerie Queen . . . Arthur is therefore not entirely on the wrong track. Indeed, he comes very near to voicing a prayer that sums up the whole tradition of affirmative theology; except that here the prayer 'This also is Thou, neither is this Thou' passes into 'O that this were Thou, o that Thou were this.' Unless Arthur only means 'O that I were now really finding Thee,' it is a dangerous sentiment. . . . But there is something like it in Plotinus: 'Those to whom the divine *eros* is unknown may guess at it by the passions of earth, if they remember how great a joy the possession of a beloved person is, and also remember that these earthly beloveds are mortal and harmful and that our love of them is a wooing of images' (Enneads VI, ix, 9)." C. S. Lewis, *Spenser's Images of Life*, ed. Alastair Fowler (Cambridge: Cambridge University Press, 1967), 133–4.

[9] Following his claim that "Poets have said more about [spiritual longing] than philosophers," Lewis asserted that "[spiritual longing] is there in bits of the Odyssey, in Pindar, in some of the choruses of Euripides, in Lucretius's bit about the home of the gods, in the Anglo-Saxon *Seafarer*." C. S. Lewis to Corbin Scott Carnell, Dec. 10, 1958, in *The Collected Letters of C. S. Lewis, Vol. III: Narnia, Cambridge, and Joy 1950–1963*, ed. Walter Hooper (New York: HarperCollins, 2007), 995–6. Nevertheless, no poet writing before the time of Plato worked out a theory of spiritual longing, and so Plato is properly seen as the originator of this idea.

[10] C. S. Lewis, *Surprised by Joy*, in *C. S. Lewis: Selected Books* [Long Edition] (London: HarperCollins, 1999), 1247.

of his life, including during the time he was writing his first major works: *The Quest of Bleheris*[11] and *Dymer*.[12]

From the myths told in both Plato's *Phaedrus* and *Symposium*, we can gather seven points related to this desire. First, since *eros* always wants something—since there is always a "Beloved" as Lewis would say—Platonic *eros* is the innate desire or appetite for Beauty. Second, since Platonic *eros* or love is always for something it knows about but lacks, the soul has some knowledge of true Beauty but lacks complete knowledge of it; hence, Platonic *eros* is the son of Poverty (a mortal who is always wanting) and Contrivance (an immortal god who, in virtue of his immortality, lacks nothing, including knowledge).[13] Third, since "wisdom is one of the most beautiful things, and Love is love of Beauty, it follows that Love must be a lover of wisdom;"[14] that is, Platonic *eros* is a love of Truth because it loves the Beauty in Truth; indeed, it is from this that we get the concept of the philosopher, who is a lover of Truth. Fourth, since what is good is the same as what is beautiful, the soul, lacking the Good, also desires it.[15] Fifth, because without the Good, the soul cannot be happy, the soul, by desiring Goodness (and Beauty and Truth), also desires happiness: "'And what will have been gained by the man who is in possession of the good?' 'I find that an easier question to answer; he will be happy.'"[16] Sixth, since the soul's home—its goodness and happiness—consists in the soul contemplating

---

[11] In his 1916 novel *The Quest of Bleheris*, Lewis described how the hero of the novel, Bleheris, had a perfect life and yet still longed for something more: "'What ails me now? Is it an evil thing that I shall wed with the love of my desire and all men have me in envy? Or shall a man long for drink, and then thrust away a cup that one giveth him?' And he *cursed himself*, for the joy that would not grow in his heart. . . . [H]e too had his dreams, and thought *that surely he should do great things in the world, and fight and love as mightily as the heroes of old song* (italicized text was underlined in the original). But now it seemed that his life was but a short space, a [of] little worth: that he should marry and live at ease and beget sons to live also at ease, as others did before him, and at the latter end to [grow] old and die, with all his dreams yet hidden a soft jerkin that none might know him from another." C. S. Lewis, *The Quest of Bleheris* (Unpublished novel [1916?]; The Marion E. Wade Center, Wheaton College), 10, 11.

[12] In a rough draft of *Dymer*, Lewis wrote the following: "Because of this land only did we love / The horizon, when in earth. Our sweet disease / Of longing. Our huge hope we fabled of / Our Apple-islands and Hesperian trees / Were but the faint stir of the laden breeze / Soft blowing from this coast, and for one breath / Of that breeze men went mad and longed to death." C. S. Lewis, "*Dymer* Rough Draft," in "Henry More and Dymer, MS-170" (Unpublished draft [1924?]; The Marion E. Wade Center, Wheaton College), 160. Cf. Michael Slack, "Sehnsucht and the Platonic Eros in *Dymer*," *CSL: The Bulletin of the New York C. S. Lewis Society* 11 (August 1980): 3–7.

[13] Plato, *Symposium*, 202a, 203b.
[14] Ibid., 204d.
[15] Ibid., 200e.
[16] Ibid., 204d.

Beauty (and Truth), the soul, by desiring after Beauty, Truth, Goodness and happiness, also desires after its true home. And seventh, while all people desire after Beauty, Truth, Goodness, happiness, and their true home, most fail to find these because they mistake images or copies of these Forms for the Forms themselves; indeed, instead of using the images or copies of the Forms in this world of flux as signposts that point beyond themselves to the Real World, most settle for loving the imperfect images. Only the true philosopher sees objects of beauty in the lower physical world as markers that help the soul remember true Beauty.

Lewis was familiar with all of this from very early on, but his knowledge of it grew considerably around 1922, when he, though still an atheist, first read Boethius's *Consolation of Philosophy*, which presented Platonic *eros* in a Christianized form. Mythical elements aside, Boethius's understanding of Platonic *eros* and its relation to Beauty, Truth, Goodness, happiness, and home was virtually the same as Plato's. However, there were two important differences: (1) Boethius accepted Plotinus's assessment that "the soul in its nature loves the One and longs to be one with Him;"[17] that is, Boethius agreed with the Father of Neoplatonism that the *eros* in the soul is a desire not simply for knowledge of the One (Plato), but also union with the One (Plotinus); however, (2) while Plotinus's doctrine of the soul's mystical union with the One carried with it connotations that Christians were often uncomfortable with, Boethius knew that Jesus himself spoke in similar terms (e.g. the union of the Father, Son, and believers), and so, following Augustine, argued that the *eros* in the soul is a desire for Perfect Happiness, which also happens to be Perfect Goodness, and since "nothing better than God can be conceived of," Boethius equated God with Perfect Goodness, which in turn he equated with Perfect Happiness and the true Home of the soul.[18]

Nevertheless, as Lewis himself confessed even when he read Boethius's Christian account of Platonic *eros*, he, like Boethius's "drunken man [who] cannot find by what path he may return home,"[19] did not immediately associate his own longings with Platonic *eros* and the desire for God.

Sehnsucht

The second species of spiritual longing is *Sehnsucht*. The origin of this German word has been lost to time, but we know that it was a word that was

---

[17] Plotinus, *The Enneads*, 6.9.9.
[18] Boethius, *The Consolation of Philosophy*, 3.10.25–35.
[19] Ibid., 3.55. Cf. C. S. Lewis, *The Discarded Image: An Introduction to Medieval and Renaissance Literature* (New York: Cambridge University Press, 1998), 84.

in vogue in the eighteenth and nineteenth centuries especially with the great Austrian and German composers, such as Mozart, Beethoven, and Schubert, and the early and late German Romantic writers, such as Goethe, Schiller, and Novalis. Lewis had read, or had tried to read, Goethe and Novalis in German while studying with Kirkpatrick between 1914–17; however, given Lewis's poor proficiency in German and relative neglect of the language throughout his life, it is just as likely as not that his appropriation of the word *Sehnsucht* came from sources other than the German romantics.[20] For instance, we know Lewis encountered this word in William James's *Varieties of Religious Experience*, which he read in 1922,[21] and it is very possible that Lewis's first appropriation of this word came after a deeper study of English Romantics like Wordsworth or Coleridge (who were heavily influenced by Goethe) or George MacDonald (who was heavily influenced by Novalis). Whatever the case may be, Lewis strongly believed that "[p]oets have said more about it than philosophers."[22]

Nevertheless, since Lewis himself did not begin to use the word (in print at least) until the 1940s,[23] it is clear that *Sehnsucht*, despite having become the title of the newest peer-reviewed journal dedicated solely to Lewis studies,[24] was not the Oxford don's preference when discussing spiritual longing.

While Platonic *eros* aims at Beauty, *Sehnsucht* aims more generally at "seeing the sublimity of nature," "longing for the unattainable," and "dreaming of fantasy worlds," all of which it picked up from its association

---

[20] "I . . . read a good deal in an English translation of Goethe's *Dichtung und Wahrheit*—wh I began to read in the original with Kirk a long time ago." C. S. Lewis, *All My Road Before Me: The Diary of C. S. Lewis; 1922-1927*, ed. Walter Hooper (San Diego: Harcourt Brace, 1991), 307 [March 28, 1924]. "I have again begun my German and do half an hour every morning before beginning my other work. I am still at Novalis—you will wonder how I have not finished it long ago, and even to myself I seem to have been reading it almost all my life. . . . Novalis is perhaps the greatest single influence on MacDonald." C. S. Lewis to Arthur Greeves, Aug. 13, 1930, in *The Collected Letters of C. S. Lewis, Vol. I: Family Letters 1905-1931*, ed. Walter Hooper (London: HarperCollins, 2000), 922.

[21] "Called at the Union . . . to take out W[illiam] James's *Varieties of Religious Experience*. I have been reading this most of the afternoon, a capital book." Lewis, *All My Road Before Me*, 48 [June 11, 1922]. "An excellent old German lady, who had done some traveling in her day, used to describe to me her *Sehnsucht* that she might yet visit 'Philadelphia,' whose wondrous name had always haunted her imagination." William James, *The Varieties of Religious Experience: A Study in Human Nature*, ed. Martin Marty (Toronto: Penguin, 1982), 383.

[22] C. S. Lewis to Corbin Scott Carnell, Dec. 10, 1958, *Collected Letters III*, 995–6.

[23] C. S. Lewis, "Christianity and Culture," in *C. S. Lewis: Essay Collection & Other Short Pieces*, ed. Lesley Walmsley (London: HarperCollins, 2000), 80.

[24] *Sehnsucht* is a peer-reviewed journal started in 2007 by the Arizona C. S. Lewis Society.

with "the Blue Flower" motif as found in the medieval Scandinavian ballads *Längtans Bläa Blomma*[25] and German literature, especially Novalis's *Heinrich von Ofterdingen*.[26] In fact, *Sehnsucht*'s broad attraction to the sublime and mysterious means that it is directed at both the shining and the sinister supernatural; thus, in a 1940 essay, "Christianity and Culture," Lewis says frankly, "The dangers of romantic *sehnsucht* are very great."[27]

However, Lewis still thought this term valuable particularly since it is probably best understood as a kind of spiritual "nostalgia." This, of course, reinforces the connection with Platonic *eros*, which for Plato was the desire resulting from the soul's preexistent state in which the immortal soul contemplated Beauty and thus experienced a happiness it no longer possesses. Although neither the Romantics nor Lewis were committed to Plato's doctrine of the transmigration of the souls, *Sehnsucht*'s nostalgia is more than nostalgia for a remembered past in this life. Lewis spoke of the "*Sehnsucht*, awakened by the past, the remote, or the (imagined) supernatural;"[28] he mentioned photos of an American landscape that "raise extreme *Sehnsucht*;"[29] and he talked, in very spiritual terms, of "our lifelong nostalgia."[30]

Thus, in general we can say that *Sehnsucht* connects with Platonic *eros* under the umbrella of spiritual longing in affirming a feeling of loss or lack and so attraction for something Distant and Profound that might satisfy.

"Joy"

The third species of spiritual longing is what Lewis called "Joy." He first used this term in his 1924 poem "Joy"[31] and then employed it again in his 1955 autobiography, *Surprised by Joy*, which in turn got its name from the poem "Surprised by Joy" by the romantic poet Wordsworth.[32] Joy, for Lewis, is a desire that brought him "into the region of awe ... [to] a road right out

---

[25] Corbin Scott Carnell, *Bright Shadow of Reality: Spiritual Longing in C. S. Lewis* (Grand Rapids, MI: Eerdmans, 1999), 22.
[26] Novalis, *Heinrich von Ofterdingen*, in *The Collected Works of Novalis*, ed. Hans-Joachim Mähl, vol. I (Munich: Hanser, 1978), 237–413.
[27] Lewis, "Christianity and Culture," 80.
[28] Ibid.
[29] C. S. Lewis to Mary Van Deusen, June 10, 1952, *Collected Letters III*, 199.
[30] C. S. Lewis, "The Weight of Glory," in *C. S. Lewis: Essay Collection & Other Short Pieces*, ed. Lesley Walmsley (London: HarperCollins, 2000), 104.
[31] C. S. Lewis, "Joy," *The Beacon* 3 (May 1924): 444–51. Cf. "The speed [of the motorbike], the sunlight, and the sense of coming home put me into an unusually prolonged fit of 'joy.'" Lewis, *All My Road Before Me*, 317 [April 26, 1924].
[32] Lewis, *Surprised by Joy*, 1253.

of the self, a commerce with something . . . the naked Other, imageless, unknown, undefined, desired."³³ Like Platonic *eros* and *Sehnsucht*, Joy also expresses the duality of loss (which results in pain) and desire:

> It is that of an unsatisfied desire which is itself more desirable than any other satisfaction. I call it Joy, which is here a technical term and must be sharply distinguished from both Happiness and Pleasure. Joy (in my sense) has indeed one characteristic, and one only, in common with them; the fact that anyone who has experienced it will want it again.³⁴

Although Lewis explicitly denies a strong connection between Joy and happiness, I think he, more in his rhetorical than philosophical mode, overstates his case, for the connection between Joy and happiness would have been so clear to wordsmiths like Wordsworth and Lewis, and so misleading if these were not more strongly connected than Lewis says here, that we should probably push Lewis a bit. My suggestion is that Lewis downplays happiness as the object of Joy because too many of his readers would have thought of happiness in a more trivial or worldly sense, such as the happiness of drinking a beer, reading a good book or even falling in love. In the spirit of Platonic *eros*, Lewis probably wants to say that Joy is not satisfied with such happy things, but longs for the Happiness that stands behind them. Joy feels dissatisfied with happiness *qua* earthly happiness, and so longs for a kind of death that will allow it to go deeper and further in its pursuit of the Happiness that will truly satisfy: the Happiness of Home. Certainly, he believed that we have "an appetite for beatitude"³⁵ and that we have been "made for infinite happiness,"³⁶ and

---

[33] Ibid., 1372.
[34] Ibid. During his absolute idealist phase, Lewis understood "Joy" to be the painful pleasure that arises as a result of at once desiring unity with Spirit and then realizing that such a unity can never take place since an Appearance must forever remain either an Appearance *qua* Spirit (and thus be separated from Spirit, which is Spirit *qua* the totality of all Appearances) or be dissolved into Spirit (and thus lose any individuality). C. S. Lewis, *Clivi Hamiltonis Summae Metaphysices Contra Anthroposophos Libri II* (November 1928 Unpublished "Great War" document; The Marion E. Wade Center, Wheaton College), 51. For more on this see, Adam Barkman, *C. S. Lewis and Philosophy as a Way of Life* (Allentown, PA: Zossima, 2009).
[35] Lewis, *Discarded Image*, 94.
[36] C. S. Lewis, *The Great Divorce*, in *C. S. Lewis: Selected Books* [Long Edition] (London: HarperCollins, 1999), 1057. Cf. "The process of being turned from a creature into a son would not have been difficult or painful if the human race had not turned away from God centuries ago. They were able to do this because He gave them free will: He gave them free will because a world of mere automata could never love and therefore

in *Till We Have Faces*, the Joy that desires the death that will lead to true Happiness is clear:

> "I have always—at least, ever since I can remember—had a kind of longing for death."
>
> "Ah, Psyche," I said, "have I made you so little happy as that?"
>
> "No, no, no," she said. "You don't understand. Not that kind of longing. It was when I was happiest that I longed most. It was on happy days when we were up there on the hills, the three of us, with the wind and the sunshine . . . where you couldn't see Glome or the palace. Do you remember? The colour and the smell, and looking across at the Grey Mountain in the distance? And because it was so beautiful, it set me longing, always longing. Somewhere else there must be more of it. Everything seemed to be saying, Psyche come! But I couldn't (not yet) come and I didn't know where I was to come to. It almost hurt me. I felt like a bird in a cage when the other birds of its kind are flying home . . . .—my country, the place where I ought to have been born. Do you think it all meant nothing, all the longing? The longing for home? For indeed it now feels not like going, but like going back. All my life the god of the Mountain has been wooing me."[37]

Thus, on top of sharing some emphasis on happiness with Platonic *eros*, Joy properly belongs to the genus of spiritual longing insofar as it bespeaks deep spiritual emptiness and profound desire for mysterious, divine satisfaction.

"Romanticism"

In *Surprised by Joy*, Lewis says that throughout his childhood, and indeed, throughout his entire life, neither of his parents "ever listened for the horns of elfland"[38]—a phrase which he borrowed from Tennyson's poem "The Princess" and one which both he and J. R. R. Tolkien[39] thought captured

---

know infinite happiness. The difficult part is this. All Christians are agreed that there is, in the full and original sense, only one 'Son of God.'" C. S. Lewis, *Mere Christianity*, in C. S. Lewis: Selected Books [Long Edition] (London: HarperCollins, 1999), 438.

[37] C. S. Lewis, *Till We Have Faces*, in C. S. Lewis: Selected Books [Long Edition] (London: HarperCollins, 1999), 888-9.

[38] Lewis, *Surprised by Joy*, 1246.

[39] C. S. Lewis to Arthur Greeves, March 25, 1933, *Collected Letters II*, 103.

an important aspect of the best sort of romanticism: not of "'[t]itanic characters,'" the macabre, revolution, dangerous adventures, egoism nor nature, but of the preternatural:

> The marvelous is "romantic," provided it does not make part of the believed religion. Thus magicians, ghosts, fairies, witches, dragons, nymphs, and dwarfs are "romantic"; angels, less so. Greek gods are "romantic" in Mr James Stephens or Mr Maurice Hewlett; not so in Homer and Sophocles. In this sense Malory, Boiardo, Ariosto, Spenser, Tasso, Mrs Radcliffe, Shelley, Coleridge, William Morris, and Mr E. R. Eddison are "romantic" authors.[40]

Nevertheless, while this is the kind of romantic *literature* Lewis liked best (both when he was very young and very old), it was not what he meant when he wrote a subscript under *The Pilgrim's Regress*, which reads: "An allegorical apology for Christianity, Reason and *Romanticism*."

What Lewis meant by "Romanticism" in 1932, "was a particular recurrent experience which dominated [his] childhood and adolescence and which [he] hastily called 'Romantic' because inanimate nature and marvelous literature were among the things that evoked it."[41] This "recurrent experience," Lewis said, is one of "intense longing,"[42] "immortal longings,"[43] or "strenuous longing."[44] Romanticism, I believe, is nearly identical to both *Sehnsucht* and Joy, but differs slightly from Platonic *eros*. Certainly the two concepts belong to same genus of spiritual longing in that both are desires that lead the soul past false homes on to its true Home or "the Island;"[45] however, they are separated by two things.

---

[40] C. S. Lewis, the preface to the third edition of *The Pilgrim's Regress*, in *C. S. Lewis: Selected Books* [Short Edition] (London: HarperCollins, 2002), 6.
[41] Ibid., 7.
[42] Ibid.
[43] Lewis, *Surprised by Joy*, 1341.
[44] "Hope died—rose again—quivered, and increased in us / The strenuous longing. We re-embarked to find / That genuine and utter West." C. S. Lewis, "The Landing," in *Poems* by C. S. Lewis, ed. Walter Hooper (San Diego: Harcourt Brace Jovanovich, 1964), 27–8 [lines 33–5].
[45] Lewis, *Pilgrim's Regress*, 22. Compare this to *The Last Battle*, in which Jewel the unicorn says upon arriving in the New Narnia, "'I have come home at last! This is my real country! I belong here. This is the land I have been looking for all my life, though I never knew it till now. The reason why we loved the old Narnia is that it sometimes looked like this.'" C. S. Lewis, *The Last Battle* (London: Fontana, 1985), 162. Also, in *The Horse and His Boy*, Shasta expresses this same sentiment: " 'Oh hurrah!' said Shasta. 'Then we'll go North [to Narnia]. I've been longing to go to the North all my life.' 'Of course, you have,' said the Horse. 'That's because of the blood that's in you.'" C. S. Lewis, *The Horse and His Boy* (London: Fontana, 1985), 20.

First, while Platonic *eros* is the desire for Beauty, Romanticism, as with *Sehnsucht* and Joy, was never absolutely linked to it. That is, while some beautiful objects, copies of true Beauty, ignited desire in Lewis, not all beautiful objects did; indeed, it seems that only objects that Lewis specifically identified as romantic (e.g. "the noise of falling waves" or "the title of *The Well at the World's End*"[46]) and not other beautiful objects (e.g. a new car) stirred the Oxford don.

Second, whereas for Platonic *eros* the feeling itself is beside the point (the object of the *eros* being all that matters), Lewis says that the Romantic experience, as with the Joyful experience, though certainly aimed at something outside of itself, is felt to be valuable for its own sake; as Lewis says, "the mere wanting is felt to be somehow a delight."[47]

The *numinous*

The final species of spiritual longing that Lewis encountered was Otto's *numinous*. Corbin Scott Carnell, who engaged in a written correspondence with Lewis and later wrote a book about spiritual longing in Lewis's thought, directly links *Sehnsucht* and the *numinous*.[48] While, as we shall see, I agree with this connection, Corbin himself does not give us a lot of confidence for this suggestion since he wrongly says that Otto's book "made a profound impression on Lewis in the 1920's," despite the fact that Lewis almost certainly only read *The Idea of the Holy* in English, meaning he could only have read it in 1936 (the evidence for this claim is both that Lewis, in his letters or publications, never mentioned Otto before 1936, and also that we have Lewis's English edition of *The Idea of the Holy*, which is heavily marked up, suggesting a first, rather than a second or third, encounter). Both Joe Christopher[49] and Colin Duriez[50] are more careful than Carnell in

---

[46] Lewis, preface to the third edition of *Pilgrim's Regress*, 9.
[47] Ibid.
[48] Carnell, *Bright Shadows of Reality*, 15.
[49] "It is tempting to see this argument from the numinous [in *The Problem of Pain*] to be parallel to Lewis's personal accounts of *Sehnsucht*, just as the emphasis on natural law obviously ties to Lewis's intellectual reasons for conversion to theism. It *may* be . . . [But Otto's awe] sounds far stronger than the romantic longings that Lewis describes for himself." Joe Christopher, "The Apologist," in *C. S. Lewis*, ed. Harold Bloom, 115–28 (New York: Chelsea House, 2006), 117.
[50] "Rudolf Otto's *The Idea of the Holy* is a phenomenological study of the sacred which deeply influenced Lewis's understanding of the *numinous*, and similar experiences of otherness such as 'Joy.'" Colin Duriez, "In the Library: Composition and Context," in *Reading the Classics with C. S. Lewis*, ed. Thomas Martin, 349–70 (Grand Rapids, MI: Baker, 2000), 357.

linking the *numinous* with *Sehnsucht* or Joy respectively, yet both admit, in the language I am using here, that they belong to the same family.

Be that as it may, Otto's *numinous* is unique in the study of Lewis's understanding of spiritual longing in that it is the only species of spiritual longing that we have looked at that he engaged with *after* he became a Christian. Moreover, what is interesting about Lewis listing *The Idea of the Holy* as one of the books that most influenced him is that we do not see, in fact, a lot of evidence for this important influence, particularly insofar as Otto's most important idea—the nonrational experience of *numinous*—is very similar to ideas that Lewis was previously familiar with, namely, Platonic *eros*, *Sehnsucht*, Joy, and Romanticism. Of course, to defend this claim, we first need to understand Otto's theories a bit better, and also see, in Lewis's work, what specifically he liked in Otto.

The Idea of the Holy is, as the subtitle says, "an inquiry into the non-rational factor in the idea of the divine and its relation to the rational." For Otto, the rational and nonrational are not so much about a contrast between thinking and feeling as between what can be predicated, or univocally spoken, of the *Numen*, Divine, Holy, or God, and what cannot be predicated, but only equivocally or analogically spoken, of. Whatever can be conceptually thought of in respect to God, such as that He is Love, is a rational aspect of God (from the point of view of the creature), and whatever cannot be so thought of conceptually, such as the Dying-God or Jesus's claim that "the Father and I are one," is nonrational. This language, we should pause to note, is not the language that Lewis himself will use. Lewis, who received a philosophical training, more properly will say that things that rational creatures cannot conceptually understand about God are not, in fact, nonrational—as if to imply that we could never understand them—but are, in fact, "supra-rational,"[51] meaning that if God were to give us superior powers of rationality (as we know He will in the next life), then such things could then be rationally understood (just as God rationally understands all that He Himself is). The nonrational, for Lewis, but not for Otto, is a term used of things that are truly incapable of rationality.

Nevertheless, linguistic differences aside, Lewis agreed with Otto that God is both knowable and unknowable and that it is dangerous to confuse these. For instance, Lewis agreed with Otto, who maintained that Christian theologians like Luther and Calvin often put too much emphasis on "rational" doctrines, such as unconditional election, when, in fact, God's

---

[51] C. S. Lewis, "Priestesses in the Church?" in *C. S. Lewis: Essay Collection & Other Short Pieces*, ed. Lesley Walmsley (1948 essay reprint; London: HarperCollins, 2000), 401.

will in this respect is more mysterious or supra-rational than a Luther or Calvin suspect. Lewis writes:

> What I *think* is this. Everyone looking back on *his own* conversion must feel—and I am sure the feeling is in some sense true—"It is not *I* who have done this. I did not choose Christ: He chose me. It is all free grace, wh. I have done nothing to earn." That is the Pauline account: and I am sure it is the only true account of every conversion *from the inside*. Very well. It then seems to us logical & natural to turn this personal experience into a general rule "All conversions depend on God's choice."
>
> But this I believe is exactly what we must not do: for generalizations are legitimate only when we are dealing with matters to which our faculties are adequate. Here, we are not. *How* our individual experiences are *in reality* consistent with (a) Our idea of Divine justice, (b) The parable [of the sheep and goats: Matt. 25:30–46, in which "all depends on works"] . . . is not clear. What is clear is that *we* can't find a consistent formula. I think we must take a leaf out of the scientists' book. They are quite familiar with the fact that, for example, Light has to be regarded *both* as a wave in the ether and as a stream of particles. No one can make these two views consistent. Of course reality must be self-consistent: but till (if ever) we can see the consistency it is better to hold two inconsistent views than to ignore one side of the evidence.[52]

When St Paul talks about election, both Otto and Lewis would maintain that St Paul is uttering meaningful words (indeed, words inspired by God and formed in the imagination), yet the complete truth of these words, for

---

[52] C. S. Lewis to Mrs. Emily McLay, Aug. 3, 1953 in *Collected Letters III*, 354–5. Furthermore, while it is not wrong for theologians to try to explain the Atonement, Lewis agreed with George MacDonald that such theologians are always on dangerous ground because *how* Christ's death takes away sin is not as important as *that* it does. George MacDonald, *Unspoken Sermons: Series I, II, III* (Boston, MA: IndyPublish, n.d.), 304 [3.7]. It is for this reason that while most who read *The Lion, the Witch, and the Wardrobe* probably get the impression Lewis is being perfectly Anselmian in regard to Aslan's sacrifice for Edmund, these same people are often surprised when they read Lewis's letters and discover that he wavered unconcernedly between the Anselmian model and the Christus Victor model, the Oxford don regulating the *how* of Christ's death, which is the theological question, as subordinate to the *that*—"the Deeper Magic," the mythical, transcendent fact. C. S. Lewis, *The Lion, the Witch and the Wardrobe* (1950 reprint; London: Fontana, 1985), 148.

Otto and Lewis, cannot be fully understood or assessed by reason since we lack some knowledge that only God has.

In this respect, Lewis also agreed with Otto, who resisted "rational" (but in fact irrational) efforts to reduce divine mystery, in Otto's phrase, to "trivial allegories." [53] This, Otto says, is "a sign of decay," and Lewis, in his edition of Otto's *The Kingdom of God and the Son of Man*, happily agrees.[54] Indeed, though it is impossible to get into the details here, Lewis's entire theory of myth is based on the current nonreductive nature of myth and the suprarational. He thought that people were better off simply enjoying a myth, "simply swallowing the story," rather than contemplating the myth and "trying to find an allegorical, separable *significacio*."[55] Myth, and the things that attract the *numinous*, are not reducible, even to moral principles: "The Numinous is not the same as the morally good," says Lewis, paraphrasing Otto approvingly.[56] Consequently, Lewis, like Otto, had little sympathy with modernist interpretations of scripture—"Stoic allegorisations of the myths standing to the original cult rather as Modernism to Christianity"[57]— because he insisted that by totally contemplating or allegorizing myths, something inexplicable and mysterious is actually lost,[58] for while *all* myths *can* be interpreted allegorically—where you are given, at least according to Lewis's narrow view of allegory, "one thing in terms of another"[59]—myths, at their best, resist being put in strict "conceptual terms"[60]: "But it remains true that wherever the symbols are best, the key is least adequate. For when allegory is at its best, it approaches myth, which must be grasped with the

---

[53] Rudolf Otto, *The Kingdom of God and the Son of Man: A Study in the History of Religion*, trans. Floyd Filson and Bertram Woolf (London: Lutterworth, 1938), 376.
[54] Ibid.
[55] C. S. Lewis to Eliza Marian Butler, Aug. 23, 1940, *Collected Letters II*, 441.
[56] C. S. Lewis, *The Problem of Pain* (New York: HarperCollins, 2001), 10.
[57] C. S. Lewis to Clyde S. Kilby, Feb. 10, 1957, *Collected Letters III*, 830. Also consider the fact that in *Till We Have Faces*, Lewis made the Fox a person who represents Stoicism: "The Fox expresses *neither* Anthroposophy *nor* my views, but Stoicism." Ibid., March 26, 1963, 1419. And then later Lewis said the Stoic Fox is an embodiment of a "shallow 'enlightenment,'" much like modernist demythologizing of the Bible. Ibid., Nov. 1962, 1382.
[58] C. S. Lewis, *An Experiment in Criticism* (Cambridge: Cambridge University Press, 1999), 45.
[59] C. S. Lewis, "The Vision of John Bunyan," in *Selected Literary Essays*, by C. S. Lewis, ed. Walter Hooper (1962 essay reprint; Cambridge: Cambridge University Press, 1969), 148. In this same essay Lewis went on to explain how an allegory should be used: "We ought to be thinking 'This green valley, where the shepherd boy is singing, represents humility;' we ought to be discovering, as we read, that humility is like that green valley. That way, moving always into the book, not out of it, from the concept to the image, enriches the concept. And that is what allegory is for." Ibid., 149.
[60] Lewis, *Collected Letters II*, 438 [Aug. 18, 1940].

imagination, not with the intellect.... It is the sort of thing you cannot learn from definition: you must rather get to know it;"[61] this is to say that myth points to an essentially nonconceptual, supra-rational thing: "In poetry the words are the body and the 'theme' or 'content' is the soul. But in myth the imagined events are the body and something *inexpressible* is the soul."[62] As a result of their elusive, supra-rational nature, myths, like "manna" (which "is to each man a different dish and to each the dish he needs"),[63] are often opened to a variety of readings, whereas allegories are not: "[A] good myth (i.e. a story out of which ever varying meanings will grow for different readers and in different ages) is a higher thing than an allegory (into which *one* meaning has been put). Into an allegory a man can put only what he already knows: in a myth he puts what he does not yet know and cd. not come to know in any other way."[64] Myths are instances of "transposition" or the Divine adapting something "from a richer to a poorer medium."[65]

Is it likely, then, that Lewis's extremely important theory of myth was significantly influenced by Otto's *The Idea of the Holy*? Almost certainly not; by the time Lewis came to Otto, his theory of myth was largely in place, having been formed throughout the 1920s in his "Great War" with Owen Barfield, and having been baptized by Chesterton, Tolkien, and others in the early 1930s. We need to go deeper, then, into the idea of the Holy, in order to see where Otto's apparent important influence lies.

From the word *numen* or holy, Otto derived the word "*numinous*," from which he then spoke of a *numinous* category of value which is always present when an individual is in a *numinous* state of mind. "This mental state," Otto wrote, "is perfectly *sui generis* and irreducible to any other; and therefore, like every absolutely primary and elementary datum, while it admits of being discussed, it cannot be strictly defined."[66] Nevertheless, despite Otto's initial insistence that the *numinous* is absolutely basic and unique, later on

---

[61] Lewis, preface to the third edition of *Pilgrim's Regress*, 12. Cf. "The mere fact that you *can* allegorise the work before you is of itself no proof that it is an allegory. Of course you can allegorise it. You can allegorise anything, whether in art or real life." C. S. Lewis, "On Criticism," in *C. S. Lewis: Essay Collection & Other Short Pieces*, ed. Lesley Walmsley (London: HarperCollins, 2000), 550. This is an incomplete essay that appears to have been written fairly late in Lewis's life.
[62] C. S. Lewis, "The Language of Religion," in *C. S. Lewis: Essay Collection & Other Short Pieces*, ed. Lesley Walmsley (1960 essay reprint; London: HarperCollins, 2000), 262 (emphasis mine).
[63] C. S. Lewis, "Shelley, Dryden and Mr. Eliot," in *Selected Literary Essays*, by C. S. Lewis, ed. Walter Hooper (Cambridge: Cambridge University Press, 1969), 205.
[64] C. S. Lewis to Father Peter Milward, Sept. 22, 1956, in *Collected Letters III*, 789–90.
[65] C. S. Lewis, "Transposition," in *C. S. Lewis: Essay Collection & Other Short Pieces*, ed. Lesley Walmsley (London: HarperCollins, 2000), 271.
[66] Otto, *Idea of the Holy*, 7.

not only did he concede that the *numinous* is intimately related to Kant's sublime, but also that it is, though he did not say so in so many words, broadly related to other forms of spiritual desire. However, before any of these connections can be made, it is important to be clear about the nature of the *numinous*.

According to Otto, the *numinous* is the feeling that overcomes the mind when the individual "is submerged and overwhelmed by its own nothingness."[67] This feeling, in turn, is always accompanied by a sense of complete dependence on the Divine.[68] However, this feeling of dependence is not merely a natural feeling of dependence, such as insufficiency resulting from a difficult circumstance; rather, it is a deep, existential sense of dependence, like the dependence Abraham felt when he pled with God for the men of Sodom: "Behold now, I, who am but dust and ash, have taken upon me to speak unto the Lord."[69] Otto called this kind of dependency the "creature-feeling,"[70] and Lewis "the shame of being mortal."[71] Whether Lewis's "shame" is directly influenced by Otto's "creature-feeling" is unclear especially since one could easily see such a feeling in Platonic *eros*, which speaks of "poverty," for example; nevertheless, the possibility remains and may even be probable if the biblical accounts of the *numinous* that Lewis gives in chapter one of *The Problem of Pain* are any indicator.

Be that as it may, while the *numinous* is broadly identified with "creature-feeling" (or "shame"), Otto claimed that this can be divided into two key elements: (1) the feeling of *mysterium tremendum*, and (2) fascination. For the sake of systematization, I will begin with *mysterium tremendum*, and then move on to fascination.

When an individual experiences *mysterium tremendum*, he feels he is in the presence of something which is at once awful, august, majestic, overpowering, living, urgent, wholly different, pulsating, and uncanny.[72] The feeling of *mysterium tremendum* may "burst in sudden eruption up from the depths of the soul with spasms and convulsions, or lead to the

---

[67] Ibid., 10.
[68] Ibid., 25.
[69] Genesis 28:27.
[70] Otto, *Idea of the Holy*, 8.
[71] When Psyche met Cupid for the first time, she said, "'When I saw the Westwind I was neither glad nor afraid (at first). I felt ashamed ... Ashamed of looking like a mortal; ashamed of being a mortal. . . . This shame . . . It's the being mortal; being, how shall I say it? . . . insufficient.'" Lewis, *Till We Have Faces*, 910, 911. Also consider one of Lewis's favorite quotations from Thomas Browne which reads: "I am not so much afraid of death as ashamed thereof." Thomas Browne, *Religio Medici*, in *The Harvard Classics*, ed. Charles W. Elliot (New York: P. F. Collier & Sons, 1937), 291 [1.40].
[72] Otto, *Idea of the Holy*, 13–30.

strongest excitements, to intoxicated frenzy, to transport, and to ecstasy"; in itself, this feeling, like *Sehnsucht*, may be either demonic or angelic, something wild and grisly or beautiful and pure.[73] Yet in whatever mode this feeling takes, it always makes the mind shudder and the individual think of himself as less than nothing since he feels himself to be in the presence of something that is nonhuman, Wholly Other and yet pulsating with an energy and life more real than his own.

Lewis himself rejected Otto's language of the "Wholly Other," calling it "meaningless" presumably because a thing that is wholly other is nothing that can be talked about conceptually or nonconceptually.[74] Nevertheless, Otto's description of the *mysterium tremendum*—its awfulness and its distinction "*from that of being afraid*"[75]—is, if annotations in Lewis's edition of *The Idea of the Holy* and Lewis's own published work are any indicator, probably something of a theoretical influence on Lewis. For instance, in "Is Theism Important?" Lewis directly discusses Otto and awe, writing, "We have in English an exact name for the emotion aroused by the Numinous, which Otto, writing in German, lacked; we have the word Awe—an emotion very like fear, with the important difference that it need imply no estimate of danger."[76] In *The Problem of Pain*, the first chapter of which Lewis engages in a fairly detailed discussion of Otto's *numinous*, Lewis suggests later on that on the New Earth or in Heaven, "the lion, when he has ceased to be dangerous, will still be aweful."[77] In *An Experiment in Criticism*, Lewis says that one element of myth is that it is "awe-inspiring."[78] And in *The Lion, the Witch, and the Wardrobe,* the four Pevensie children experience awe upon hearing the name "Aslan."[79] However, as I said, we must not exaggerate Otto's influence, even the influence of a theoretical

---

[73] Ibid., 12–13.
[74] C. S. Lewis, *Prayer: Letters to Malcolm*, in *C. S. Lewis: Selected Books* [Long Edition] (1964 reprint; London: HarperCollins, 1999), 565.
[75] C. S. Lewis, underlining (in italics) in his edition of *The Idea of the Holy: An Inquiry in to the Non-Rational Factor in the Idea of the Divine and Its Relation to the Rational*, by Rudolf Otto, trans. John W. Harvey (Oxford: Oxford University Press, 1936; The Rare Book Collection, The University of North Carolina at Chapel Hill), 13.
[76] C. S. Lewis, "Is Theism Important?" in *God in the Dock* by C. S. Lewis, ed. Walter Hooper (Grand Rapids, MI: Eerdmans, 1970), 174.
[77] Lewis, *The Problem of Pain*, 147. "In all developed religion we find three strands.... The first of these is what Professor Otto calls the experience of the *Numinous*.... This feeling may be described as awe, and the object which excites it as the *Numinous* .... A modern example may be found ... in *The Wind in the Willows* where Rat and Mole approach Pan on the island. 'Rat,' he found breath to whisper, shaking, 'Are you afraid?' 'Afraid?' murmured the Rat, his eyes shining with unutterable love. 'Afraid? of Him? O, never, never. And yet—and yet—O Mole, I am afraid.'" Ibid., 5, 7.
[78] Lewis, *An Experiment in Criticism*, 44.
[79] Lewis, *The Lion, the Witch, and the Wardrobe*, 65.

understanding of *numinous* awe, on Lewis, for way back in his unpublished 1916 romance, *The Quest of Bleheris*, Lewis wrote tellingly:

> "In God's name," said Bleheris, "speak to me plain, and riddle not." So the churl, looking yet once again at the dark stairway, put his haggard face close to the youth, and whispered so low that it was scarcely to be heard, "Bethrelladoom." At the sound of that word, Bleheris felt on a sudden *strange terror come upon him: yet not in truth an honest fear*, as he had felt towards the Lumpher of the Sunken Wood, but rather *a shrinking awe as a savage might feel towards the frightful god of his imaginings.*[80]

In addition to awe, eeriness or a sense of the uncanny is central to *mysterium tremendum* in particular and the *numinous* in general. Eeriness is a vital part of this concept since it points to the unlimited, nonnatural and indeterminate nature of the *numinous*. Otto himself compared this element of the *numinous* to Kant's sublime, for while neither are concerned with Beauty per se, both are concerned with the mysterious, the maddening, the daunting, the unformed, and the boundless[81] (although, of course, Kant's sublime has to do with aesthetics, whereas Otto's *numinous* has to do with religion; hence, Otto said Kant's sublime is "a pale reflexion of" the *numinous*).[82] These common elements in the *numinous* and the sublime are also shared with *Sehnsucht*, Joy, and Romanticism, for they are not, as Platonic *eros* is, concerned with Beauty as such, but with the wonderful, the marvellous, the elusive, and the haunting. Hence, the *numinous*, not to mention *Sehnsucht*, Romanticism, and Joy, can be incited by things like romantic literature, fairy stories and, most importantly, myths; as Otto says, "But the fairy-story proper only comes into being with the element of the 'wonderful,' with miracle and miraculous events and consequences, i.e. by means of an infusion of the *numinous*. And the same holds good in an increased degree of *myth*."[83]

---

[80] Lewis, *The Quest of Bleheris*, 29 (emphasis mine).
[81] For Kant, emotion is irrelevant to beauty, but not to the sublime. Moreover, while beauty has to do with quality, the formed, the finite, and the natural, the sublime has to do with quantity, the unformed, the infinite, and the nonrational. Immanuel Kant, *Critique of Judgement*, trans. J. H. Bernard (1790 reprint; New York: Hafner, 1961) [2.23]. It should be noted that the division between the sublime and the beautiful did not originate with Kant, for Kant himself derived this idea from Edmund Burke's *On the Sublime and Beautiful* (not Longinus's *On the Sublime*). However, since Otto dealt with Kant and not Burke, I have restricted my comments to Kant. Cf. Edmund Burke, *On the Sublime and Beautiful* (1756 reprint; New York, P. F. Collier & Son, 1937), 101 [3.27].
[82] Otto, *Idea of the Holy*, 40.
[83] Ibid., 122.

In addition to the *mysterium tremendum* (with its awfulness and eeriness), "fascination" is the other major element in Otto's understanding of the *numinous*. This sensation occurs in the individual as a result of his experiencing the mysterious and unknown. Awe, it is true, brings the individual to his knees, but desire to see and understand the mystery—indeed, fascination and "love" for the mystery[84]—causes him to raise his eyes. And what he sees when he raises his eyes causes him to be overcome with a kind of madness, but it is the madness of the finite looking into the infinite,[85] and in this sense, it bears some resemblance to Platonic *eros*, which speaks of the need for the soul to be possessed by divine *eros* in order to ascend into the heavens. Consequently, the individual who experiences the *numinous* feels at once terrified of, and attracted to, the haunting mystery; such a person sees it, as the Priest in *Till We Have Faces* does of the perfect sacrifice, as "both the best and the worst."[86]

In sum, then, we could say the *numinous* is not exactly synonymous with Platonic *eros*, since it has little to do with Beauty, Truth, the Good, Happiness, or Home,[87] nor is it synonymous with *Sehnsucht*, Joy, and Romanticism since the *numinous* places greater emphasis on the "creature-feeling" and "shame." However, all four concepts belong to the general category of spiritual longing in virtue of two things: first, the individual is aware of his poor state in comparison to the Divine, and second, the individual subsequently becomes fascinated with, or desirous of, the Divine.

Hope and the end of the matter

In *A Grief Observed*, Lewis points out the connection between mystery, awe, and hope.[88] Of the latter, he writes in *Mere Christianity*, "Hope is one of the Theological virtues. This means that a continual looking forward to the eternal world is not (as some modern people think) a form of escapism or wishful thinking, but one of the things a Christian is meant to do."[89]

---

[84] Ibid., 41.
[85] Ibid., 29.
[86] Lewis, *Till We Have Faces*, 875.
[87] Otto said that *numen* or "the Holy" is analogous to, but not synonymous with, Beauty and the Good. Otto, *Idea of the Holy*, 51.
[88] C. S. Lewis *A Grief Observed* (Toronto: Bantam, 1976), 35–6.
[89] Lewis, *Mere Christianity*, 406, 408. Cf. "Nothing is more likely to destroy a species or a nation than a determination to survive at all costs. Those who care for something else more than civilization are the only people by whom civilization is at all likely to

It seems likely that Lewis envisioned hope as a kind of amplification or honing of spiritual longing in general, a kind of supernatural grace that elevates the natural desires of Platonic *eros*, *Sehnsucht*, Joy, Romanticism, and the *numinous*.

Given, then, that Lewis would have worked with not four, but five forms of spiritual longing before, and as, he read Rudolf Otto's *The Idea of the Holy*, I think it is too much to say that Otto's book and his understanding of the numinous was a significant influence on Lewis. James Como, again, suggests that Lewis "would have learned" all that Otto taught of the numinous with or without Otto.[90] I am inclined to think he is right. Thus, when Lewis said variously that *The Idea of the Holy* was a major influence, we should try to understand this in a less literal sense. Perhaps Lewis, being put on the spot, could not remember another book that was a more important influence (I might suggest a few). Or perhaps more likely what Lewis meant is that *The Idea of the Holy* was the best theoretical explanation of spiritual longing that he had read—the best account of an experience that he had both felt profoundly and read about deeply. We will probably never know, but either way we would do well to take Lewis's suggestion to read, to our profit, Otto's great book.

Bibliography

Augustine. *Confessions*. (This and other classic works listed below are available in many editions.)

Bundy, Murray Wright. *The Theory of Imagination in Classical and Medieval Thought*. Urbana, IL: University of Illinois Press, 1927.

Burke, Edmund. *On the Sublime and Beautiful*. 1756. Reprint, New York: P. F. Collier & Son, 1937.

Carnell, Corbin Scott. *Bright Shadow of Reality: Spiritual Longing in C. S. Lewis*. Grand Rapids, MI: Eerdmans, 1999.

Descartes, René. *Meditations on First Philosophy*, vol. 2, *The Philosophical Writings of Descartes*. Translated by John Cottingham, Robert Stoothoff, and Dugald Murdoch. Cambridge: Cambridge University Press, 1999.

---

be preserved. Those who want Heaven most have served Earth best. Those who love Man less than God do most for Man." C. S. Lewis, "On Living in an Atomic Age," in *C. S. Lewis: Essay Collection & Other Short Pieces*, ed. Lesley Walmsley (1948 essay reprint; London: HarperCollins, 2000), 365–6.

[90] James Como, *Branches to Heaven: The Geniuses of C. S. Lewis* (Dallas: Spense, 1998), 92.

Holyer, Robert. "C. S. Lewis on the Epistemic Significance of the Imagination." *Soundings* 74, no. 1 and 2 (1991).
Hyatt, Douglas. "Joy, the Call of God in Man: A Critical Appraisal of Lewis's Argument from Desire." In *C. S. Lewis: Lightbearers in the Shadowlands; the Evangelistic Vision of C. S. Lewis*, edited by Angus Menuge, 305–28. Wheaton, IL: Crossway, 1997.
James, William. *The Varieties of Religious Experience: A Study in Human Nature*, edited by Martin Marty. 1902. Reprint, Toronto: Penguin, 1982.
Kant, Immanuel. *Critique of Judgement*. Translated by J. H. Bernard. 1790. Reprint, New York: Hafner, 1961.
Lewis, C. S. Underlining in his edition of *The Idea of the Holy: An Inquiry in to the Non-Rational Factor in the Idea of the Divine and Its Relation to the Rational*, by Rudolf Otto. Translated by John W. Harvey. Oxford: Oxford University Press, 1936. The Rare Book Collection, University of North Carolina at Chapel Hill.
—. "Joy." *The Beacon* 3 (May 1924): 444–5.
—. *The Pilgrim's Regress*. In *C. S. Lewis: Selected Books* [Short Edition]. 1933. Reprint, London: HarperCollins, 2002.
—. *The Problem of Pain*. New York: HarperCollins, 2001.
—. *The Quest of Bleheris*. 1916 Unpublished novel. The Marion E. Wade Center, Wheaton College.
—. *Surprised by Joy*. In *C. S. Lewis: Selected Books* [Long Edition]. 1955. Reprint, London: HarperCollins, 1999.
—. *The Voyage of the Dawn Treader*. 1952. Reprint, London: Fontana, 1984.
Otto, Rudolf. *The Idea of the Holy: An Inquiry into the Non-rational Factor in the Idea of the Divine and Its Relation to the Rational*. Translated by John W. Harvey. Oxford: Oxford University Press, 1958.
Plato. *Phaedo*.
—. *Phaedrus*.
—. *Symposium*.
Porphyry. *Life of Plotnius*.
Slack, Michael. "Sehnsucht and the Platonic Eros in *Dymer*." *CSL: The Bulletin of the New York C. S. Lewis Society* 11 (August 1980): 3–7.
Virgil. *The Aeneid*.

Suggestions for further reading

Burke, Edmund. *On the Sublime and Beautiful*. 1756. Reprint, New York: P. F. Collier & Son, 1937.
  A classic book, that would have had some influence on Lewis, concerning the connection between the sublime and spiritual desires.
Carnell, Corbin Scott. *Bright Shadow of Reality: Spiritual Longing in C. S. Lewis*. Grand Rapids, MI: Eerdmans, 1999.
  The first great secondary source on spiritual longing in Lewis's thought.

Hyatt, Douglas. "Joy, the Call of God in Man: A Critical Appraisal of Lewis's Argument from Desire." In *C. S. Lewis: Lightbearers in the Shadowlands; the Evangelistic Vision of C. S. Lewis*, edited by Angus Menuge, 305–28. Wheaton, IL: Crossway Books, 1997.
Explores a bit of how spiritual longing relates to the argument from desire. Lewis's subjective experience gets the philosophical treatment.

James, William. *The Varieties of Religious Experience: A Study in Human Nature*, edited by Martin Marty. 1902. Reprint, Toronto: Penguin, 1982.
Another classic that loosely connects religious experience and spiritual desire.

Kant, Immanuel. *Critique of Judgement*. Translated by J. H. Bernard. 1790. Reprint, New York: Hafner, 1961.
Another book that Lewis knew which connects the sublime and longing.

Otto, Rudolf. *The Idea of the Holy: An Inquiry into the Non-rational Factor in the Idea of the Divine and Its Relation to the Rational*. Translated by John W. Harvey. Oxford: Oxford University Press, 1958.
Obviously a must-read both for its own illuminating comments on spiritual longing, but also for how the *numinous* connects to spiritual longing in the thought of Lewis.

Plato, *Symposium*.
Along with Augustine's confessions, this is a must-read for those interested in ancient accounts of spiritual longing and desire. This was a book that Lewis knew well and recommended to others.

Slack, Michael. "Sehnsucht and the Platonic Eros in *Dymer*." *CSL: The Bulletin of the New York C. S. Lewis Society* 11 (August 1980): 3–7.
A nice essay linking one notion of spiritual longing (Plato's) with another (the Romantics).

Virgil. *The Aeneid*.
A fantastic poem, but also an important treatise on the complex relation between duty and longing.

7

Boethius, *The Consolation of Philosophy*

Chris Armstrong

He was a philosopher first, and then a master of literature, with his Christianity informing both. He grew up surrounded by and saturated with books, and his greatest work demonstrates his amazing capacities of recall, organization, logic, and synthesis. He was perhaps the best-educated man of his generation—and that generation found itself already gathering speed as it rolled down into a valley of forgetfulness and ignorance, heedless of the rich traditions that had nurtured its parents and grandparents. He became to that dark generation a public intellectual and educator of huge popular impact—an impact that continued after his death.

His greatest pedagogical work he did not do in the classroom, but in writing fiction, poetry, allegory. He was at heart a popularizer. He wrote accessible theological works of an orthodox sort—content to pass on, to those less erudite than he, the wisdom of tradition. For him, however, that tradition most certainly included the best of the pagan philosophers; he wove their wisdom into his writings; and indeed, he revered Plato, Aristotle, and their ilk so highly that some questioned his commitment to the Christian faith. Nonetheless, many devout Christians who came after him called his name blessed (even "sainted") and tried (with varying degrees of success) to repeat his arguments and make use of his literary techniques.

He was sensitive to people's existential troubles and emotional states; in fact, when passing on the wisdom of the ancients, he started at just that point. He was foremost a moral philosopher, not only in his treatises, but also in his imaginative work. He took no comfort in the doctrine of predestination; as a moralist, he valued human free will too much to go with Augustine in that great African's extreme monergism. And he understood that God's omniscience does not create a situation where all our actions are determined.

He valued happiness highly, but he knew better than to rest his hope in earthly happiness or believe the world owed it to him. But he was no fatalist: he knew that what from a human perspective looks like bad fortune is often, indeed always, the guiding, correcting, disciplining hand of God. His philosophy had more than a little Stoicism in it—the "stiff upper lip" needed in a troubled time. When the going got tough, he learned not to demand an explanation from God, knowing that the only answer he would get would be the one Job got. He learned to rest in the knowledge that God's ways are higher than our ways. And as a remedy and salve for life's ordinary pains, he learned to turn to prayer. And when this great Christian philosopher-poet came to the attention of C. S. Lewis, it changed Lewis's life.

I write, as the chapter's title already reveals, of Anicius Manlius Severinus Boethius, who lived from AD 480 to 524 or 525. But if my list of descriptors sounded like someone else, then I may already be starting to make my point. This essay will begin to unpack the nature of Boethius's influence on Lewis—an influence suggested, I think, by some of the qualities in both men that I have listed. The essay starts simply, with the fact that when in 1962, *The Christian Century* magazine asked Lewis the question, "What books did most to shape your vocational attitude and your philosophy of life?"[1] the single medieval book this accomplished medievalist included in his top ten was Boethius's *The Consolation of Philosophy.*

What, then, brought to Lewis's mind Boethius—not Dante, whom he perhaps imitated more in his writings; nor Chaucer, whom he wrote about more; nor the great spiritual writers such as Julian of Norwich or Walter Hilton or the author of *The Cloud of Unknowing*, who shaped his spiritual life more and whom he recommended more to those seeking spiritual growth? What was the nature of Boethius's influence on Lewis?

First, I will assume in what follows that Lewis's debt was *not* limited to the holding of certain Boethian ideas. Like any good school child, Lewis would have paid careful attention to the wording of the question *The Christian Century* set for him. They had asked him not "Whose ideas do you admire the most," or "who influenced your literary style?" Rather, they asked about the shaping of Lewis's very vocation and philosophy of life. Those are deep sorts of influence, indeed. And I will take these two sorts of influence as a structure for what follows.

The clues to Lewis's debt to Boethius are scattered throughout his writings. In *The Discarded Image* he gave 16 pages of discussion to Boethius's *The Consolation of Philosophy*. He said it was one of the most influential books in medieval literature, and added, "until about two hundred years ago it would, I think, have been hard to find an educated man in any European country

---

[1] C. S. Lewis, "Ex Libris," *Christian Century* 79 (June 6, 1962): 719.

who did not love it."[2] Furthermore, he noted it was the most translated book in the Middle Ages. Alfred the Great, Chaucer, and, later, Queen Elizabeth I were among its translators. Its philosophical arguments and their allegorical form guided everyone from the Carolingians to Aquinas to Chaucer. (The latter, in *Troilus and Cressida*, had Pandarus recount the entire argument of *The Consolation*.)

And then, probably Lewis's loftiest endorsement of *The Consolation:* "To acquire a taste for it is almost to become naturalised in the Middle Ages."[3] And for Lewis, Boethius was not some antiquarian taste, like collecting old spoons. He believed the great Roman still had important things to say to the people of his own day. Repeatedly in responding to letters seeking his advice, Lewis listed Boethius among authors beneficial to read. In an essay describing the ideal English school, Lewis recommended the reading of "the authors who have really affected us deeply and over long periods."[4] He pushed to the fore of this list "the Romans," and especially "those . . . who enjoyed the same degree and nearly the same kind of prestige both before and after the Renaissance."[5] Ovid was among these. Virgil put in his appearance, naturally. But the greatest and first on Lewis's list was Boethius.

Vocation

The discussion of Boethius in *The Discarded Image* and the references scattered about *The Allegory of Love* and various scholarly essays could, however, mislead us. They might seem to indicate that Lewis's debt to the great Roman was primarily a scholarly one—a matter of sorting out influences and understanding lineages of thought. There is much to recommend this view. For one thing, it is consistent with how Lewis himself described his motivations when he first read Boethius in 1922: "I myself was first led into reading the Christian classics," he wrote, "almost accidentally, as a result of my English studies. Some, such as Hooker, Herbert, Traherne, Taylor and Bunyan, I read because they are themselves great English writers; others,

---

[2] C. S. Lewis, *The Discarded Image: An Introduction to Medieval and Renaissance Literature*, 1964 Canto Edition, rep. and ed. (Cambridge: Cambridge University Press, 1994), 75.
[3] Ibid.
[4] C. S. Lewis, "The idea of an 'English School,'" in *Image and Imagination: Essays and Reviews*, Canto Classics Edition, ed. Walter Hooper (New York: Cambridge University Press, 2013), 9.
[5] Ibid.

such as Boethius, St. Augustine, Thomas Aquinas and Dante, because they were 'influences.'"[6]

But there is in *The Allegory of Love* a clue to something else that Lewis found in Boethius—something that changed his life. In the *Allegory*, Lewis uses a certain glowing epithet for Boethius. He called him "the divine popularizer."[7] That single phrase clues us into a different sort of Boethian influence in the life of the twentieth-century Oxford don—one that goes back to the wording of *The Christian Century*'s question: "Which books shaped your *vocational attitude*," they had asked him.

In a 2010 essay, Samuel Joeckel explores Lewis's vocation as a "public intellectual."[8] That is to say, "a figure who defends religious, political, or ideological beliefs in a manner that requires the expertise of a scholar, possessing the learning and critical acumen to engage with proficiency a wide range of complex issues, and the communicative skills of a journalist, capable of making those complex beliefs understandable to the layperson."[9] Thus a public intellectual must be a "philosopher-poet"—possessing both subtlety and depth of rational thinking and the rhetorical skill to communicate that thinking powerfully and winsomely.

Significantly for both the case of Boethius and that of Lewis, Joeckel tells us that the public intellectual serves a "translative" function. To speak intelligibly to a diverse company, "patrician and plebian, bourgeoisie and proletariat, rich and poor, educated and semi-educated, specialist and nonspecialist,"[10] he or she must use a language they all understand—the vernacular. Aside from the *Consolation*, the work of Boethius that most shaped the Middle Ages was his labor translating the wisdom of the ancient Greeks, which he read in their original language, into the vernacular of his day, Latin. And Lewis of course both was master of many languages and could "translate" the most complex philosophical ideas not just into clear radio addresses for the masses, but into the imaginative, concrete world of children's books.

The public intellectual also, says Joeckel, stands at a time of radical cultural change.[11] Certainly this was true of Boethius, to the degree that

---

[6] C. S. Lewis, "On the Reading of Old Books," in *C. S. Lewis: Essay Collection & Other Short Pieces*, ed. Lesley Walmsley (London: HarperCollins, 2000), 440.
[7] C. S. Lewis, *The Allegory of Love: A Study in Medieval Tradition* (Oxford: Oxford University Press, 1971).
[8] Samuel Joeckel, "C. S. Lewis, Public Intellectual," in *Sehnsucht* 4 (2010): 43–66.
[9] Ibid., 44.
[10] Ibid.
[11] C. S. Lewis, "C. S. Lewis, Public Intellectual," *Sehnsucht* 4 (2010): 44.

he has been interpreted[12] as the Last Educated Man standing against an encroaching barbarism. This image is made vivid, of course, by the nature of his end. This cultured philosopher was first imprisoned by barbarians—the Ostrogothic king Theodoric and, as Lewis put it, his "huge, fair-skinned, beer-drinking, boasting thanes"—until "presently they twisted ropes round his head till his eyes dropped out and finished him off with a bludgeon."[13] What a tempting symbol of the death of the old Roman culture and the dawning of the Dark Ages. Yet, Boethius's death did not, in fact, terminate the influence—of that classical culture—not by a long shot. The blood of this martyr was the seed of Christian culture. For Boethius was something unkillable: a 100,000-megawatt transmitter of tradition.

It is hard to think of an apter description, in fact, of C. S. Lewis. Though like Boethius, Lewis was not *just* a transmitter but also a thinker of great originality, when in 1954 Lewis described his *vocation* to the audience gathered at Cambridge University to witness his installation to the Chair of Medieval and Renaissance Literature, he turned to this function of cultural transmission.

First, he framed the cultural moment: "We have lived," he says "to see the second death of ancient learning. In our time something which was once the possession of all educated men has shrunk to being the technical accomplishment of a few specialists."[14] As he had written almost a decade before in his book *Miracles* (1947), "All over the world, until quite modern times, the direct insight of the mystics and the reasonings of the philosophers percolated to the mass of the people by authority and tradition; they could be received by those who were no great reasoners themselves in the concrete form of myth and ritual and the whole pattern of life."[15] But now the West had become cut off from its traditions, and the results, Lewis was sure, would be dire: "a society where the simple many obey the few seers can live: a society where all were seers could live even more fully. But a society where the mass is still simple and the seers are no longer attended to can achieve only superficiality, baseness, ugliness, and in the end extinction."[16] Lewis wanted, as much as did Boethius, to stand in the gap of that cataclysmic loss, to bring the tradition back to the people. He told his Cambridge audience, "I myself belong far more to that Old Western order than to yours. . . . I read

---

[12] "Over-interpreted," says Marenbon. John Marenbon, *Boethius (Great Medieval Thinkers)* (New York: Oxford University Press, 2003), 7.
[13] Lewis, *Discarded Image*, 76.
[14] C. S. Lewis, "De Descriptione Temporum," in *Selected Literary Essays*, Canto Classics Edition, 1969, ed. Walter Hooper (Cambridge: Cambridge University Press, 2013), 4.
[15] C. S. Lewis, *Miracles* (New York: Macmillan, 1960), 42.
[16] Ibid., 43.

as a native texts that you must read as foreigners.... That way, where I fail as a critic, I may yet be useful as a specimen."[17]

What, exactly, did Lewis feel was being lost in this new Dark Ages? Not "just" tales and songs, myths, and poems, but the very wisdom that, following Barfield's work in *Poetic Diction,* he felt was inextricably embodied in and inseparable from that lost literature. What wisdom? The Christian Gospel? Well, yes, that. But more deeply, the particular complex, perceptive, philosophically sophisticated and morally robust appropriation of the gospel to the pagan mind that Boethius epitomized. After all, Lewis said, "Christians and Pagans had much more in common with each other than either has with a post-Christian. The gap between those who worship different gods is not so wide as that between those who worship and those who do not."[18]

In fact, this point about the wisdom of the pagans is an important one that occurs throughout Lewis's writings and joins him even more firmly to Boethius. In response to those who argue that the modern world is lapsing into paganism, Lewis responded, in essence, "If only we would!" For there is wisdom in pagan culture that we need (a "consolation" of philosophy). Lewis always felt more affinity for a thoroughgoing pagan pursuing virtue by pagan lights than for a godless modern, and he returned again and again throughout his writing life to the wisdom of the ancients (as did Boethius—thus, he is Boethian in this). But alas, in this new Dark Ages, Lewis lamented, "The post-Christian is cut off from the Christian past and therefore doubly from the Pagan past."[19]

Much ink has been spilled on the question of why Boethius, imprisoned, exiled, his goods scattered, and awaiting execution, turned not to the consolation of *religion,* but rather the consolation of *philosophy.* Certainly there are Christian elements in his book that none of his pagan sources would have recognized: his recommendation of prayer and his portrayal of God in personal terms are just two. The first thing to say here is that modern scholarship has shown with no reasonable doubt that Boethius *was* a Christian, of an orthodox and a committed sort. The second is that Lewis, who taught philosophy before he taught literature, and who read the classics voraciously under Kirkpatrick before coming to Christianity, joined Boethius in feeling the power of such consolation.

---

[17] Lewis, *"Descriptione Temporum,"* 14.
[18] Ibid., 5.
[19] Ibid., 10.

That the Narnia Chronicles turn out, if we believe Michael Ward, to hang on an elaborate secret scaffolding of pagan planetary mythology,[20] or that the *Abolition of Man* and *Mere Christianity* ransack Aristotelian virtue ethics and natural law theory for their ethical understanding, or that his favorite of his own novels, *Till We Have Faces,* was a reworked pagan myth—Lewis saw none of this as contradicting his Christianity. Like medievals from Boethius to the Beowulf author to Dante, Lewis was a happy syncretist, at least in the typical medieval sense of "plundering the Egyptians" for usable material while maintaining a firm Christian intellectual framework. In Lewis's words: "For one reference to Wade or Weland we meet fifty to Hector, Aeneas, Alexander, or Caesar. For one probable relic of Celtic religion . . . a score of references to Mars and Venus and Diana."[21]

And indeed, Lewis believed—as Boethius seems also to have believed—that it is within a Christian framework that the classical materials truly come into their own. As he wrote to Bede Griffiths on April 4, 1934:

> [I]t is only since I have become a Christian that I have learned really to value the elements of truth in Paganism and Idealism. I *wished* to value them in the old days; now I really do. Don't suppose that I ever thought myself that certain elements of pantheism were incompatible with Christianity or with Catholicism.[22]

In a 1944 address to the Socratic Club at Oxford, he made the point more emphatically:

> Theology, while saying that a special illumination has been vouchsafed to Christians and (earlier) to Jews, also says that there is some divine illumination vouchsafed to *all* men. The Divine light, we are told, "lighteneth every man." We should, therefore, expect to find in the imagination of great Pagan teachers and myth makers some glimpse of that theme which we believe to be the very plot of the whole cosmic story—the theme of incarnation, death, and rebirth.[23]

---

[20] Michael Ward, *Planet Narnia: The Seven Heavens in the Imagination of C. S. Lewis* (New York: Oxford University Press, 2008),
[21] Lewis, *Discarded Image*, 8.
[22] C. S. Lewis to Dom Bede Griffiths, April 4, 1934, in *The Collected Letters of C. S. Lewis, Vol. II: Books, Broadcasts, and the War 1931-1949*, ed. Walter Hooper (New York: HaperCollins, 2004), 133–44.
[23] C. S. Lewis, "Is Theology Poetry?" in *The Weight of Glory and Other Addresses*, ed. Walter Hooper, rev. and exp. (New York: Macmillan, 1980), 83.

Obscuring the divine light for many, the nature of modernity's shadow in Lewis's eyes is well enough known: materialism, utilitarianism, subjectivism—all conspired to destroy the wisdom that had made it all the way from the ancients to the time of Jane Austen and Sir Walter Scott. Now, especially in the face of cataclysmic world wars, even Oxford's students were wondering to themselves, Why study philosophy? In his address "Learning in War Time," Lewis gave the answer:

"Good philosophy must exist, if for no other reason, because bad philosophy needs to be answered." And where is that good philosophy to be found? "Most of all . . . we need intimate knowledge of the past."[24] Of course he recognized, and no doubt understood that Boethius also recognized, that there are limits to all merely human philosophy. But its power could be great nonetheless. In his essay "Christianity and Culture," Lewis reflected: "[C]ulture is a storehouse of the best (sub-Christian) values. These values are in themselves of the soul, not the spirit. But God created the soul. Its values may be expected, therefore, to contain some reflection or antepast of the spiritual values."[25]

> "There is another way," he wrote, "in which it [that is, culture, especially literature] may predispose to conversion. The difficulty of converting an uneducated man nowadays lies in his complacency. Popularized science, the conventions or 'unconventions' of his immediate circle, party programmes, etc., enclose him in a tiny windowless universe which he mistakes for the only possible universe. There are no distant horizons, no mysteries. He thinks everything has been settled."[26]

A tiny, windowless universe. I am reminded of Chesterton's definition of insanity: "the clean and well-lit prison of one idea."[27] Our modern prison is well lit by the bare bulb of science. But of what lies beyond, we see nothing. Like the children in *The Silver Chair*, trapped underground with the witch, we cannot even reason from the light bulb to the sun of heaven. For that, we would need to open the windows of culture. Lewis continues:

> A cultured person, on the other hand, is almost compelled to be aware that reality is very odd and that the ultimate truth, whatever it may be, *must* have the characteristics of strangeness—*must* be something

---

[24] Ibid., 28.
[25] C. S. Lewis, "Christianity and Culture," in *Christian Reflections*, ed. Walter Hooper (Grand Rapids, MI: Eerdmans, 1967), 23.
[26] Ibid.
[27] G. K. Chesterton, *Orthodoxy* (New York: John Lane, 1908), 38.

that would seem remote and fantastic to the uncultured. Thus some obstacles to faith have been removed already.[28]

What better description can we find than this of Boethius's *Consolation*? Boethius the character starts the book grieving hysterically in the small, blind room of his own bad fortune. Slowly, gently, Lady Philosophy opens the windows, allowing Boethius to see that his happiness cannot and *must* not rest in the things on earth that fortune both gives and takes away. This is a *Platonic* insight as well as a Christian one: a classical philosophical foretaste of an important Truth given fully only in the Christian Gospel. Lady Philosophy is bringing Boethius to a "pre-evangelistic" realization, by which, as Lewis says of culture in general, "some obstacles to faith have been removed already." And remember, by the way, that Lewis first read the *Consolation* in 1922—nearly a full decade before his conversion to Christianity.

This pre-evangelistic realization of Boethius's is a close cousin to the "argument from desire" so often used by Lewis—indeed, used as the framework for his artful story, *Surprised by Joy*, about his own conversion. It does, it must, start with the existential: the miserable reality of our own sense of the wrongness of the world and our own inability to find happiness in it. Then it slowly comes to conclude, as Lady Philosophy leads Boethius to conclude, that if one's happiness rests only in earthly fortune, then that happiness can never be secure. I will return to this point in a bit.

Lewis concludes that "culture has a distinct part to play in bringing certain souls to Christ."[29] Without doubt, he would have said that one of these "certain souls" was himself. It seems almost certain that Boethius's *Consolation* had a role in that philosophical journey, which is told in outline in *Surprised by Joy* and in great detail in the *The Pilgrim's Regress*. But whether it did or not, this vocational understanding that Lewis had of himself as a Boethian public intellectual, preserver of tradition, and conduit of culture was surely made even more powerful by the fact that he shared Boethius's faith and, like Boethius, adeptly wove that faith into the garment even of writings that seemed purely "cultural"—"philosophical"—"poetical."

Philosophy of life

Now I'd like to turn in more detail to Lewis's debt to Boethius on the second matter in *The Christian Century*'s question: philosophy of life. But let's start

---

[28] Lewis, "Christianity and Culture," 23.
[29] Ibid., 24.

with a point about Boethius's influence on Lewis that is so obvious we might miss it. That is: Lewis, like Boethius, and like that poet's great medieval protégé, Dante, had fallen in love with Lady Philosophy. Though tempted, perhaps, in his youth to read philosophy as an intellectual exercise, a "dabbling," he soon turned the corner. You'll remember the story he told on himself in *Surprised by Joy*, of how he one day made the mistake of referring to philosophy as "a subject," and was pulled up short by Owen Barfield, who said with some heat, "It wasn't a *subject* to Plato . . . it was a *way*."[30] Lewis thought philosophically because he wanted to come to answers that were important for his life. One must imagine, then, that when he began to read the *Consolation*, which begins with Boethius thrashing about in the thickets of theodicy, he decided pretty quickly that he had found a friend.

What would have appealed to Lewis even more was that Boethius was not only one for whom philosophy was a *way*, not a subject, but also, standing at the hinge point from the ancient to the medieval world, he treated the wisdom of the pagan philosophers of the classical period on its own merits. Boethius did not find it necessary, even in his hour of greatest need, to apply to Plato, Aristotle, and the rest, a heavy-handed Christian filter to make it useful.

This sort of appreciation for pagan thought had deep roots in Lewis's training as a scholar. From age 16 to 18, he had studied with the former headmaster of an Irish college, William T. Kirkpatrick, who observed that Lewis read more classics than any boy he had taught. When he proceeded to apply for admission to Oxford, "E. F. Carritt, the University College don who interviewed him . . . said that Lewis was the best read applicant he had ever examined."[31] This early training in the classics prepared Lewis to find in "old books" not only aesthetic pleasures but meaning for living. And before he became a professor of English literature, C. S. Lewis was "an Oxford graduate looking for a fellowship not in literature or theology but in philosophy."[32] This was 1922, again the year of his first reading of the

---

[30] Owen Barfield, *Owen Barfield on C. S. Lewis*, ed. G. B. Tennyson (Middleton, CT: Wesleyan University Press, 1989), 10. Owen Barfield believes that Lewis's memory failed him here. Referring to this very passage in *Surprised by Joy*, Barfield writes: "Well, flattering as this passage may be to my self-esteem, I am bound to say, and I am rather glad at having this opportunity to say it, that it is, as far as my recollection goes, pure applesauce, unless of course Lewis is using the word 'frivolity' in a highly specialized and limited sense." CF. C. S. Lewis, *Surprised by Joy: The Shape of My Early Life* (New York: Harcourt Brace & World, 1955), 225.

[31] James Patrick, "The Heart's Desire and the Landlord's Rules: C. S. Lewis as a Moral Philosopher," in *The Pilgrim's Guide: C. S. Lewis and the Art of Witness*, ed. David Mills (Grand Rapids, MI: Eerdmans, 1998), 78.

[32] Ibid., 70.

Consolation. Trying for that fellowship, he submitted an essay positing the existence of natural law, the subject of his later work *The Abolition of Man.*

Now, this "meaning for life" that philosophy provided did take a turn Lewis had not expected. As it turned out, Lady Philosophy in fact *led Lewis to Christianity,* though not by a direct or swift path. (I think it's fair to say, as Adam Barkman does, that "Lewis's early readings in Plato, Aristotle, and Boethius" had the nature of "a seed planted in Lewis's mind that took years to develop.")[33] First, we should see how unlikely that would have seemed to Lewis: "As a boy, he had been told by his schoolmasters that Christianity was 100 per cent correct and every other religion, including the pagan myths of ancient Greece and Rome, was 100 per cent wrong."[34] As Michael Ward reminds us, Lewis was already so convinced of the value of classical philosophy that he "found that this statement, rather than bolstering the Christian claim, undermined it and he abandoned his childhood faith 'largely under the influence of classical education.'"[35]

An inauspicious beginning. Yet, when Lewis was asked to write the story of his conversion, he protested that he had come to Christian faith down such a thoroughly philosophical path, that any recounting of his journey could hardly be useful to the great mass of the population.[36] Despite that protest, when he first wrote of his conversion in *The Pilgrim's Regress,* it was in unapologetically, and like the *Consolation, allegorically* philosophical terms. Not only does the *Regress* use allegory, as the *Consolation* does, but also, in fact, Lewis places on the *Regress*'s first page twin quotations from Plato and the *Consolation,* which together make the same point about how people on the path to truth proceed.

First Plato: "This every soul seeketh and for the sake of this doth all her actions, having an inkling that it is; but *what* it is she cannot sufficiently

---

[33] Adam Barkman, *C. S. Lewis & Philosophy as a Way of Life* (Allentown, PA: Zossima, 2009), 109.
[34] Ward, *Planet Narnia,* 28.
[35] Ibid.
[36] Barkman, *Lewis & Philosophy,* 245. "Whenever Lewis was asked to write about his conversion to xnty, he always pointed out that his, like Justin Martyr's, was 'almost [a] purely philosophical [conversion]' which came about as the result of a *philosophical journey,* "I gave up Christianity at about fourteen. Came back to it when getting on for thirty. Not an emotional conversion: almost purely philosophical," C. S. Lewis, "Autobiographical Note," prepared by the Macmillian [sic] Company in 1946 (Marion E. Wade Center, Wheaton College), 1]. Thus, to one inquirer he wrote, "My own history was so mixed up with technical philosophy as to be useless to the general [public]," C. S. Lewis to Eric Fenn, April 12, 1943, *Collected Letters II,* 568; and to another, "The details of my own conversion were so technically philosophical on one side, and so intimate on the other that they can't be used in the way you suggest," C. S. Lewis to Mr Young, May 20, 1943, ibid., 575.

discern, and she knoweth not her way, and concerning this she hath no constant assurance as she hath of other things."[37]

Then Boethius: "Whose souls, albeit in a cloudy memory, yet seek back their good, but, like drunk men, know not the road home."[38]

He concludes his opening triad of quotations with Hooker, whose quotation does two things: First, it provides a relatively modern English and indeed Anglican lens for the Boethian philosophical-religious quest he is about to narrate. And second, it surfaces the eudaemonism—the classical philosophy grounded in the desire for and pursuit of happiness—that came to the modern Christian West from Plato, through the Neoplatonists, via Boethius's Christianizing version.

Here's Hooker: "Somewhat it seeketh, and what that is directly it knoweth not, yet very intentive desire thereof doth so incite it, that all other known delights and pleasures are laid aside, they give place to the search of this but only suspected desire."[39] This is particularly reminiscent, for me, of Boethius's late great protégé Dante, who in his *Convivio*, recounted his passionate early courtship with Lady Philosophy in language whose eroticism echoes the Song of Solomon.

This language of desire, of *eros*, would become crucial for Lewis's developing Christian apologetic. Indeed, when he honed the story of his own conversion for a wider audience, in *Surprised by Joy*, in the process radically compressing his philosophical path, this Platonic-Boethian language of desire and its fulfillment remained prominent. Again, more on this shortly.

But a final comment to make here is that Lewis not only shared Boethius's approach to philosophy as a way of life, he also saw Boethius's *Consolation* as itself a consummate *Praeparatio evangelii*. He says, "[*The Consolation of Philosophy's*] philosophy is a profoundly religious philosophy. It might be described as prolegomena to any of the great religions; it teaches the insufficiency of the world and points on to the Eternal—after that the various religions can have their say as to the nature of the Eternal and the means of approaching it. We need not doubt that Boethius passed through this philosophy preliminary and reached that particular religion described in his *De Fide*."[40] I would add, he may well have come by the path described in the *Consolation*—by being gradually weaned away from the incomplete

---

[37] C. S. Lewis, *The Pilgrim's Regress* (Grand Rapids, MI: Eerdmans, 1974), 19.
[38] Ibid.
[39] Ibid.
[40] C. S. Lewis, review of *Boethius: Some Aspects of His Times and Works*, by Helen Barrett, *Medium Aevum* 10, no. 1 (February 1941): 33, cited in Barkman, *Lewis & Philosophy*, 176.

(and therefore tenuous, unreliable) earthly satisfactions of the desire for the source of all Good: God.

Lewis believed, in other words, that the *Consolation* and the classical philosophical wisdom to which it pointed, while not themselves the *evangelium,* start a reader down the road to that fuller truth. From a boyhood in which he was told that philosophy and faith were absolutely incompatible, Lewis came to believe that "the only possible basis for Christian apologetics is a proper respect for Paganism." "If Paganism could be shown to have something in common with Christianity," Lewis concluded, "'so much the better for Paganism,' not 'so much the worse for Christianity.'"[41] In his fine essay, "The Weight of Glory," echoing Lady Philosophy's insistence on the insufficiency of worldly goods, Lewis said: "[Y]ou and I have need of the strongest spell that can be found to wake us from the evil enchantment of worldliness which has been laid upon us for nearly a hundred years. Almost our whole education has been directed to silencing this shy, persistent, inner voice [that is, our *Sehnsucht,* longing for that which truly satisfies but which we recognize lies beyond this world]; almost all our modern philosophies have been devised to convince us that the good of man is to be found on this earth" [precisely what Lady Philosophy sets out to show the distraught Boethius is *not* the case!]. "And yet," he concludes, "it is a remarkable thing that such philosophies of Progress or Creative Evolution themselves bear reluctant witness to the truth that our real goal is elsewhere."[42]

The role of desire and happiness (eudaemonism)

Now I want to return for a moment to that key theme in the *Consolation* of the role of desires and happiness in that philosophical journey which leads to God. The preface to the third edition of *Pilgrim's Regress* may prove a good contextualizing device for the relationship between affect and intellect in Lewis's thought: he affirms both, while cautioning of the pitfalls of both; I take it to be doing that (and more) in his distinction between "North" and "South" in that preface and throughout the book.

See also his serious (and I take it, Aristotelian, virtue-ethical) treatment, in *The Abolition of Man,* of our affective lives as something that must receive a moral shape if we are to behave ethically. He further argues that training in moral virtue is a matter of training the aesthetic judgment for practical

---

[41] Ward, *Planet Narnia*, 28.
[42] Lewis, "Weight of Glory," 8–9.

purposes. And he adduces Coleridge, Traherne, Augustine, Aristotle, Plato, and Confucius as people who taught that it is possible to have just sentiments—that is, responses to nature and events that are appropriate to the object or situation—but that such responses are not natural.[43] They have to be learned, and students learn them through training that emphasizes the creation of habitual responses. And what faculty must be trained in that learning? The emotions, passions, desires. Here is Lewis:

> The head rules the belly through the chest—the seat, as Alanus tells us, of Magnanimity, of emotions organized by trained habit into stable sentiments. The Chest—Magnanimity—Sentiment—these are the indispensable liaison officers between cerebral man and visceral man. It may even be said that it is by this middle element that man is man: for by his intellect he is mere spirit and by his appetite mere animal.[44]

Conversion from earthly desires

In *The Abolition of Man* Lewis contents himself with making the case for natural law, observing that the moral law is not the exclusive domain of Christianity, but belongs to everyone, as its axioms may be found in all the world's great cultures and religions (which he enumerates in the appendix to that work).

But Lewis's reading of Boethius, quite a while before his Christian conversion, revealed to him a particularly Christian (to be more precise, an Augustinian, Neoplatonic, and eudaemonistic), understanding of the role of our desires in the path to God. Fully formed, that understanding would later become the basis in Lewis of his particular formulation of one traditional apologetic argument for Christianity: the argument from desire. Put simply, this argument insists that the very fact we find ourselves yearning for a happiness beyond what the world can provide (a yearning configured by Lewis as "Joy" or romantic *Sehnsucht*) indicates that such otherworldly happiness must exist—as the thirst of a man in the desert indicates that he is the sort of creature that requires water, and that such a thing as water exists to slake his thirst.

How does Boethius handle this notion of desire for an otherworldly good? In a nutshell, Boethius, the character in the allegory, begins the book in a very agitated state. His fortunes have turned for the worse, he has been

---

[43] C. S. Lewis, *The Abolition of Man* (New York: Macmillan, 1955), 25–8.
[44] Ibid., 34.

accused of perfidy, his goods have been confiscated, he is under arrest. And with the righteous fervor of a Job and the melancholy of a psalm of lament, he says, "I seem to see the wicked haunts of criminals overflowing with happiness and joy."[45] How is it that the wicked can be enjoying themselves, and he, who has lived an upright life as a faithful servant of Theodoric, has had happiness snatched away from him?

Now, again, Lady Philosophy spends much of the first half of the book convincing Boethius that the things he thinks will bring him secure happiness—money, fame, power, pleasure—are actually will-o'-the-wisps, or pale shadows of true happiness. But she does not disagree with Boethius's premise: that happiness is our proper end. That is the classical teaching of eudaemonism.

We see this in Book III, which begins with Boethius's expression of a kind of ecstasy at Lady Philosophy's argument—in song form—about the mutability and ultimate uselessness of all worldly goods: "She had stopped singing, but the enchantment of her song left me spellbound. I was absorbed and wanted to go on listening."[46]

And here again in Book III, Lady Philosophy says her goal is eudaemonistic. "'[Y]ou are eager to hear more. You would be more than eager if you knew the destination I am trying to bring you to.'" Boethius asked what this was, and she answered "'true happiness.'"[47] She is going to move him from false happiness to true happiness—which is the proper end, the *telos,* of human beings, for which we yearn as the caged bird yearns for the woods.

Barkman is right that what Boethius teaches us here, and it seems clear taught Lewis, is a Christianized Platonic understanding of the purpose and end of human beings. The Platonists had taught that the real and perfect essence of each of us "first exists as an Idea in God's mind." This idea is "a Platonic form" which is also our *end,* our *telos,* our *perfection,* and thus also the measuring stick "by which all creatures are individually judged and measured."[48]

Even more important for Lewis's reading, and I might say ingestion, of Boethius's *Consolation* is that when created things are given existence—when God's Ideas are actualized in creation—they are instilled with Platonic

---

[45] Boethius, *Consolation of Philosophy,* trans. with an intro. by V. E. Watts (Middlesex, England: Penguin, 1981), I.IV, 46.
[46] Ibid., III.I, 78.
[47] Ibid.
[48] Barkman, *C. S. Lewis & Philosophy as a Way of Life* (Allen Town, PA: Zossima, 2009), 245.

eros, which causes them to desire to be whole or to become like the Idea God has of them: "Everything," Lewis summarized in the margins of his copy of King Alfred's translation of the *Consolation* "desires to realize its own proper nature."[49]

As Barkman shows us that Lewis himself argues in *The Problem of Pain,* "all creatures become more themselves—attain more happiness and are more fully actualized—the more they look to, and act like, God; that is, the more they exercise 'creaturely participation in Divine attributes.'"[50] And as Lady Philosophy will argue, this time drawing from the Neoplatonists more than Plato himself, that we can achieve that realization of our nature only through union with the sum of all good and the source of all happiness—God himself. Thus God is the true end of the desires that we pursue in partial and flawed ways through money, high office, fame, pleasure, and beauty.

As a footnote, an important corollary of this teaching about human fulfillment, and one that owes something to Aristotle, is that the *farther* we get from God, the *less* human we become—indeed we become bestial. This Lewis shows us in the endragoned Eustace, as George MacDonald had shown it in Curdie's power to feel, at a handshake, the hoof or paw hidden within the hand of decadent persons. It is also the source for one of Boethius's greatest students, Dante, when he shows us the *contrapasso*—that is, a sort of homeopathic punishment—of many inmates of hell, who appear there in various animal forms appropriate to their earthly sins.

To see how thoroughly Lewis absorbed the eudaemonism of Boethius, we need only to begin reading his sermon, "The Weight of Glory":

> If you asked twenty good men today what they thought the highest of the virtues, nineteen of them would reply, Unselfishness. But if you had asked almost any of the great Christians of old, he would have replied, Love. You see what has happened? A negative term has been substituted for a positive, and this is of more than philological importance. The negative idea of Unselfishness carries with it the suggestion not primarily of securing good things for others, but of going without them ourselves, as if our abstinence and not their happiness was the important point. I do not think this is the Christian virtue of Love. The New Testament has lots to say about self-denial, but not about

---

[49] Ibid. [n. 102: C. S. Lewis, marginalia in his edition of *King Alfred's Old English Version of Boethius' De Consolatione Philosophiae* by Boethius, trans. King Alfred, ed. Walter John Sedgewick, 4.3].

[50] Ibid., 245–6 [n. 105: Lewis, *Problem of Pain,* 496].

self-denial as an end in itself. We are told to deny ourselves and to take up our crosses in order that we may follow Christ; and nearly every description of what we shall ultimately find if we do so contains an appeal to desire. If there lurks in most modern minds the notion that to desire our own good and earnestly to hope for the enjoyment of it is a bad thing, I submit that this notion has crept in from Kant and the Stoics and is no part of the Christian faith. Indeed, if we consider the unblushing promises of reward and the staggering nature of the rewards promised in the Gospels, it would seem that Our Lord finds our desires not too strong, but too weak. We are half-hearted creatures, fooling about with drink and sex and ambition when infinite joy is offered us, like an ignorant child who wants to go on making mud pies in a slum because he cannot imagine what is meant by an offer of a holiday at the sea. We are far too easily pleased.[51]

A more Boethian account of the human quest for happiness is hard to imagine.

Fortune

Finally, I want to turn from eudaemonism to fortune. One of the ways Lady Philosophy leads Boethius out of his brown funk and into the light of truth is to show him that, properly speaking, there is no bad fortune. Though from an earthly perspective, fortune wavers back and forth, blessing evil men and cursing good ones, from a divine perspective (which, granted, we are not given to have, but may come partially to share as we are gradually sanctified on earth) there really is no such thing as bad fortune. In everything that happens to us, we are made stronger and brought closer to God, if we allow it. God uses tremendous evil as an instrument of tremendous good. And indeed the good who experience supposed "misfortune" are already enjoying more and more the reward of sharing in the divine nature, and those evil men we envy for their supposed "good fortune" are already experiencing the evil of their own sinful decisions in their own bodies as they regress into beastly states.

We have mentioned, under that heading, the endragoned Eustace in *The Voyage of the "Dawn Treader."* When Reepicheep comes to talk to Eustace, he does so, as Michael Ward points out, in Boethian mode, relativizing the

---

[51] Lewis, "Weight of Glory," 3–4.

seeming goods and evils of the Wheel of Fortune (an image that the TV game show, and all of Western culture, owes to Boethius):

> [H]e would explain that what had happened . . . was a striking illustration of the turn of Fortune's wheel, and that if he had Eustace at his own house in Narnia . . . he could show him more than a hundred examples of emperors, kings, dukes, knights, poets, lovers, astronomers, philosophers, and magicians, who had fallen from prosperity into the most distressing circumstances, and of whom many had recovered and lived happily ever afterward.[52]

Lewis turns this Boethian insight to pastoral use in his letter to Mary Neylan, March 26, 1940:

> The Christian view would be that every psychological situation, just like every degree of wealth or poverty, talent or stupidity etc, had its own peculiar temptations and peculiar advantages, that the worst could always be turned to a good use and the best cd. always be abused to one's spiritual ruin. In fact "all fortune is good" as Boethius said.
>
> This doesn't mean that it wd. be wrong to try to cure a [psychological] complex any more than a stiff leg: but it does mean that if you can't, then, so far from the game being up, life with a complex, or with a stiff leg, is precisely the game you have been set.[53]

The thing that is most pastoral about this insight, Lewis teaches us in his brief review of Boethius's thought in *The Discarded Image*. When he comes to Lady Philosophy's famous extended argument about the "wheel of fortune," Lewis calls it biblical (consistent with passages in Job and John) and also "one of the most vigorous defences ever written against the view, common to vulgar Pagans and vulgar Christians alike, which 'comforts cruel men' by interpreting variations of human prosperity as divine rewards and punishments, or at least wishing that they were. It is an enemy hard to kill."[54]

---

[52] Ward, *Planet Narnia*, 112 [n. 38: *The Voyage of the "Dawn Treader,"* 102–3].
[53] C. S. Lewis to Mary Neylan, March 26, 1940, *Collected Letters II*, 374 [n. 172: Boethius, *The Consolation of Philosophy*, Book IV, prosa 7].
[54] Lewis, *Discarded Image*, 82.

Conclusion

I have been able in this chapter only to open a small window into the "Boethianism" of Lewis. But my own exploration of this theme has suggested the truth of Barkman's insistence that "Lewis's metaphysics, epistemology, ethics and literary style all owe something to the Last of the Romans."[55]

Bibliography

Barfield, Owen. *Owen Barfield on C. S. Lewis*, edited by G. B. Tennyson. Middleton, CT: Wesleyan University Press, 1989.
Barkman, Adam. *C. S. Lewis & Philosophy as a Way of Life*. Allentown, PA: Zossima, 2009.
Boenig, Robert. *C. S. Lewis and the Middle Ages*. Kent, OH: Kent State University Press, 2012.
Boethius. *The Consolation of Philosophy*. Reprint Edition. Translated with an introduction by V. E. Watts. Middlesex, England: Penguin, 1981.
Chesterton, G. K. *Orthodoxy*. New York: John Lane, 1908.
Joeckel, Samuel. "C. S. Lewis, Public Intellectual," *Sehnsucht* 4 (2010): 43–66.
Lewis, C. S. *The Abolition of Man*. 1947. MacMillan Paperback Edition. New York: Macmillan, 1955.
—. *The Allegory of Love: A Study in Medieval Tradition*. Oxford: Oxford University Press, 1971.
—. Review of *Boethius: Some Aspects of His Times and Works*, by Helen Barrett, *Medium Aevum* 10, no. 1 (February 1941).
—. "Christianity and Culture." In *Christian Reflections*, edited by Walter Hooper, 12–36. Grand Rapids, MI: Eerdmans, 1967.
—. *The Collected Letters of C. S. Lewis, Vol. II: Books, Broadcasts, and the War 1931-1949*, edited by Walter Hooper. New York: HaperCollins, 2004.
—. "De Descriptione Temporum," In *Selected Literary Essays*. 1969. Canto Classics Edition, edited by Walter Hooper, 1–14. New York: Cambridge University Press, 2013.
—. *The Discarded Image: An Introduction to Medieval and Renaissance Literature*. 1964. Canto Edition, New York: Cambridge University Press, 1994.
—. "Ex Libris," *Christian Century* 79 (June 6, 1962): 719.
—. "The idea of an 'English School.'" In *Image and Imagination: Essays and Reviews*, Canto Classics Edition, edited by Walter Hooper. New York: Cambridge University Press, 2013.

---

[55] Barkman, *Lewis & Philosophy*, 55.

—. "Is Theology Poetry?" In *The Weight of Glory and Other Addresses,* rev. and exp., edited by Walter Hooper. New York: Macmillan, 1980.

—. *Miracles.* New York: Macmillan, 1960.

—. "On the Reading of Old Books." In *God in the Dock: Essays on Theology and Ethics,* edited by Walter Hooper, 200–7. London: HarperCollins, 2000.

—. *Pilgrim's Regress.* Grand Rapids, MI: Eerdmans, 1974.

—. *That Hideous Strength.* New York: MacMillan, 1971.

Patrick, James. "The Heart's Desire and the Landlord's Rules: C. S. Lewis as a Moral Philosopher." In *The Pilgrim's Guide: C. S. Lewis and the Art of Witness,* edited by David Mills, 70–85. Grand Rapids, MI: Eerdmans, 1998.

Ward, Michael. *Planet Narnia: The Seven Heavens in the Imagination of C. S. Lewis.* New York: Oxford University Press, 2008.

Suggestions for further reading

Barkman, Adam. *C. S. Lewis & Philosophy as a Way of Life.* Allentown, PA: Zossima, 2009.
This is the most comprehensive portrait I know of Lewis as moral philosopher and public intellectual. Especially intriguing are the thorough tracing of Lewis's debts to Neoplatonism and Pseudo-Dionysius, and the anatomizing of his Christian eudaemonism (philosophical focus on happiness and desire as crucial categories for understanding life).

Boenig, Robert. *C. S. Lewis and the Middle Ages.* Kent, OH: Kent State University Press, 2012.
The title might mislead: this is *not* a full-orbed study of Lewis's medievalism (personal, literary, devotional, spiritual, churchly, etc.). Boenig, himself a medievalist, does conclude early in the book that "the medieval is not only [Lewis's] emotional center, but it is also the center of his professional life" (17)—a conclusion I heartily share. But the book's central task is more modest: a literary-critical analysis of medieval method (less so *theme*) in Lewis's imaginative fiction—particularly his "medieval" habit of writing stories that draw in, argue with, or elaborate upon other books. An informative, enjoyable, and at times eye-opening read.

Boethius. *The Consolation of Philosophy.* 1969, Reprint Edition. Translated with an introduction by V. E. Watts. Middlesex, England: Penguin, 1981.
Of course Boethius's classic itself bears reading today, as it has ever since Boethius's day. Here you find not only a masterful and engaging allegorical tale, but also a penetrating philosophical commentary by a first-rate Christian mind on such subjects as fortune, time, and the good life. Its legacy today goes far beyond Boethius's image of the "wheel of fortune," and its influence on the thought of the medieval period cannot be overstated. As Lewis said, to read it is almost to become "naturalized" in that period.

Lewis, C. S. *The Abolition of Man*. 1947. MacMillan Paperback Edition. New York: Macmillan, 1955.
I have come to the conclusion that in almost all of his fictional work (with the possible exception of *Till We Have Faces*), Lewis wrote first of all in his primary vocation as a moral philosopher—and only second as a literary artist. (This may be why the consummate literary artist Tolkien didn't think much of his friend's literary works.) In this essay you find Lewis at the peak of that primary vocation. If you want to see some of these same arguments worked out in fictional form, you should turn to the next work in this list.

Lewis, C. S. *That Hideous Strength*. New York: MacMillan, 1971.
Here Lewis imagines vividly a world (or at least a quasi-scientific cabal) in which the consequences of utilitarianism have been played out to their death-dealing end. As he says in his preface, "This is a 'tall story' about devilry, though it has behind it a serious 'point' which I have tried to make in my Abolition of Man." In contrast to the evil of the National Institute for Coordinated Experiments (N.I.C.E.), we find the ordinary virtues attractively painted in a sort of intentional Christian community called St Anne's. The book, a stylistic homage to his friend Charles Williams, also contains a correction and "re-medievalization" of T. H. White's portrait of Merlyn in *The Once and Future King,* and appearances by more than one of the Ptolemean planets in medieval moral garb (for more on this, see Michael Ward's book below).

Lewis, C. S. "*De Descriptione Temporum*." In *Selected Literary Essays*. 1969. Canto Classics Edition, edited by Walter Hooper, 1–14. New York: Cambridge University Press, 2013.
Here is Lewis's "manifesto" as an intuitive medievalist—one who wants to see not only the morality and spirituality but also many other aspects of the Middle Ages revivified in his own age.

—. *The Discarded Image: An Introduction to Medieval and Renaissance Literature*. 1964. Canto Edition. New York: Cambridge University Press, 1994.
This work summarizes many years of Lewis's lectures at Cambridge. Mere mortals without the benefit of Lewis's thorough education and astounding memory will find the welter of classical and medieval references somewhat bewildering, but the book is still a must-read for anyone interested in how Lewis *saw* the medieval world, and what he regretted that modern people had lost from that era. It also contains a complete section devoted to Boethius.

Ward, Michael. *Planet Narnia: The Seven Heavens in the Imagination of C. S. Lewis*. New York: Oxford University Press, 2008.
With penetrating insight, sensitive analysis, and wit, Ward explores what might well be described as the "discarded image pattern" behind and

beneath Lewis's most famous fictional stories—The Chronicles of Narnia. Ward's now famous argument is that Lewis amused himself by creating a hidden structure that ties together the seven books of that series: the planets of the Ptolemean cosmos, as each was understood in moral, allegorical terms by medieval thinkers. Whether you become convinced or not (I have), you will enjoy both Ward's many insights into the medieval material behind Lewis's story cycle, and his clear, sparkling prose.

8

James Boswell, *The Life of Samuel Johnson*

Paul Tankard

In Lewis's list, James Boswell's *Life of Samuel Johnson* (1791) stands out for a number of reasons. It is one of the few narrative works, and of those few it is the only one that is not a novel. It appears to be an entirely secular work, not a book of ideas or a work of the imagination: to people for whom everything to do with C. S. Lewis connotes vivid imagery and deep spirituality, the *Life of Johnson* seems disappointingly prosaic. Yet it is perhaps the most widely read of all the books on the list, and has never been out of print, and in acknowledging its influence, Lewis aligns himself with an enduring element of English literary and national culture. It is also by far the longest book on the list: it is a text of almost offensive materiality. This all-too-obvious characteristic is sometimes mentioned in disparaging terms; but the *Life of Johnson* is also the funniest book on Lewis's list—and if something is funny, who would want it shorter? Nevertheless, its presence among this particular top ten, with nine more serious, sublime and dignified texts, needs some explaining.

The Life of Johnson was published seven years after the death in 1784 of its subject, Samuel Johnson: the poet, journalist, lexicographer, essayist, editor, biographer, critic—and more besides—who was regarded as the preeminent man of letters of his day. Almost since the moment of publication, Boswell's *Life of Johnson* has been regarded as the first and best of modern biographies. Thomas Macaulay's famous assessment of 1831— which should be read in full—was that "Boswell is the first of biographers. He has no second."[1] Indeed, the persuasive power of the book has meant that it has—among scholars as well as general readers—tended to overshadow the literary work of its protagonist. Soon after its publication, Johnson's friend, the philosopher and statesman Edmund Burke, is reported to have

---

[1] Thomas Macaulay, *Boswell's Life of Johnson*, ed. R. F. Winch (London, 1896), 21. It was first published in the *Edinburgh Review* of September 1831, as a review of J. W. Croker's edition of the *Life*. The full text is readily findable on the internet.

said that Boswell's *Life* was "a greater monument to Johnson's fame, than all his writings put together."[2] It is hard to exaggerate how well known the book was, at least until quite recently. A critic of the very early twentieth century, John Bailey, says, "in his lifetime Johnson was chiefly thought of as a great writer. To-day we think of him chiefly as a great man. This is the measure of Boswell's genius."[3]

I won't say much about James Boswell, although he is fascinating in his own way. He was not perhaps a very great or admirable man, but he was a very great writer. His major works in his own time were his *Account of Corsica* (1768) and his two books about Samuel Johnson.[4] In the twentieth century he has become well known for his voluminous "Private Papers": his journals, correspondence, and other writings of which almost 30 volumes have been published since 1950, with many more to come. He was also a busy contributor to the periodical press, writing at least 600 pieces for newspapers and magazines.[5] But the *Life of Johnson* was his self-described *magnum opus*. It was based on conscientious research; he wrote to at least 120 people for firsthand information about Johnson,[6] and no doubt spoke to many more. But his great gift, and his uniquely powerful biographical method—a method which no subsequent biographer of Johnson (or anyone else) has been able to replicate—is intimately connected with his own lifelong practice of journal keeping. From his early twenties, through a disciplined habit, supported by a remarkable memory, and (it must be said) a talent for mimicry, Boswell kept a full and detailed record of his own daily life. During the summers he spent in London, in breaks from his own career as a lawyer in Edinburgh, his journal includes a convincing and seemingly verbatim account of Johnson's conversation, which—incorporated into the *Life of Johnson*—brings an image of the sage vividly before us.

It has often been pointed out that the book is in many ways unbalanced; that the first two thirds of Johnson's life takes up only the first fifth of Boswell's gigantic book. Where the book comes alive for its readers is at

---

[2] Qtd. in James Boswell, *The Life of Samuel Johnson, LL.D.*, ed. George Birkbeck Hill, rev. L. F. Powell, 6 vols. (Oxford: Clarendon Press, 1934–64), 1:10 n.1.
[3] John Bailey, *Dr. Johnson and His Circle*, 2nd ed. (London: Oxford University Press, 1947), 123. The book was first published in 1913 and much reprinted.
[4] The first of which was *A Journal of a Tour to the Hebrides with Samuel Johnson*, published in 1785, as a taster for the *Life*.
[5] My own edition of these materials, most of them reprinted for the first time in over 200 years, is published as *Facts and Inventions: Selections from the Journalism of James Boswell*, ed. Paul Tankard (New Haven: Yale University Press, 2014).
[6] "List of Correspondents," in *The Correspondence and Other Papers of James Boswell Relating to the Making of the "Life of Johnson,"* ed. Marshall Waingrow, 2nd ed.; corr. and enl. (Edinburgh: Edinburgh University Press; New Haven, CT: Yale University Press, 2001).

the point when, on May 16, 1763, the 53-year-old Samuel Johnson steps into the back parlor of the bookseller and actor Tom Davies, and is introduced to a visitor from Scotland, his future biographer, the 22-year-old James Boswell.

> [W]hen I was sitting in Mr. Davies's back-parlour, after having drunk tea with him and Mrs. Davies, Johnson unexpectedly came into the shop ... Mr. Davies mentioned my name, and respectfully introduced me to him. I was much agitated; and recollecting his prejudice against the Scotch, of which I had heard much, I said to Davies, "Don't tell him where I come from."—"From Scotland," cried Davies, roguishly. "Mr. Johnson, (said I) I do indeed come from Scotland, but I cannot help it." ... [W]ith that quickness of wit for which he was so remarkable, he seized the expression "come from Scotland," which I had used in the sense of being of that country; and, as if I had said I had come away from it or left it, retorted, "That, Sir, I find, is what a very great many of your countrymen cannot help."[7]

From that moment, for the next 20 years and 1,000 pages, the reader accompanies Boswell into the domestic and social life of a fascinating circle of people, to enjoy their ideas and savor the quality of their friendships.

Lacking a plot or an argument, the *Life of Johnson* is a difficult book to summarize. Boswell's scheme was "to write Dr. Johnson's *Life* in Scenes";[8] that is, to give—from the record of his contemporaneous journals—as full an account as possible of the occasions when he was in Johnson's company, in particular of his conversation, and to paint these scenes on the backdrop of a narrative woven around Johnson's doings derived from his publications, his letters, and anecdotes supplied by others. The result is a book in which—through letters and conversation—the hero frequently appears, as it were, in real time and in his own words. Johnson comes across as a figure of immense intellectual energy and moral power, which qualities are rendered convincing and sympathetic by the frank depiction of his human frailties and eccentricities, and by a great vein of wit and humor. Nevertheless, for an audience unacquainted with Johnson the man or Boswell the book, some summary of his life and achievements is probably required.

Samuel Johnson was born in 1709 in the English provincial city of Lichfield, a city in those days of about 3,000 people, the son of a bookseller. His mother was 40 and his father 10 years older; he was their first child.

---

[7] Boswell, *Life*, 1:392.
[8] Waingrow, *Correspondence*, li.

Johnson attended the grammar school in Lichfield, and when a small legacy came to the family, he went for 13 months to Pembroke College, Oxford, which he left without a degree, having run out of money. He worked for periods in his father's shop, and as a private tutor. In 1735 he married a woman 20 years his senior and used her small fortune to set up a school. When this collapsed, he set out for London to try to find a living as a writer. He contacted the editor of the recently established monthly, the famous *Gentleman's Magazine*, and quickly made himself indispensible, writing poems, lives, translations, reviews, and parliamentary reports. His energy and knowledge attracted a consortium of booksellers—the eighteenth-century equivalent of a publishing house—to commission him to prepare a thorough and scholarly English dictionary. This huge work was published after seven years' labor, in 1755. During this same period he wrote his series of periodical essays, *The Rambler* (1750–2). His next project was to edit his own journal, the *Literary Magazine*, which he did for three years, and he also commenced work on an edition of Shakespeare. He embarked on another series of essays, *The Idler* (1758–60) and his little novel, *Rasselas* (1759). In 1762 his hand-to-mouth way of life changed when he was granted a £300 annual pension. The following year he met the young James Boswell, and in 1764 he and his great friend, the renowned portrait painter Sir Joshua Reynolds, founded the (Literary) Club, for dining and conversation. His edition of Shakespeare was published in 1765. In 1773 he was persuaded to spend three months with Boswell, traveling around Scotland, a trip which gave rise to two literary classics: Johnson's own *Journey to the Western Islands* (1775) and—after Johnson's death—Boswell's *Journal of a Tour to the Hebrides with Samuel Johnson* (1786). In the late 1770s, Johnson embarked on his last great work, *The Lives of the Most Eminent English Poets*, which was published in 1779–81. After suffering a stroke in June 1784, he died at home in London in December that year.

This is, in a sense, what the *Life of Johnson* is about. But if a collection of facts about the life of one dead Englishman—even a very great writer—was all it was about, no one (much less C. S. Lewis) would ever have read it, much less reread it.

There has been much discussion among literary scholars in the late twentieth century over the proposition—forcefully argued by, in particular, Donald Greene—that to give Johnson his due as a writer requires that he be rescued from Boswell.[9] It is argued that Boswell trivializes Johnson: that

---

[9] Donald Greene pursued this supposedly revisionist criticism most vigorously in a number of essays, notably "Reflections on a Literary Anniversary," in *Twentieth-century Interpretations of Boswell's "Life of Johnson,"* ed. James Clifford (Englewood Cliffs: Prentice-Hall, 1970), 97–103; and " 'Tis a Pretty Book, Mr. Boswell, But—,"

the book depicts Johnson as an ogre or a buffoon, and that in preparing to write the *Life*—as the book testifies—Boswell manipulated Johnson in social situations to make him more interesting or extravagantly peculiar. Certainly Boswell has his own "angle" on Johnson and he emphasizes aspects of Johnson's character and opinions—particularly political ideas—that are most in accord with his own. But this argument seems to me to promulgate a false dichotomy: in fact, because Boswell's great work includes so much of Johnson's spoken wisdom, its overwhelming moral or didactic tendency is substantially the same as that of Johnson's own writing. And in any case, from a practical point of view, it seems now as if something like parity has been reached between readers of Johnson and readers of Boswell's *Johnson*: that is to say, there are more scholarly people reading Johnson, and fewer nonscholarly people reading Boswell (or anything else). Johnson is now as much read as Boswell, and Boswell is as much studied as Johnson—though higher levels of study and readership of both writers is greatly to be desired.

Lewis meets Johnson

Although C. S. Lewis was reading Boswell's *Life of Johnson* from the age of 17 at least, he never wrote about it as such (apart from an occasion that I will mention shortly) and the evidence for its influence on him is not to be found in his books and essays, but—in a sense—in his own biography: particularly if we include his letters as part of his biography. The first mention that I find of Boswell is in October 1916, when Lewis wrote from the home of his crammer in Surrey, to his lifelong friend and confidante Arthur Greeves, of having "dipped often into Boswell's 'Life of Johnson.' Being entirely made up of conversation I don't think it is a book to be read continuously," and a few weeks later he told his father that he is "dipping into" the book and liking it "better and better."[10]

He seems to have started reading the book in earnest as a soldier in France on the Western Front, after having requested his father send him the two-volume "Everyman" edition.[11] He must have started reading it in the

---

and "Boswell's *Life* as 'Literary Biography'," both in *Boswell's "Life of Johnson": New Questions, New Answers*, ed. John A. Vance (Athens, GA: University of Georgia Press, 1985), 110–46; 161–71. In the latter book, Greene's essays are responded to by a number of other scholars.

[10] C. S. Lewis to Arthur Greeves, Oct. 4, 1916, in *The Collected Letters of C. S. Lewis, Vol. I: Family Letters, 1905-1931*, ed. Walter Hooper (London: HarperCollins, 2004), 228; C. S. Lewis to Albert Lewis, Oct. 12, 1916, ibid., 234.

[11] It would be interesting to know where Lewis's own copy is now.

trenches, for by the time he found himself in a field hospital, on February 1, 1918, he was into volume two. He says, "it is the ideal book to read out here and to keep me in touch with all the quiet literary pleasant things in the world—one feels so cut off at times among all these godless philistines."[12] (Of course, the "godless philistines" to whom he refers are not the enemy, but his comrades in arms.) The critic Paul Fussell has described how, for British soldiers in the Great War, "eighteenth-century writing was popular [because it] offered an oasis of reasonableness and normality, a place one could crawl into for a few moments' respite from the sights, sounds and smells of the twentieth century."[13] By February 22, Lewis was still in hospital and "still at Boswell."[14]

It is some time before he next mentions Boswell's *Johnson* in his letters, but virtually all future mentions of it (there are at least 50) signify that he is not, in the usual sense, reading the book—and certainly not doing so for the first time—but rather that he *knows* it, and can call upon it in letters and conversations for apposite quotations and allusions. Furthermore, his familiarity with the book is frequently renewed, as signified by the casualness of his mentions of it. In his autobiography, he described the routine of his teenage days under his private tutor, a routine that he ever afterwards thought of as his normal day (whilst lamenting how rare such days were):

> eating and reading are two pleasures that combine admirably. Of course not all books are suitable for mealtime reading. It would be a kind of blasphemy to read poetry at table. What one wants is a gossipy, formless book which can be opened anywhere. The ones I learned so to use at Bookham were Boswell, and a translation of Herodotus, and Lang's *History of English Literature*. *Tristram Shandy*, *Elia* and the *Anatomy of Melancholy* are all good for the same purpose.[15]

So much for doing Sudoku or the crossword over lunch. In other words, Lewis found—like many readers before and since—that the *Life of Johnson* is not just a book to read: it is a book to inhabit. Lewis was a great one for rereading, and this was for him not just a preference, but a matter of principle, as he once explained, using telling examples:

---

[12] C. S. Lewis to Arthur Greeves, Feb. 2, 1918, *Collected Letters I*, 353.
[13] Paul Fussell, *The Great War and Modern Memory* (New York: Oxford University Press, 1975), 162. I am grateful to Austin Gee for drawing this to my attention.
[14] C. S. Lewis to Albert Lewis, Feb. 22, 1918, *Collected Letters I*, 362.
[15] C. S. Lewis, *Surprised by Joy: The Shape of My Early Life* (London: Geoffrey Bles, 1955), 136.

An unliterary man may be defined as one who reads books once only. There is hope for a man who has never read Malory or Boswell or *Tristram Shandy* or Shakespeare's *Sonnets*: but what can you do with a man who says he "has read" them, meaning he has read them once, and thinks that settles the matter?[16]

But for a man with such a retentive memory, rereading (and just reading) means that the books he knows in that way become part of his intellectual and imaginative furniture. Throughout his life Lewis seems to have taken a certain pleasure in having minor illnesses that stopped him from working but still allowed him to read, and on one of these occasions, in February 1932, when he was in bed for a week with 'flu, he wrote to a friend of having "had an orgy of Scott"; he read (or reread) four of Sir Walter Scott's novels, and says that "*The Antiquary* I have read over and over again, and old Oldbuck is almost as familiar to me as Johnson."[17] Here Lewis compares Johnson, not as a writer or with Scott himself, but with Scott's Jonathan Oldbuck: in other words, the "Johnson" with which he is so familiar is Johnson the character, Johnson as depicted by Boswell—and the clear implication of this passage is that the *Life of Johnson* is virtually his touchstone of literary familiarity: there is no book that he knows better.

One of the features of the book that renders it so attractive and habitable is in fact its great length—that however well one knows it, as Lewis observed in a letter to his brother, one can't "spend an hour on Boswell without finding something new."[18] Reading and rereading Boswell is a bit like revisiting an old friend. And while it is Johnson and the representation of his conversation that is attractive to readers, and Johnson whom we imagine and whom we quote, it is James Boswell who is responsible for this unique work of literary creation, and Lewis was happy to give him due credit. In May 1925, Lewis read a paper on the subject of "Boswell" to the Martlets, an undergraduate literary society in Oxford, and in this paper (according to the minutes of the meeting) he says that

> Johnson while purporting to have historical reality actually has the reality of art. We treat him as a living man, we quarrel with him & are reconciled again. All this is Boswell's work . . . Boswell in recording

---

[16] C. S. Lewis, "On Stories," in *Of Other Worlds: Essays and Stories*, ed. Walter Hooper (London: Geoffrey Bles, 1966), 17.
[17] C. S. Lewis to Arthur Greeves, Feb. 1932, in *The Collected Letters of C. S. Lewis, Vol. II: Books, Broadcasts and War, 1931-1949*, ed. Walter Hooper (London: HarperCollins, 2004), 53.
[18] Feb. 3, 1940, ibid., 337.

conversation showed the unconscious selection of memory & the conscious selection of the great artist.[19]

Writing to his brother, Lewis commented, "If one had not experienced it, it wd. be hard to understand how *a dead man out of a book* can be almost a member of one's family circle."[20] This strong expression shows Lewis's keen appreciation of Boswell's achievement.

So, having established the fact of the book's influence on Lewis, how was that influence manifest? We could just trawl through those 50 references to the book in his letters, but that might be a trifle too dull. In the first year of his acquaintance with Boswell's Johnson—as I said earlier—he said that the book was perfect to read in a trench on the Western Front, "to keep me in touch with all the quiet literary pleasant things in the world."[21] Twenty-two years later, during another world war, in a letter to his brother he described the book as

> All very ordinary and obvious . . . but . . . full of sense and leisure and happiness. Does it occur to you that people have written of that sort of thing in almost all ages but our own? I begin to suspect that the world is divided not only into the happy and the unhappy, but into those who *like* happiness and those who, odd as it may seem, really don't.[22]

"Sense and leisure and happiness": what an accurate formula by which to describe the qualities of Boswell's *Life of Johnson*. And Lewis is right of course about people disliking happiness. The early nineteenth-century writers of the romantic movement, who so esteemed their own precious and unique imaginations, and of whose subjectivism we are still heirs today, made a cult of melancholy, and reified their emotional lives over common sense in a way that Johnson—and Lewis, for all his credentials as a romantic himself—would have regarded as dangerously self-indulgent.

Boswell's portrait of Johnson of course has its limitations. We do not in the *Life of Johnson* see Johnson at work. We do not see Johnson alone. We see Johnson at leisure and in company: not doing nothing, but meeting people of all kinds, talking, eating, arguing, traveling. He is sometimes in the company of many people, sometimes just a few, sometimes in mixed

---

[19] Qtd. in Walter Hooper, "To the Martlets," in *C. S. Lewis: Speaker and Teacher,* ed. Carolyn Keefe (Grand Rapids, MI: Zondervan, 1971), 53. The paper itself was not published, and no MS or typescript has been discovered.
[20] C. S. Lewis to Warren Lewis, Dec. 1939, *Collected Letters II*, 305 (my emphasis).
[21] C. S. Lewis to Arthur Greeves, Feb. 2, 1918, *Collected Letters I*, 353.
[22] C. S. Lewis to Warren Lewis, Jan. 28, 1940, *Collected Letters II*, 334–5.

company, though often just with men—some of those as talented and eminent as himself; and sometimes he is only in the company of one other person, the one other person without whom the book would not have been written: James Boswell. The milieu that is depicted in the book is characterized by a particular form of literary and intellectual sociality, which will remind many readers of this essay of another such group: of course, I mean the Inklings. It is not surprising that a book of conversation should enter into and stimulate conversations, or that a book about friendship—in particular male friendships—should itself inspire and stimulate friendships. In fact, on just about any given weekend, in some very unpredictable parts of the world, there are people meeting formally and informally to discuss Johnson and/or Boswell's *Johnson*. There are (or have been) Johnson societies in London, and Lichfield in the United Kingdom; New York, Los Angeles, and the Great Lakes, Midwest, and Northwest regions of the United States; Brisbane and Melbourne in Australia; Japan; and no doubt more besides.

The Johnsonian Lewis

Of course, Lewis (like most readers) was attracted not only to the milieu of the book, but to the subject of the biography, Samuel Johnson himself. Most often, when Johnson is mentioned in relation to Lewis, it is in regard to the perceived physical and temperamental resemblances between the two men. Many people who had read Boswell, and then met Lewis—particularly his scholarly colleagues and students—made such observations. Richard Ladborough said "he had many affinities" with Johnson.[23] Leo Baker referred to "his Johnsonian intelligence."[24] Derek Brewer described Lewis replying to a question in "his most Johnsonian manner."[25] Bede Griffiths recalled that "once when I spoke disparagingly of Dr. Johnson how vehement was Lewis's reaction. Dr. Johnson was a hero to him, and Lewis himself has often been compared to Johnson."[26] Jack Bennett wrote that Lewis's "unique combination of different kinds of learning" led one to think "of him as a Johnsonian Colossus."[27] Nevill Coghill said that Lewis was "formidable in

---

[23] Richard W. Ladborough, "In Cambridge" in *Remembering C. S. Lewis: Recollections of Those Who Knew Him*, ed. James T. Como (San Francisco: Ignatius Press, 2005), 194.
[24] Leo Baker, "Near the Beginning," ibid., 70.
[25] Derek Brewer, "The Tutor: A Portrait," ibid., 138.
[26] Bede Griffiths, "The Adventure of Faith," ibid., 81.
[27] J. A. W. Bennett, "'Grete Clerk'," in *Light on C. S. Lewis,* ed. Jocelyn Gibb (London: Geoffrey Bles, 1965), 47.

appearance, rather as Dr Johnson (to judge [from the portraits of him] by Sir Joshua Reynolds) was formidable. There were many echoes of Johnson in Lewis. Both were formidable in their learning and in the range of their conversation, both had the same delight in argument, and in spite of their regard for truth, would argue for victory."[28]

Other resemblances would be apparent to readers familiar with the biographies of both men, such as their fondness for walking, and tea drinking. Johnson described himself as "a hardened and shameless tea-drinker, who has, for twenty years, diluted his meals with only the infusion of this fascinating plant, whose kettle has scarcely time to cool, who with tea amuses the evening, with tea solaces the midnight, and, with tea, welcomes the morning."[29] Lewis is recorded as having remarked, "You can't get a cup of tea large enough or a book long enough to suit me."[30] This mention of the quintessential English beverage also suggests the quality of "Englishness" that is represented in and by both writers, that Lewis certainly identified in Johnson,[31] and that with pubs, old libraries, Anglican liturgy, Oxford, dry humor, pipe-smoking, country lanes, etc., is part of the "charm" of the Lewis milieu for his many American readers.

A deeper vein of resemblance between the two men is identified by Lewis's one-time student, the poet and novelist, John Wain. If I may lapse into autobiography for a moment: it was through Wain (and thus through Lewis) that I became a Johnsonian. I did not come across Johnson when studying for my undergraduate degree in English. I read Wain's 1974 biography of Johnson mainly because I knew of John Wain as a junior Inkling.[32] I have read the book perhaps four times (twice out loud, with friends): it is a warm and powerfully moving book. Wain also wrote an

---

[28] Nevill Coghill, "The Approach to English," ibid., 57.
[29] Jonas Hanway, "Review of *A Journal of Eight Days' Journey*," in *Samuel Johnson: The Major Works*, ed. Donald Greene (Oxford: Oxford University Press, 2000), 509.
[30] Reported by Walter Hooper, in the Preface to *Of Other Worlds* by C. S. Lewis.
[31] In his *Samuel Johnson and the Culture of Property* (Cambridge: Cambridge University Press, 1999), 61 ff., Kevin Hart has artfully surveyed many of the ways in which Johnson is "associated with a cultural nationalism" (61), including Boswell's repeated descriptions of him as "a true-born Englishman" and a "John Bull," John Bailey's opening chapter which considers him as a "national institution" and describes him as "the embodiment of the essential features of the English character," and that copies of Boswell's *Life of Johnson* were in 1943 sent as gifts from the King and Queen to British prisoners of war in Europe (which reminds us of Lewis reading the book in the trenches in the previous world war). And we could add that both he and Lewis have recently been included for commemoration in the Anglican liturgical calendar. Cf. C. S. Lewis to Warren Lewis, Aug. 2, 1928, *Collected Letters I*, 773, where he remarks on the "Englishness" of Johnson's *Lives of the Poets*.
[32] John Wain, *Samuel Johnson* (London: Macmillan, 1974); there were second and third editions, in 1980 and 1994.

autobiography, called *Sprightly Running*, in which he describes his tutor at Oxford, Lewis, and the character of the gatherings of the Inklings that he attended. In this book he reflects on the various people—Lewis, Charles Williams, Nevill Coghill, the theologian Donald MacKinnon—who made the strongest impact on him at Oxford; and I would like to quote a longish passage.

> All these people I admired—Lewis, Williams, Heath-Stubbs, Coghill, MacKinnon—had one thing in common that bridged their differences. They were all dramatic personalities, making a strong impact. None of them bore any resemblance to the ordinary, commonplace, faceless citizen. Each had a characteristic style, not merely a style of writing or thinking but a style of presenting himself to the outside world . . . They attracted me because in their different ways they all treated life as if it were art. I do not mean that they posed. They simply recognized, intuitively, that the presence of other people, even the humblest and fewest, constitutes an audience, and towards an audience one has certain duties.
>
> The older I grow, the more clearly I see that this is one of the ways in which the human race can be divided up. Some people give the impression of being exactly the same in company as they are when alone. The same raw, untreated personality which serves them for solitary meditation, country walks, cleaning their teeth, casting their accounts, has to do duty in public too. They respond to other people, but they do so artlessly, much as animals might. Such people are often likeable, but my lifelong preference happens to have been for the opposite type, those for whom the presence of even one other person is a perpetual stimulus to character-creation. They are always giving a performance in the rôle for which they have cast themselves, making up the play as they go along, and tacitly inviting others to collaborate. That, indeed, is one reason why such people seek one another out; they enjoy being together because the very zest with which A plays his rôle puts B on his mettle to excel in his . . . By the mere fact of our birth, we have been cast for certain parts in the great play that is always going on, and we must act those parts with energy and imagination, making the most of every line. . . .
>
> If any reader still thinks I am referring to empty self-dramatizing and Narcissism, I must leave him at this point. Ultimately, the matter cannot be explained to those who do not understand it already. I doubt if even great literature can help much. Such a person could probably

read [. . . and here I pause for dramatic effect . . .] Boswell's *Life of Johnson* and take it simply as a compendium of anecdote and aphorism, not noticing that what gives the book its vitality is exactly this delight taken by the principal characters in the fine performances they give as themselves. Johnson had a heightened appreciation of the possibilities of being Johnson because Boswell was so delightedly Boswell.

Such people are in fact instinctively fulfilling a moral duty. The Creator . . . has equipped them with a certain identity, and they are all the time delightedly aware of this identity and out to get, and to give, as much fun as possible with it.[33]

Like Wain, Lewis himself was aware—what reader of Boswell could not be?—that Johnson was a very particular (and a rather uncommon) type of person. In a letter of March 1958, Lewis makes the actually quite profound observation that not all Christians are one kind of person, and he gives Johnson as one example.[34] There are a great many Christian circles in which Samuel Johnson, and even C. S. Lewis, would not personally, culturally, or temperamentally "fit in." I am put in mind of a homemade bumper sticker—legendary in our family—that read, "Be Nice—be a Christian." Samuel Johnson was learned, highly principled, orthodox, compassionate, witty. But he was often not nice. He was dogmatic, combative, melancholic, did not wash very often, and had very indecorous table manners. He could be very rude when faced with impertinence or foolishness. Yet, in another letter Lewis includes "even burly old Dr. Johnson" in a very short list of "shining examples of human holiness."[35] That "even" signifies Lewis's hint that we frequently err by imagining holiness to be manifest only in quiet, pale incorporeality: or naïveté, a fixed smile and hushed voices—or unrelenting cheerfulness. One of the reasons for which Lewis loved Johnson was that he was a holy man.

Two middle-aged moralists

But Johnson's character, and the Johnsonian aspects of Lewis's character, while endearing and picturesque, are in the end less interesting and less important than the fact that Samuel Johnson—as a writer and as a

---

[33] John Wain, *Sprightly Running: Part of an Autobiography* (London: Macmillan, 1962), 154–7; (ellipses and interpolation mine).
[34] C. S. Lewis to William P. Wylie, Mar. 28, 1958, *The Collected Letters of C. S. Lewis, Vol. III: Narnia, Cambridge, and Joy 1950–1963*, ed. Walter Hooper (London: HarperCollins, 2007), 929.
[35] C. S. Lewis to Arthur Greeves, Dec. 11, 1944, *Collected Letters III*, 1555.

biographical subject—was for C. S. Lewis an object lesson in how to be the kind of writer he wanted to be. I believe that Lewis included Boswell's *Life of Johnson* on this particular list because of its role in shaping—to use the actual terms of the question he was asked—his "vocational attitude." In his famous talk on "The Inner Ring," Lewis advised his audience, "When you invite a middle-aged moralist to address you, I suppose I must conclude, however unlikely the conclusion seems, that you have a taste for middle-aged moralizing."[36]

Samuel Johnson was also a middle-aged moralist. He was a scholar (though not, like Lewis, a professional scholar), and one who—like C. S. Lewis—wrote for the common reader (which was a term which Johnson himself coined).[37] He was what is now sometimes called a "public intellectual." He was in particular—and also like Lewis—a moral and didactic writer who recognized and addressed the peculiar challenges of that calling. Moral writing takes its place in the world alongside conventional "literature" on the one hand, and the text of the author's life on the other—and may be compromised by either relationship. Boswell's version of Johnson's character and opinions shows him manfully negotiating these complexities in ways that many readers have over two centuries found attractive and inspirational.

More than any other kind of writing, avowedly didactic writing of the kind practiced by Johnson and Lewis must supply the perceived needs of its readers. Instruction in how to slim one's tummy or download a software program poses no real problems in this regard, for the reader enters into the relationship with a specific focus on agreed terms. But the writer of moral literature—literature concerning right and wrong behavior, the motives of thought and action, the management of time and social relationships, and Life in General, and which is intended not for a narrowly religious readership but for a general audience—has no more pressing dilemma than that of finding a language in which to both dictate and amuse, to be both authoritative and companionable. Persuading the readers of particular ideas may be such a writer's goal, but such a goal will in practical terms be of secondary importance to persuading them to simply keep reading. Moral writing is not intended to fulfill the readers' immediate perceived needs. Frequently the moralist has to convince readers of the reality of certain

---

[36] C. S. Lewis, "The Inner Ring," *Transposition, and Other Addresses* (London: Geoffrey Bles, 1949), 55.

[37] Writing, in the Life of Thomas Gray, of Gray's famous "Elegy Written in a Country Churchyard," Johnson said, "I rejoice to concur with the common reader [. . . by whom] must be finally decided all claim to poetical honours." *The Lives of the English Poets*, ed. George Birkbeck Hill, 3 vols. (Oxford: Clarendon, 1905), 3:441.

unperceived needs, often against their own immediate interest in (for instance) mental complacency, physical indolence, or sensual gratification. If a reader feels too much rebuked by a text, and is not under some obligation to read it, he will put the book down and go and watch television. Johnson is well aware of this difficulty. He says, in one of the essays in his series, *The Rambler*:

> Advice is offensive, not because it lays us open to unexpected regret, or convicts us of any fault which had escaped our notice, but because it shows us that we are known to others as well as to ourselves; and the officious monitor is persecuted with hatred, not because his accusation is false, but because he assumes that superiority which we are not willing to grant him, and has dared to detect what we desired to conceal.[38]

In fact, I would argue that *The Rambler* is actually about the difficulty of giving advice. Time and time again in his essays, Johnson returns to this theme. The narrator figure, Mr Rambler, attempts to enlist the sympathy and cooperation of the (actual) reader by presenting and addressing portraits of various imagined readers, by whose faults and failings the reader is invited to be warned and amused. Many of the essays are in the form of supposed letters from readers,[39] who misunderstand him or who ask foolish questions, and Mr Rambler implicitly asks the real reader: aren't you and I glad we're not this silly? The real reader is not the direct object of Mr Rambler's advice, mockery or scorn, but still gets the message.

Lewis was one of the real readers of Johnson's essays. In August 1928, he told his brother, "I have read a good deal of the Rambler last term,"[40] and goes on to examine and commend Johnson's style in that series and the *Lives of the Poets*. On June 1930 he wrote to Arthur Greeves, "I personally get more pleasure from the *Rambler* than from anything else of his & at one time I used to read a Rambler every evening as a nightcap. They are so *quieting* in their brave, sensible dignity."[41] He calls Johnson's style "magnificent," and says, "I find Johnson very *bracing* when I am in my slack, self pitying mood. The amazing thing is his power of stating platitudes—or what in anyone

---

[38] Samuel Johnson, *Rambler* no. 155 in *The Rambler*, ed. W. J. Bate and Albrecht B. Strauss, 3 v. *The Yale Edition of the Works of Samuel Johnson*, vv. 3–5 (New Haven and London: Yale University Press, 1969), 5:61.

[39] Fifty-nine of the 208 essays are in the form of letters from correspondents, and toward the end of the series (no. 193) the narrator cheerfully acknowledges that this is a literary device.

[40] C. S. Lewis to Warren Lewis, Aug. 1928, *Collected Letters I*, 772–3.

[41] C. S. Lewis to Arthur Greeves, June 22, 1930, ibid., 909.

else wd. be platitudes—so that we really believe them at last and realise their importance."[42]

Moral and didactic writing does not fit into our usual literary categories, partly because we associate literature with leisure and freedom, whereas advice or instruction we associate with the opposite conditions.[43] The moral writer might be thought of as a species of critic. Lewis and Johnson brought to criticism a distrust of ideological positions and a delight in particular detail. In the case of their criticism of literature, this was based on a faculty which—at least in the pre-digital era—would have been a chief qualification for being a critic: that is, a phenomenal memory for text.

Two memorable critics

Boswell said that Johnson "never forgot anything that he either heard or read,"[44] and gives us in his book many instances of Johnson's prodigious memory.[45] Such anecdotes are consistent with the image of Johnson as a titan, of extraordinary intellectual and physical power, and Boswell and other biographers of Johnson relish retelling them—as do I.

> Of the power of his memory, for which he was all his life eminent to a degree almost incredible, the following early instance was told me in his presence at Lichfield, in 1776, by his step-daughter, Mrs. Lucy Porter, as related to her by his mother. When he was a child in petticoats, and had learnt to read, Mrs. Johnson one morning put the common prayer-book into his hands, pointed to the collect for the day, and said "Sam, you must get this by heart." She went up stairs, leaving him to study it: but by the time she had reached the second floor, she heard him following her.

---

[42] Ibid.
[43] Modern "self-help" books are, by contrast with traditional moral writing, thoroughly secular and egocentric, and their immense contemporary popularity feeds a hunger for circumstantial and functional success, rather than for selfunderstanding or moral improvement.
[44] Boswell, *Life*, 1:48. This section about Johnson's memory reflects ideas developed in my essay, "Samuel Johnson's *History of Memory*," *Studies in Philology* (Winter 2005), 102:1.
[45] His editors—their own imaginations apparently captivated by this aspect of Johnson's abilities—have been moved to add as footnotes many more. Most of these may be found in the index to the Hill-Powell, *Life*, 6:205. To be precise, Boswell gives six anecdotes of Johnson's memory in the *Life* and the *Tour*, Malone points out another, Hill adds a further three in the notes, and Powell in the index identifies a further five stories in Boswell's text as examples of Johnson's extraordinary memory (and omits a further story identified by Hill in the 1st ed. of the index).

"What's the matter?" said she. "I can say it," he replied; and repeated it distinctly, though he could not have read it more than twice.[46]

After that, we are often told of Johnson recalling passages of text, of verse and prose, in Latin, Greek, and Italian as well as English, of minor and ephemeral writing as well as of significant literature, frequently after having only seen them once and briefly, often years earlier. I shall restrict myself to another two such stories.

G. B. Hill gives in a footnote a story John Nichols related about Johnson's "Life of Rowe": "This *Life* is a very remarkable instance of the uncommon strength of Dr. Johnson's memory. When I received from him the MS he complacently observed that the criticism was tolerably well done, considering that he had not read one of Rowe's plays for thirty years."[47]

Another example concerns Johnson's famous letter to Lord Chesterfield, in which he rejected that nobleman's paltry and belated offer of patronage of his *Dictionary*. The fact of the letter was a matter of public knowledge, and its contents were the subject of much contemporary curiosity. Johnson dictated a version of it from memory to Guiseppi Baretti, then, some years later (on June 4, 1781), he again dictated it from memory to Boswell.[48] Baretti's version (with Johnson's handwritten corrections) eventually surfaced from among Johnson's papers, and was the version that Boswell used in the *Life of Johnson*.[49] Boswell tells us that the variations between the two versions are "slight," but it was not possible for scholars to compare them until the copy which had been dictated to him emerged in the mid-twentieth century from his papers at Yale.[50] When the two texts are compared, it appears that in the approximately 460 words of the letter there are between them a total of 22 phrasal or verbal differences, 13 of them differences of a single word.[51]

---

[46] Boswell, *Life*, 1:40.
[47] Ibid., 4:36 n.3.
[48] Ibid., 4:128.
[49] Ibid., 1:260–3.
[50] Boswell says that "I have deposited both the copies in the British Museum" (*Life* 1, 263 n.2). Powell found the Baretti version there, but not Boswell's (Boswell, *Life* 1:540, App. G). In the final stages of preparing his 1952 edition of Johnson's *Letters*, R. W. Chapman was able to see the Boswell version, and the printer's copy made from it, and describes them in a preface; see *The Letters of Samuel Johnson, with Mrs. Thrale's Genuine Letters to Him*, ed. R. W. Chapman, 3 vols (Oxford: Clarendon Press, 1952), 1:xxxi–xxxv.
[51] Twenty of these variations are to be seen in Redford's edition of Johnson's letters. Marshall Waingrow notes two more in his edition of the MS of the *Life*. See *The Letters of Samuel Johnson*, ed. Bruce Redford, 5 vols (Princeton, NJ: Princeton University Press, 1992–4) I, 94–7 (Feb. 7, 1755). See *James Boswell's Life of Johnson: An Edition of the Original Manuscript*, vol. 1, ed. Marshall Waingrow (Edinburgh: Edinburgh University Press; New Haven: Yale University Press, 1994), 444 (n. 14 on p. 188, and n. 3 on p. 189).

None of them could be called anything other than a minor variation. What is particularly impressive is that the structure of the paragraphs, indeed, the rhythms of the sentences, are exactly the same in both versions.

Some years ago I collected similar tales about C. S. Lewis, drawn from over a dozen writers who observed him at first hand, one of which I shall limit myself to retelling here. This story was related by Canadian professor John Leyerle, at the time a student of Lewis's, who dated the occasion to November 1954:

> Lewis was asked about his current writing and grumbled a bit about having found that he was concluding many of his paragraphs with iambic pentameter.
>
> Seated near him was an American Rhodes scholar, Richard Selig, a poet of energetic mind and considerable spirit. He responded in [a] pressing manner to the remark.
>
> Selig asked, "If you *will* end your paragraphs in iambic pentameter, why do you grumble about it, sir?"
>
> Lewis replied, "As usual, Selig, you missed the point. The difficulty is that I remember everything I've ever read and bits pop up uninvited."
>
> "Surely not *everything* you've ever read, Mr. Lewis?"
>
> "Yes everything, Selig, even the most boring texts."
>
> Selig got to his feet and went to the College library, which was open late in term, and took out a volume of the long and little-read poem.[52] He returned and opened the volume. He read a few lines.
>
> "Stop!" said Lewis who lifted his eyes toward the ceiling and recited the poem in his rich and modulated public voice. He stopped after ten lines or so and looked at Selig, now very silent. Conversation was slow to resume at that end of the table.[53]

In addition to this remarkable gift that both Lewis and Johnson brought to the role of literary criticism, there are the literary strategies

---

[52] John Leyerle left out of this account the detail of the name of the text. My colleague Chris Ackerley heard Prof. Leyerle tell this story, and on that occasion he said the book was the fifteenth-century poem in Middle English, *The Fall of Princes*, by John Lydgate (c.1370–c.1451), and that Lewis had said he had last looked at it 40 years earlier (personal communication).

[53] John Leyerle, Letter to *The Canadian C. S. Lewis Journal*, rpt. in *In Search of C. S. Lewis*, ed. Stephen Schofield (South Plainfield, NJ: Bridge, 1983), 164. For other testimony to Lewis's memory, see Paul Tankard, "William Empson on C.S. Lewis's Memory and Reading," Notes and Queries, N.S. 61:4 (December, 2014), doi: 10.1093/notesj/gju181.

that they employ themselves, as writers. There is something significant about their deployment of a wide range of literary genres; unlike the greatest literary writers—Shakespeare wrote no novels, Jane Austen no plays, Dickens no poems—Johnson and Lewis were very versatile. I think this was because they thought less about literary art than about how to say what they wanted to say in ways adapted to the needs of their potential audiences. They do not wish to write only for one sort of person, because the things they have to say are (or ought to be) of profound concern to everyone. And even if we exclude from our consideration their fiction, poetry, plays and literary criticism, and concentrate only on their moral and didactic writing, we find them both deploying closely related strategies to deal with the difficulty of giving advice. I mean, in particular, the use of satire.

Two charitable satirists

Walter Jackson Bate has written very persuasively of Samuel Johnson's qualifications as a satirist.[54] Johnson is undoubtedly a satirist in a perfectly straightforward sense, in that two of his major works, *London* and *The Vanity of Human Wishes*, are long poems in imitation of *Satires* by the classical Roman poet Juvenal. Describing the equipment Johnson brings to satirical writing, Bate instances "the range and readiness of his humour,"[55] his "readiness and aggressive militance of reply,"[56] "the power of *reductionism*,"[57] his "deeply pessimistic conviction of the frightening and unsleeping strength of human egotism and vanity,"[58] and "those prolonged outbursts of laughter ... where Johnson's intellect sees through the pretenses and self-delusions that fill up so much of life."[59] However, despite this display of evidence, Bate concluded that Johnson is not a satirist, but what he calls a "satirist *manqué*,"[60] that is, a *foiled* satirist: he has all the equipment for being a satirist, but out of "charity and justice"[61] he blunts the force of his satire with explanation and sympathy.

---

[54] W. J. Bate, "Johnson and Satire Manqué," *Eighteenth-Century Studies: In Honor of Donald F. Hyde* (New York: The Grolier Club, 1970), 145–60.
[55] Ibid., 146.
[56] Ibid.
[57] Ibid., 147.
[58] Ibid., 149.
[59] Ibid., 150.
[60] Ibid., 151.
[61] Ibid.

In a similar way, Peter Schakel has considered C. S. Lewis's deployment of satire.[62] He asserts that "Lewis himself wrote no satires" (and hence, I suppose, that he cannot be called a satirist). Certainly, Lewis is not known to have imitated the *Satires* of Juvenal. However, Schakel tells us that Swift's "*Gulliver's Travels* could be considered a satire, since its main focus and purpose is the humorous exposure and undercutting of folly and evil."[63] On precisely that basis, I would argue, Lewis's *Screwtape Letters* could be considered a satire. The trouble is that, aside from the Roman verse satires of Juvenal and Horace, *satire* is not really a genre but a mode of expression. Generically, *The Screwtape Letters* is a novel, just like *Gulliver's Travels*. But both are so satirical that it makes sense to call them satires.

Lewis said of the book, "Though I had never written anything more easily, I never wrote with less enjoyment."[64] Why should this be? It was easy because all that is required to see human behavior from Screwtape's point of view is to consider one's own actions and motives—and those of one's neighbors—from a consistently uncharitable perspective. Lack of charity comes to us very easily and, with regard to most of us for much of the time, it is not actually unfair to put a negative construction on our motives; and so, when we read the result in the *Screwtape Letters*, and find our own motives exposed, the book strikes us as a work of great moral insight. But if we always thought the worst of each other conventional social relations would scarcely be possible, and so we are polite and respectful, often when we'd like to be otherwise, and believe the situation might warrant it. The character Screwtape is allowed this freedom, because he's not one of us; but Lewis found that it did him no good at all to indulge himself in this way of thinking, even for imaginative purposes. Both Johnson and Lewis are attracted to satire as a natural means of giving literary form to the didactic impulse. Both are sensitive to the dangers of satire, and modify its effects in different ways.

A. N. Wilson described *Screwtape* as a "cruel" book,[65] but he fails to see that the reason Lewis uses a double plot is to avoid exactly that risk. Lewis makes his satirical narrator, Screwtape—who mocks, manipulates, and scolds his human patients—an object of satire himself. The book is a satire on humanity, like *Gulliver's Travels*—think of the portraits of

---

[62] Peter Schakel, "The Satiric Imagination of C. S. Lewis," *Studies in the Literary Imagination*, 22:2 (Fall, 1989), 129–48.
[63] Ibid., 129.
[64] C. S. Lewis, "Preface," *The Screwtape Letters and Screwtape Proposes a Toast* (London: Geoffrey Bles, 1961), 12.
[65] A. N. Wilson, *C. S. Lewis: A Biography* (London: Collins, 1990), 177.

the clergymen, or the patient's mother—but it is just as much a satire on demons. We see our own frailties and self-deceptions laid bare, but we also see Screwtape himself turn into a caterpillar, and of course his hapless nephew is by the end of the book a tasty tidbit for his uncle's consumption. And the book has a happy ending: the patient himself has been snatched out of the devilish clutches by being killed by a bomb. The use of the literary device of the "unreliable narrator" does not detract from the power of the book to instruct and warn its human readers.

In fact, in both Lewis's *Screwtape* and Johnson's *Rambler* essays, this device of the double audience is used to deflect the directness and what Johnson called the offensiveness of the didacticism. I have already mentioned some of the strategies by which Johnson's moral essays avoid moralism, by at least partially constructing a fictitious narrator, by the use of fictitious correspondents, by the use of anecdotes and stories, and by seeming to address a narratee other than the actual readers.

Something of the same kind occurs in Boswell's *Life of Johnson*. The book contains a great deal of moral teaching, but it is conveyed in the form of dramatized conversation. It is not Boswell, but Samuel Johnson the literary character ("a dead man out of a book," as Lewis said) whom we admire and learn from, and whose wit and wisdom we quote. But because we see and hear Johnson only through the mediating eye and voice of Boswell, we are enabled to keep a certain critical distance. Boswell keeps up both a presence (as a character) within the diegesis, and a commentary (as the narrator) outside it, which ensures that Johnson does not overwhelm us. We are amused by the book, but also—so it seems to us—by Johnson himself; and if on occasion he says offensive or brusque things, they are not things that offend us as readers. None of the advice in the book is directed at us, so we have no cause to be offended by it. We smile, but we also increase in wisdom.

Conclusion

James Boswell's genius is such that he makes us not only admire Johnson, but love him, and love him as much for his wisdom as for his humanity. This is a great gift. It is right and good that we should love that which is admirable. Boswell's *Life of Samuel Johnson* is readable and rereadable; it is vivid, memorable, browsable, and quotable. It has the literary qualities that Johnson strove for in his own writing, so that wisdom might not be too august, or heavy or remote, but fresh, approachable, and companionable.

For over two centuries Boswell's *Life of Johnson* has gained for these two writers many lifelong companions, including C. S. Lewis, who as all of his own readers can testify, learned its lessons well.

Bibliography

Bailey, John. *Dr. Johnson and His Circle*, 2nd ed. London: Oxford University Press, 1947.
Baker, Leo. "Near the Beginning." In *Remembering C. S. Lewis: Recollections of Those Who Knew Him*, edited by James T. Como. San Francisco: Ignatius, 2005.
Bate, W. J. "Johnson and Satire Manqué." In *Eighteenth-Century Studies: In Honor of Donald F. Hyde*. New York: Grolier Club, 1970.
Bennett, J. A. W. "'Grete Clerk'." In *Light on C. S. Lewis*, edited by Jocelyn Gibb. London: Geoffrey Bles, 1965.
Boswell, James. *James Boswell's Life of Johnson: An Edition of the Original Manuscript*, vol. 1, edited by Marshall Waingrow. Edinburgh: Edinburgh University Press; New Haven: Yale University Press. 1994.
—. *A Journal of a Tour to the Hebrides with Samuel Johnson*, n.p., 1785.
—. *The Life of Samuel Johnson, LL.D.*, edited by George Birkbeck Hill, revised by L. F. Powell, 6 vols. Oxford: Clarendon, 1934–64.
—. "List of Correspondents." In *The Correspondence and Other Papers of James Boswell Relating to the Making of the "Life of Johnson,"* edited by Marshall Waingrow, 2nd ed.; corr. and enl. Edinburgh: Edinburgh University Press; New Haven, CT: Yale University Press, 2001.
Brewer, Derek. "The Tutor: A Portrait." In *Remembering C. S. Lewis: Recollections of Those Who Knew Him*, edited by James T. Como. San Francisco: Ignatius, 2005.
Coghill, Nevill. "The Approach to English." In *Light on C. S. Lewis*, edited by Jocelyn Gibb. London: Geoffrey Bles, 1965.
Fussell, Paul. *The Great War and Modern Memory*. New York: Oxford University Press, 1975.
Greene, Donald. "Reflections on a Literary Anniversary." In *Twentieth Century Interpretations of Boswell's Life*, edited by James L. Clifford, 97–103. Englewood Cliffs, NJ: Prentice-Hall, 1970.
Hart, Kevin. *Samuel Johnson and the Culture of Property*. Cambridge: Cambridge University Press, 1999.
Hooper, Walter. Preface to *Of Other Worlds: Essays and Stories*, by C. S. Lewis, edited by Walter Hooper. London: Geoffrey Bles, 1966.
—. "To the Martlets." In *C. S. Lewis: Speaker and Teacher*, edited by Carolyn Keefe. Grand Rapids, MI: Zondervan, 1971.

Johnson, Samuel. *The Letters of Samuel Johnson, with Mrs. Thrale's Genuine Letters to Him,* edited by R. W. Chapman, 3 vols. Oxford: Clarendon, 1952.
—. "The Life of Thomas Gray." *The Lives of the English Poets,* edited by George Birkbeck Hill, 3 vols. Oxford: Clarendon Press, 1905.
—. *The Rambler,* edited by W. J. Bate and Albrecht B. Strauss. The Yale Edition of the Works of Samuel Johnson, vols 3–5. New Haven and London: Yale University Press, 1969.
—. "Review of [Jonas Hanway], A Journal of Eight Days' Journey." In *Samuel Johnson: The Major Works,* edited by Donald Greene. Oxford: Oxford University Press, 2000.
Ladborough, Richard W. "In Cambridge." In *Remembering C. S. Lewis: Recollections of Those Who Knew Him,* edited by James T. Como. San Francisco: Ignatius, 2005.
Lewis, C. S. *The Collected Letters of C. S. Lewis, Vol. I: Family Letters 1905–1931,* edited by Walter Hooper. London: HarperCollins, 2004.
—. *The Collected Letters of C. S. Lewis, Vol. II: Books, Broadcasts and War, 1931–1949,* edited by Walter Hooper. London: HarperCollins, 2004.
—. *The Collected Letters of C. S. Lewis, Vol. III: Narnia, Cambridge, and Joy 1950–1963,* edited by Walter Hooper. London: HarperCollins, 2007.
—. "The Inner Ring." In *Transposition, and Other Addresses.* London: Geoffrey Bles, 1949.
—. "On Stories." In *Of Other Worlds: Essays and Stories,* edited by Walter Hooper. London: Geoffrey Bles, 1966.
—. *Surprised by Joy: The Shape of My Early Life.* London: Geoffrey Bles, 1955.
Leyerle, John. Letter to *The Canadian C. S. Lewis Journal.* Reprinted in *In Search of C. S. Lewis,* edited by Stephen Schofield. South Plainfield, NJ: Bridge, 1983.
Macaulay, Thomas. *Boswell's Life of Johnson,* edited by R. F. Winch. London: n.p., 1896.
Schakel, Peter. "The Satiric Imagination of C. S. Lewis." *Studies in the Literary Imagination* 22, no. 2 (Fall 1989): 129–48.
Tankard, Paul, ed. *Facts and Inventions: Selections from the Journalism of James Boswell.* New Haven: Yale University Press, 2014.
—. "Samuel Johnson's *History of Memory.*" *Studies in Philology* 102, no. 1 (Winter 2005): 110–42.
Vance, John A., ed. "Boswell's *Life* as 'Literary Biography'." In *Boswell's "Life of Johnson": New Questions, New Answers,* 161–71. Athens, GA: University of Georgia Press, 1985.
—, ed. " 'Tis a Pretty Book, Mr. Boswell, But—." In *Boswell's "Life of Johnson": New Questions, New Answers.* 110–46. Athens, GA: University of Georgia Press, 1985.
Wain, John. *Samuel Johnson.* London: Macmillan, 1974.
—. *Sprightly Running: Part of an Autobiography.* London: Macmillan, 1962.
Wilson, A. N. *C. S. Lewis: A Biography.* London: Collins, 1990.

Suggestions for further reading

Stop what you are doing, and start reading James Boswell's *The Life of Samuel Johnson, LL. D.* (1791).

Boswell, James. *Life of Johnson, Including Boswell's Journal of a Tour to the Hebrides and Johnson's Diary of a Journey into North Wales,* edited by George Birkbeck Hill; revised by L. F. Powell, 6 vols. Oxford: Clarendon, 1934–64.
This is the standard edition for the purposes of scholarly reference.
The edition that Lewis owned was the "Everyman's Library" edition (2 vols; London: Dent, 1906), in which famous series it was the first title (nos 1 and 2 of the series), and many times reprinted. In 1949, the series adopted a new edition, with an Introduction by S. C. Roberts, and a comprehensive index (London: Dent, 1949).

The best and most readily available contemporary editions of the complete text are (1) the Oxford edition, prepared in 1950 by R. W. Chapman, revised by J. D. Fleeman, 1970, and published since 1998 as an Oxford World's Classic paperback, with an introduction by Pat Rogers; and (2) a completely new edition of the complete text, edited by David Womersley (London: Penguin Classics, 2008). For those who do not wish at first to tackle the complete text (1536 pp. in Oxford; 1408 pp. in Penguin), Penguin seems to be keeping in print their abridged edition, 384 pp., ed. Christopher Hibbert (Harmondsworth: Penguin Classics, 1979; many reprints), which omits much material, including Johnson's letters, and divides the text into chapters.

Johnson, Samuel. *The Journal of a Tour to The Hebrides with Samuel Johnson, LL.D.* (1785).
Readers of Boswell's great book will also want to acquaint themselves with his first foray into Johnsonian biography, his blow-by-blow account of the trip the pair made to Scotland in 1776. There are many reputable editions.

Wain, John. *Samuel Johnson.* London: Macmillan, and New York: Viking, 1974.
Johnson continues to fascinate biographers. The modern biography that first enlisted me as a Johnsonian is that by C. S. Lewis's student and fellow Inkling John Wain. This rich and engaging book was reprinted with revisions and new prefatory material in 1980 and 1994. There are new biographies every decade or so (three were published for the 300th anniversary of his birth, in 2009).

Bate, Walter Jackson. *Samuel Johnson.* New York: Harcourt Brace Jovanovich, 1977.
I would also strongly recommend this near contemporary biography.

Johnson, Samuel. *The Rambler*, 1750–2 and *The Idler*, 1758–9.
Readers may sample Johnson's essays in the following two publications: *Selected Essays*, edited by David Womersley. London: Penguin Classics, 2003. Donald Greene, ed. *Samuel Johnson: The Major Works*. Oxford: Oxford University Press, 2000.
This book is the supreme selection of his wide-ranging work.

—. Rasselas, 1759.
Readers ready to sample the sage's own sonorous prose may approach him through this wry and philosophical novella, available in many editions, and included in full in Greene's edition of The Major Works (above).

—. *Dictionary of the English Language*, 1755.
Here is an almost inexhaustible source of interest, of which a thoughtful and manageable selection is Samuel Johnson's *Dictionary: Selections from the 1755 Work that Defined the English Language*, edited by Jack Lynch. Delray Beach, FL: Levenger, 2002 (and other editions).

9

Charles Williams, *Descent into Hell*

Holly Ordway

Charles Williams' novel *Descent into Hell* was one of the ten books that Lewis named as most influencing him[1]—although Lewis provided no commentary on these ten books and no rationale for his selection, leaving it up to readers and future scholars to puzzle out the connections.[2] This chapter traces a few of the connections between *Descent into Hell* and Lewis's work and life, keeping in mind that it is impossible to draw a sharp line between *Descent into Hell* and Williams' other work in its influence on Lewis.

Williams and Lewis first encountered each other through their writing. In the spring of 1936, Lewis picked up a copy of Williams' novel *The Place of the Lion* (1931), and was so impressed that he wrote a letter to Williams:

> A book sometimes crosses one's path which is so like the sound of one's native language in a strange country that it feels almost uncivil not to wave some kind of flag in answer. I have just read your *Place of the Lion* and it is to me one of the major literary events of my life—comparable to my first discovery of George Macdonald, G. K. Chesterton, or Wm. Morris.[3]

At the same time, Williams, working at Oxford University Press, had been reading the proofs for Lewis's *The Allegory of Love*. He wrote in admiration to Lewis, saying:

> My dear Mr. Lewis, If you had delayed writing another 24 hours our letters would have crossed. It has never before happened to me to be admiring an author of a book while he at the same time was admiring

---

[1] C. S. Lewis, "Ex Libris," *The Christian Century* 79 (June 6, 1962): 719.
[2] A very Lewisian move.
[3] C. S. Lewis to Charles Williams, March 11, 1936, in *The Collected Letters of C. S. Lewis, Vol. II: Books, Broadcasts, and the War 1931-1949*, ed. Walter Hooper (New York: HarperCollins, 2004), 183. Lewis wrote "ones" in his original letter.

me. My admiration for the staff work of the Omnipotence rises every day.[4]

From this beginning of mutual admiration of each other's writing came an immediate friendship. In 1939, during the Blitz, Oxford University Press moved its London staff to Oxford for safety; Williams was quickly made welcome by Lewis and the other Inklings. He became a popular lecturer at Oxford University, and was part of the Inklings circle until his untimely death in 1945.

Charles Williams considered himself first to be a poet; on his gravestone in Holywell Cemetery in Oxford is inscribed "Poet" and "Under the Mercy." He produced several collections of shorter poems and, most notably, the long, complex, allusive sequence "Taliessin through Logres." He was a literary biographer and a literary critic; his book *The Figure of Beatrice*, is a classic work on Dante. He wrote works of theology, most notably, *The Descent of the Dove, He Came Down from Heaven*, and *The Forgiveness of Sins*, and a number of novels that have been called spiritual thrillers: stories that bring the supernatural into contact with the modern world. It is one of these spiritual thrillers, *Descent into Hell* (1937), that C. S. Lewis counted among the ten books that most influenced him.

Descent into Hell is arguably Williams' greatest and most sophisticated novel. It is in some ways difficult to give a plot summary, since the drama is spiritual and psychological.[5] The novel features several interlocking stories centered around a play being performed by the residents of a London suburb, Battle Hill. A young woman, Pauline Anstruther, is troubled by the persistent appearance of a doppelgänger; the poet-playwright Peter Stanhope teaches her about the doctrine of substituted love, and takes on her burden of fear so that she is free to meet her other self. Colonel Wentworth, a historian, is thwarted in his desire for Adela Hunt, and, willingly being consumed by hate and jealousy, accepts as his lover a succubus formed from his own personality. Pauline's grandmother, Margaret Anstruther, slowly moves toward a grace-filled death. Meanwhile, the past overlaps the present: Battle Hill is haunted by the ghost of a workman who committed suicide on the housing site, and Pauline is drawn to the suffering of her ancestor, a Protestant martyr.

---

[4] Charles Williams to C. S. Lewis, March 12, 1936, ibid., 184.
[5] Which Lewis noted with approval: "I'm glad to have got off the amulet or 'sacred object' theme." C. S. Lewis to Charles Williams, Sept. 23, 1937 *Collected Letters II*, 219.

Descent into Hell, like Williams' other novels, has been described as a spiritual or "supernatural thriller."[6] In stark contrast to the fantasy worlds of Narnia and Middle-Earth, the setting of *Descent into Hell* is the modern world, and the characters are the sort of people one would meet in the suburbs of London: a playwright, a retired historian, cultured upper-middle-class men and women; a building worker for the estate. Even the Lilith-figure, Mrs Sammile, appears in realistic guise.

Given Lewis's interest in apologetics, it is likely that he immediately recognized the potential of Williams' novelistic style. One of the important effects of Williams' choice of genre is that it serves as a reminder that damnation and salvation are not abstract ideas, but present realities; not something that happens to other people, in far-off Bible times, but choices confronting the modern person in his or her own daily life. The shattering effect of encountering the reality of the spiritual world becomes more clear by its effect, in the story, on recognizably modern characters.

That Hideous Strength, the third book of the Ransom Trilogy, is widely recognized as Lewis's most Williams-like novel. However, the Williams influence may have already been operating in the previous novels in the trilogy. In 1936, Lewis had read and admired *The Place of the Lion*, which takes a similar approach to presenting the intersection of the spiritual and the ordinary; he read *Descent into Hell*, published in 1937, as soon as it came out.[7] *Out of the Silent Planet*, published in 1938, has certain Williams elements: the protagonist, Ransom, is an ordinary twentieth-century man who is drawn into progressively stranger and stranger events that culminate in his discovering something of how the cosmos really works on a spiritual level.[8]

Certainly *That Hideous Strength*, published in 1945, reflects the influence of Williams and in particular of *Descent into Hell*. As readers discover, often to their surprise, *That Hideous Strength* has a very different feel to it than the two preceding Ransom novels. In contrast to *Out of the Silent Planet* and *Perelandra*, whose action takes place almost exclusively on another planet (Mars and Venus, respectively), *That Hideous Strength* takes place only on Earth, and in the small area of the university town of Edgestow and

---

[6] T. S. Eliot, introduction to *All Hallows' Eve*, by Charles Williams (Vancouver, BC: Regent College Publishing, 2003), xiv.

[7] "Many thanks for the book; fortunately I had seen it announced and ordered a copy before it arrived, so that both of us have it both ways." C. S. Lewis to Charles Williams, Sept. 23, 1937, *Collected Letters II*, 218.

[8] This may account for why Lewis wrote to Williams to say "I have written a thriller about a journey to Mars on which I urgently want your opinion." C. S. Lewis to Charles Williams, Sept. 23, 1937, *Collected Letters II*, 219–20.

immediate environs, much as the action in *Descent into Hell* is restricted to the suburb of Battle Hill. Furthermore, even though *That Hideous Strength* is longer than either of the two previous volumes of the Ransom Trilogy, it is more tightly constructed in terms of time, with the plot unfolding in a relatively short span of time from the opening events to the finale—again, more like *Descent into Hell* than the relatively protracted narratives of *Out of the Silent Planet* and *Perelandra*. This tightness of construction with regard to location and time are part of what give *That Hideous Strength* an intensity similar to *Descent into Hell*.

As in *Descent into Hell*, the action in *That Hideous Strength* is heavily psychological and spiritual. To be sure, the novel ends with dramatic events, but it is notable that until then, almost nothing actually happens in terms of plot. Mark Studdock is drawn deeper into the N.I.C.E.; Jane joins St Anne's; plans are made, but no action is taken. Not until chapter 15, "The Descent of the Gods," does anything really happen, and this is more than three-quarters of the way through the novel. What Lewis has been unfolding in those 300 pages is the spiritual drama of salvation and damnation: of Jane and Mark Studdock, and the various other people at St Anne's and the N.I.C.E.

In both books, part of the internal or spiritual action involves the women characters who must come to terms with the reality of their spiritual sight. In *Descent into Hell*, Pauline is haunted by the vision of her doppelgänger, and later by recurring reflections on, and a vision of, her martyred ancestor. In *That Hideous Strength*, Jane Studdock has terrifying visions of the experiments that the N.I.C.E. are doing with a severed head. In both cases, the intrusion of the supernatural into the natural is not welcomed; in fact, it brings fear and anxiety. Likewise, both Pauline and Jane turn away from, or find themselves unable to deal with, these visions on their own. They must (and indeed do) seek out and receive help and guidance from those who are wiser than they.

For both Jane and Pauline, the encounter with the reality of transcendence through their experiences draws them to an explicit encounter with and turn toward God, and specifically Christ. As an apologist, Lewis was very interested in the experience of conversion, and how to present Christ in such a way as to help readers to make that turn toward him. Williams, on the other hand, was more of a theologian and a mystic. Thus it is not surprising that Lewis's presentation of the supernatural intersecting with the natural does so with added emphasis on the move from outside to inside. Jane is more clearly hostile to the idea of faith than Pauline; while Pauline must learn to both give and receive help in prayer, Jane must first step inside the world where such an offer is possible.

One of the most powerful aspects of *Descent into Hell* is its depiction of damnation as the soul willfully turning away from God, and the effects of that choice on the human being even before death. This powerful vision of the reality of Hell impressed Lewis greatly. In a letter to Williams written shortly after reading *Descent into Hell,* Lewis wrote:

> I find the form of evil that you are dealing with much more real than the Evil (with a big E) that appears in the other books and which, though I enjoy it, (like pantomime red fire) in a story, I do not believe in. But your Gomorrah is the real thing, and Wentworth a truly tragic study. Of course he can't in the nature of things be as good *fun* as Sir Giles Tumulty, but he's more important.[9]

It is worth looking in some detail at Williams' presentation of damnation in *Descent into Hell,* since its influence can be seen in a number of Lewis's works. The central figure for this theme is Wentworth, who by the end of the novel indeed descends into Hell, in the complete turning inward of his personality.

As is typical in all his work, Williams avoids using standard Christian terminology, choosing instead terms that are more evocative of the concept he is presenting. For instance, in *Descent into Hell,* the dominant image for Hell is the city of Gomorrah. As Stanhope describes it to Pauline, Gomorrah is Hell in the form of complete narcissism:

> "The lovers of Gomorrah are quite contented . . . They aren't bothered by alteration, at least till the rain of the fire of the Glory at the end, for they lose the capacity for change, except for the fear of hell. They're monogamous enough! and they've no children—no cherubim breaking into being or babies as tiresome as ours; there's no birth there, and only the second death. There's no distinction between lover and beloved; they beget themselves on their adoration of themselves, and they live and feed and starve on themselves, and by themselves too, for creation, as my predecessor said, is the mercy of God, and they won't have the facts of creation."[10]

Williams peels away the layers of romance about the individual, and shows the disturbing way that the individual can willfully self-deceive, choosing the false over the real, the empty over the full; he contrasts Pauline and Stanhope, as characters who choose joy, to Wentworth and Mrs Sammile, as characters who reject reality, and thus reject joy.

---

[9] C. S. Lewis to Charles Williams, Sept. 23, 1937, *Collected Letters II,* 218.
[10] Charles Williams, *Descent into Hell* (Grand Rapids, MI: Eerdmans, 1966), 174.

One of the key moments in *Descent into Hell* comes when Wentworth sees in the newspaper that a rival historian has been knighted:

> There was presented to him at once and clearly an opportunity for joy—casual, accidental joy, but joy. If he could not manage joy, at least he might have managed the intention of joy, or (if that also were too much) an effort toward the intention of joy. The infinity of grace could have been contented and invoked by a mere mental refusal of anything but such an effort.... Such honours meant nothing, but they were part of the absurd dance of the world, and to be enjoyed as such. Wentworth knew that he could share that pleasure. He could enjoy; at least he could refuse not to enjoy. He could refuse and reject damnation.
>
> With a perfectly clear, if instantaneous, knowledge of what he did, he rejected joy instead. He instantaneously preferred anger, and at once it came; he invoked envy, and it obliged him.[11]

In the end, Wentworth, having chosen himself over others, and self-deception over truth, in the end gets nothing at all. In the terrifying scene that closes the novel, he is given one last chance to be saved, when he encounters his rival at a dinner: "If he had ever hated Sir Aston because of a passion for austere truth, he might even then have laid hold on the thing that was abroad in the world and been saved . . . [Instead] He looked at Sir Aston and thought, not 'He was wrong in his facts', but 'I've been cheated'. It was his last consecutive thought."[12]

In *That Hideous Strength*, Lewis gives us several characters who experience precisely the kind of choice that Williams shows in *Descent into Hell*. First, we have the scientist Frost. Lewis's depiction of Frost's retreat from reality is different from Williams', in that Lewis chooses to emphasize the consequences of a thoroughgoing materialist philosophy,[13] but the way in which Frost chooses damnation is very much like Wentworth. At the end of the novel, Frost goes through a series of actions like an automaton that lead him to immolate himself. At that last moment, with his death now inevitable, he has a moment of clarity:

> Not till then did his controllers allow him to suspect that death itself might not after all cure the illusion of being a soul—nay, might prove the entry into a world where that illusion raged infinite and unchecked.

---

[11] Ibid., 80.
[12] Ibid., 219.
[13] Lewis explores this idea in *The Abolition of Man*.

Escape for the soul, if not for the body, was offered him. He became able to know (and simultaneously refused the knowledge) that he had been wrong from the beginning, that souls and personal responsibility existed. He half saw: he wholly hated. The physical torture of the burning was not fiercer than his hatred of that. With one supreme effort he flung himself back into his illusion. In that attitude eternity overtook him as sunrise in old tales overtakes and turns them into unchangeable stone.[14]

Particularly worth noting is that Frost, like Wentworth, barely responds at all at the very end, when his damnation is closing in on him with finality. His choices had been made so often, turning toward Hell, that it would have taken a tremendous turn of the will to reject the consequences of his choice; indeed part of the horror of the situation is that Frost and Wentworth seem hardly to realize what they are rejecting, or fear what they are embracing. They have been so corrupted, through their own action, that they willingly embrace Hell.

Interestingly, however, Lewis gives us a second, and different account of this experience of spiritual choice, in the character of Mark Studdock, who throughout the book has been going down the slippery slope of acquiescence in his involvement with N.I.C.E. Like Wentworth, he has a moment when he could choose the right, but does not. Miss Hardcastle directs him to write newspaper articles ahead of time providing coverage of a riot that she will engineer: "This was the first thing Mark had been asked to do which he himself, before he did it, clearly knew to be criminal. But the moment of his consent almost escaped his notice; certainly, there was no struggle, no sense of turning a corner."[15] As he writes the letters, rather than awakening to reason, Mark became "more and more reconciled to the job the longer he worked at it."[16]

As the N.I.C.E. seek to break him to their ends, Mark is turned over to Frost, who subjects him to a series of bizarre and disturbing tasks and experiences designed to break his moral sense. However, Mark has gained the insight that there exists such a thing as the Straight, or the Normal, over against the perversions shown to him, and he clings to that insight throughout Frost's manipulations. Here it is interesting to note that Lewis picks up on an important image from *Descent into Hell*. In Williams' novel, Pauline's grandmother, Margaret Anstruther, is dying, and in her dying is

---

[14] C. S. Lewis, *That Hideous Strength* (New York: Scribner, 2003), 355–6.
[15] Ibid., 127.
[16] Ibid., 132.

making the final movement toward God and the joy that awaits her. She experiences her dying as a kind of vision, in which she finds herself on the surface of a great mountain in the moments before dawn:

> She set herself to crawl out of that darkened corner toward the light . . . It might take hours, or days, or even years, but it was certain; as she moved, crawling slowly over the rock, she saw the light sweeping on to meet her. The moment of death was accepted and accomplished in her first outward movement; there remained only to die.[17]

In her vision, as she sees Mrs Sammile speaking to Pauline with her false but tempting offer of dreams, "Margaret Anstruther put out a hand; it touched a projection in the rock on which she was lying in her journey toward corporeal death. She clung to it, and pulled herself forward towards Pauline."[18]

In *Descent into Hell*, the mountain image remains somewhat unfocused; it may represent God, or transcendent reality, but it is certainly associated with the choice of salvation. With this in mind, we can recognize further significance in an image that Lewis uses in *That Hideous Strength* that is otherwise a bit odd: a mountain being used as an image for the Straight. For Mark:

> that idea of the Straight or the Normal . . . grew stronger and more solid in his mind till it had become a kind of mountain. He had never before known what an Idea meant: he had always thought till now that they were things inside one's own head. But now, when his head was continually attacked and often completely filled with the clinging corruption of the training, this Idea towered up above him—something which obviously existed quite independently of him and had hard rock surfaces which would not give, surfaces he could cling to.[19]

Lewis's adoption of Williams' mountain image suggests that this moment is a genuine spiritual turning point for Mark, and sets up the scene that follows, in which Mark is asked to trample on a crucifix and refuses.[20] Like Wentworth, he is offered a last chance, but here Lewis gives us a different view: that of a man who is well down the path toward damnation, but who stops, and chooses to turn around.

We can see, then, that Lewis draws on Williams' spiritual insights as well as aspects of characterization and even imagery to convey the idea

---

[17] Williams, *Descent into Hell*, 73.
[18] Ibid., 74–5.
[19] Lewis, *That Hideous Strength*, 307.
[20] Ibid., 334.

of damnation and salvation in *That Hideous Strength*. Lewis's treatment is different from Williams'; he presents in a single image or brief scene what Williams, in *Descent into Hell,* would describe in an almost stream of consciousness style. The result is that Lewis is able to present the insights of *Descent into Hell* more subtly in *That Hideous Strength*, and to integrate these insights more fully into the novel as a novel; it is part of the reason that while *Descent into Hell* is a good novel, *That Hideous Strength* is a great one.

It is also worth noting that the idea of damnation as being fundamentally a turning inward, away from reality, from others, and from God, plays an important part in several of Lewis's other works of fiction. In *The Great Divorce*, for instance, in addition to several Ghosts displaying Wentworthian selfishness, the George MacDonald character describes a particular type of damnation in very similar terms to Wentworth's hellish descent into incoherence:

> it begins with a grumbling mood ... And yourself, in a dark hour, may will that mood, embrace it. Ye can repent and come out of it again. But there may come a day when you can do that no longer. Then there will be no *you* left to criticize the mood, nor even to enjoy it, but just the grumble going on forever like a machine.[21]

Another influence of *Descent into Hell,* perhaps more subtle, is its vivid presentation of Williams' ideas on the theology of substitution and exchange. These ideas were highly influential on Lewis, both in his writing, most notably in *Till We Have Faces*, and in his own life. Lewis recognized the way that *Descent into Hell* functioned didactically, writing to one of his correspondents that "The stuff about Substitution comes in all C.W.'s books but most clearly I think in *He Came Down from Heaven* and *Descent into Hell.* It was all meant to be practical & he wd. not have admitted your contrast of 'practical' and 'poetical'."[22]

Descent into Hell has, in fact, an entire chapter called "The Doctrine of Substituted Love," and the idea is central to the plot. Williams has his character Peter Stanhope explain substitution to Pauline:

> Haven't you heard it said that we ought to bear one another's burdens? ... I think that when Christ or St. Paul, or whoever said *bear*, or whatever he Aramaically said instead of *bear*, he meant something

---

[21] C. S. Lewis, *The Great Divorce* (New York: Touchstone, 1996), 74.
[22] C. S. Lewis to June Flewett, Sept. 23, 1947, *Collected Letters II*, 805–6.

much more like carrying a parcel instead of someone else. To bear a burden is precisely to carry it instead of.[23]

He goes on to tell Pauline:

> If you want to disobey and refuse the laws that are common to us all, if you want to live in pride and division and anger, you can. But if you will be part of the best of us, and live and laugh and be ashamed with us, then you must be content to be helped. You must give your burden up to someone else, and you must carry someone else's burden.[24]

Stanhope explains that because he will carry her burden of fear, she will not feel fear: and indeed this is the case. He consciously, imaginatively enters into the anxiety and terror of her encounters with the doppelgänger, and in so doing picks up the burden; she, in turn, discovers (to her surprise) that her burden is gone: she is able to walk home and enjoy the day without her usual sense of oppression and anxiety. By the end of the novel, she willingly takes up the burden of fear from her ancestor, the martyr John Struther, and in the strange economy of prayer that is not bound by time, she thus frees him to die with complete trust in God.

While Williams' theology here may sound very strange, it has scriptural underpinnings. Williams takes as his starting point a very straightforward reading of St Paul, who writes "We then that are strong ought to bear the infirmities of the weak, and not to please ourselves."[25] Some translations, such as the ESV, have "bear with" here rather than "bear," but Paul is even more direct in his letter to the Galatians: "Bear one another's burdens, and so fulfill the law of Christ."[26] If, indeed, it is possible to bear another's burden, then one of the great paradoxes of Scripture becomes more clear. Jesus says both, "If anyone would come after me, let him deny himself and take up his cross and follow me"[27] and also "my yoke is easy, and my burden is light."[28] These two sayings seem to be opposed, but if in fact we can carry one another's burdens, and find the other's burden easier than our own, these two sayings point toward the same truth.

---

[23] Williams, *Descent into Hell*, 98.
[24] Ibid., 99.
[25] Rom. 15:1 KJV.
[26] Gal. 6:2 ESV.
[27] Mt. 16:24 ESV.
[28] Mt. 11:30 ESV.

Some critics have hedged their discussion of substitution and exchange, keeping it at arm's length as merely an interesting idea; R. J. Reilly, for instance, notes that he will discuss Williams' ideas insofar as they influenced Williams' own attitudes, but that he "cannot discuss them as a practical way of life."[29] This skepticism may be the result of a disinclination to recognize the way that the supernatural may very well interpenetrate the world of daily life more than we like to admit; unfortunately, it has the effect of directing attention away from a serious assessment of Williams' practical theology.

One well-thought-out objection to Williams' doctrine comes from Leanne Payne, who argues that substitution is unbiblical, dangerous, and wrong. Her critique centers on the action of the person who chooses to practice substitution, who "asks to take upon himself the pain, illness, fear, or even sorrow of another."[30] However, she argues, "only Christ is great and good enough to die on the Cross for mankind. Substitution is wrong."[31] Payne's warning ought to be taken seriously. The very goodness of substitutionary prayer can be a temptation to pride, putting oneself in the place of God, who only can bear the suffering of the world. Insofar as the act of substitution leads us, as Payne says, to "forget the distinction between being a savior-redeemer (something only Jesus could ever be and do) and being His disciple, a sacramental channel through whom His life is to flow"[32] it is not a properly Christian prayer, and can do harm to the person who attempts to bear what no human can bear.

However, *abusus non tollit usum*[33]; it is worth reading Williams more fully to explore the possibility that substitution and exchange may be a legitimate, if difficult, mode of prayer for Christians. We must not forget the Christian's affirmation that it is not our own strength, but Christ's,[34] upon which we must rely in the act of substitution and exchange.[35] Indeed, although Williams avoids using conventional Christian terms, he is quite clear in *Descent into Hell* that it is in and through God—"the Omnipotence"— that the substitution is done. Pauline, reflecting on Stanhope's successful

---

[29] R. J. Reilly, *Romantic Religion: A Study of Barfield, Lewis, Williams, and Tolkien* (Great Barrington, MA: Lindisfarne Books, 2006), 150.
[30] Leanne Payne, *The Healing Presence* (New York: Crossway, 1989), 218.
[31] Ibid.
[32] Ibid., 221-2.
[33] Abuse does not preclude proper use.
[34] "I can do all things through him who strengthens me" (Phil. 4:13 ESV).
[35] I am indebted to Michael Ward for this insight in particular, for his comments on the potential danger of substitution that led to the development of this section, and for bringing Payne's critique to my attention.

carrying of her fear, "hoped it was not troublesome to Peter Stanhope. He and whatever he meant by the Omnipotence would manage it quite well between them."[36] In the clearest depiction of substitution in the novel, Stanhope sets about to carry the burden of Pauline's fear of the doppelgänger:

> The body of his flesh received her alien terror, his mind carried the burden of her world. The burden was inevitably lighter for him than for her, for the rage of a personal resentment was lacking. He endured her sensitiveness, but not her sin; the substitution there, if indeed there is a substitution, is hidden in the central mystery of Christendom.[37]

That Christ as the central actor in any true act of substitution is made clearer by reference to the chapter "The Practice of Substituted Love" in *He Came Down from Heaven*. There, Williams begins his discussion of substitution focusing on Christ's self-giving on the cross, an act which makes possible all lesser substitution; "the new law of the kingdom made that substitution a principle of universal exchange."[38]

Next, it is worth noting that while Payne's critique is focused strictly upon substitution, Williams does not usually present the doctrine of substitution by itself, but in the context of both substitution and exchange. Mutuality is inherent in the act: "You must give your burden up to someone else, and you must carry someone else's burden . . . not to give up your parcel is as much to rebel as not to carry another's."[39] Further, Williams does not suggest in *Descent into Hell* that the substitution is physical; the instances of substitution in the story are all of mental or emotional suffering. In *He Came Down from Heaven*, Williams is quite direct, noting that "The body is probably the last place where such interchange is possible."[40] Even if it were possible, Williams hesitates to recommend it:

> Most men are already so committed that they ought not, whatever their goodwill, to contemplate the carrying of the burden of paralysis or consumption or even lesser things . . . Certainly it is reasonable to believe that the kind of burden might be transmuted into another equivalent kind, and in a full state of the kingdom upon earth such a

---

[36] Williams, *Descent into Hell*, 107–8.
[37] Ibid., 101.
[38] Charles Williams, *He Came Down from Heaven and the Forgiveness of Sins* (Berkeley, CA: Apocryphile, 2005), 83.
[39] Ibid., 99.
[40] Ibid., 90.

transmutation would be agreeable and natural. It remains at present an achievement of which our "faith" is not yet capable.⁴¹

Nor is the carrying permanent. Stanhope tells Pauline, "what can be easier than for me to carry a little while a burden that isn't mine?"⁴² When he takes on her burden, he does so in a specific mental act, which, having been completed, does not need to be repeated or prolonged: "In the place of the Omnipotence there is neither before nor after; there is only act."⁴³ It is here that Williams' view of time, and of the coinherence of all human beings in the body of Christ, is most relevant. Williams would, I think, have rejected the idea that substitution must be parallel in time or duration to the other person's experience.

Finally, it is worth noting that the preeminent quality of substitution and exchange in the novel is joy. The clearest example of this is Pauline's willing "carrying" of the fear experienced by her martyred ancestor. She does not carry his physical pain, nor prevent his death by fire; rather, she "carries" the fear that was about to break him and cause him to recant. Having made the substitution, she "sighed deeply with her joy . . . her heart was warm, as if the very fire her ancestor had feared was a comfort to her now."⁴⁴ At another point, she reflects that substitution and exchange means "everyone carrying everyone else's [burden], like the Scilly Islanders taking in each other's washing. Well, and at that, if it were tiresome and horrible to wash your own clothes and easy and happy to wash someone else's, the Scilly Islanders might be intelligent enough."⁴⁵

A balanced assessment of Williams' ideas about substitutionary prayer is that while they have elements of great value and are rooted in a serious attention to Scripture, they are also speculative and at least potentially harmful. It is worth noting that Williams was himself aware of the potential dangers and difficulties of the practice of substitution. In a letter written in 1933, he commented about substituted love that "None of us know—yet. After all, we only discovered it as an experiential fact, by chance, as it were; and I'm terrified out of my senses at the idea of going further."⁴⁶ In *He Came Down from Heaven*, published in 1938, Williams is more confident and specific about the functioning of substitution, but continues to stress

---

⁴¹ Ibid., 91.
⁴² Williams, *Descent into Hell*, 98.
⁴³ Ibid., 102.
⁴⁴ Ibid., 170.
⁴⁵ Ibid., 108.
⁴⁶ Charles Williams, qtd. in introduction by Anne Ridler to *The Image of the City and Other Essays* by Charles Williams (Berkeley, CA: Apocryphile, 2007), xlviii.

that "practice and intelligence"[47] are needed. Later in the chapter, he is quite direct: "It is therefore necessary (*a*) not to take burdens too recklessly; (*b*) to consider exactly how far any burden, accepted to the full, is likely to conflict with other duties. There is always a necessity for intelligence."[48]

Furthermore, the healthy boundaries of mutuality, impermanence, and nonphysical substitution seem to be more clearly expressed in *Descent into Hell* than in Williams' other writings or indeed his practice. For instance, as the founder of the "Companions of the Co-Inherence," Williams exercised authority over his disciples, including directing them to offer themselves in substitution for each other in specific instances, even to the point of ordering one disciple to offer herself for another whom she did not personally know.[49] Williams also recounts with favor a disturbing story of St Seraphim of Sarov instructing a nun to accept the burden of death in place of her sick brother.[50]

As with the literary influence of *Descent into Hell*, so with the theological influence: Lewis refines and purifies Williams' ideas in the process of drawing them into his own work. One of the places that we can see this is in Lewis's use of the "doctrine of substituted love" in his last fictional work, *Till We Have Faces*.

Till We Have Faces, a retelling of Apuleius's story of Cupid and Psyche, is a complex and multi-layered novel in which Lewis explores, above all, the nature of love. As Peter Schakel explains, the ideas from Lewis's book *The Four Loves* are "embodied in literary form in *Till We Have Faces*. The story shows how all of Orual's loves turn possessive and destructive." until finally, "By removing the veil, by dying to self, she becomes able to live for others."[51] What is notable about the ending of *Till We Have Faces* is that Orual literally carries the burden of suffering for Psyche. Orual experiences a series of terrible visions or dreams, in which she suffers greatly. After her confrontation with the gods at the end of the book, when she retracts her accusation, Orual is shown a depiction of Psyche's life in exile. Although Orual expected Psyche's life to be bitter and full of hardship, she sees that this has not been the case, because Orual herself has suffered in her place.

---

[47] Williams, *He Came Down*, 88.
[48] Ibid., 90.
[49] Lois Lang-Sims, *Letters to Lalage: The Letters of Charles Williams to Lois Lang-Sims* (Kent, OH: Kent State University Press, 1989), 53–4. For a more extended discussion of this point, see Barbara Newman, "Charles Williams and the Companions of the Co-Inherence," in *Spiritus: A Journal of Christian Spirituality* 9, no. 1 (Spring 2009): 1–26.
[50] Williams, "The Way of Exchange," in *Image of the City*, 53.
[51] Peter J. Schakel, "Till We Have Faces," in *Cambridge Companion to C. S. Lewis* (Cambridge: Cambridge University Press, 2010), 286–7.

At the very close of the book, Lewis gives us a passage that echoes Pauline's question to Stanhope about how it could be possible for her to bear the burden of fear for an ancestor who died 400 years earlier. Orual asks the Fox:

> "But how could she—did she really—do such things and go such places—and not . . . ? Grandfather, she was all but unscathed. She was almost happy."
> "Another bore nearly all the anguish."
> "I? Is it possible?"
> "That was one of the true things I used to say to you."[52]

This is a clear depiction of Williams' ideas of substituted love: just as Stanhope bears Pauline's fear, and Pauline bears the agony and fear of her ancestor, Orual literally bears the suffering of Psyche. The idea does not stand out in *Till We Have Faces* the way that it does in *Descent into Hell*, because of the mythic quality of *Till We Have Faces*, but it is central to the story.

Orual's substitution for Psyche is particularly important in that it implicitly involves Williams' understanding of how time and duration are irrelevant for an act of substitution. Orual labors in a series of dream-visions near the end of her life, and her work functions to relieve Psyche's burdens in experiences that had, in linear time, happened many years earlier and extended over a much longer period of time.

It might be easy to conclude that Lewis took the idea of substitution as an interesting idea for the story, and nothing more; however, at various points in his correspondence, Lewis explicitly endorsed Williams' doctrine of coinherence, substitution, and exchange, and recommended his works as guides to prayer: hardly something he would have done if he thought it all merely speculative. To one correspondent, writing about intercessory prayer, he recommends "Read Charles Williams on Co-inherence in almost any of his later books or plays (*Descent of the Dove, Descent into Hell, The House of the Octopus*)."[53] In another letter, quoting from Williams' *He Came Down from Heaven*, Lewis referred to "the *vicariousness* of the universe":

> Charles Williams' view that every one can help to paddle every else's canoe better than his own. We must bear one another's burdens because

---

[52] C. S. Lewis, *Till We Have Faces* (Orlando, FL: Harcourt, 1956), 262–3.
[53] C. S. Lewis to Rhona Bodle, Oct. 24, 1949, *Collected Letters II*, 988.

that is the only way the burdens can get borne: and "He saved others, himself He cannot save" is a fundamental law.⁵⁴

Williams was no theoretical theologian; as much as he could, he attempted to put his belief into practice, and his example certainly encouraged others to do likewise. The particular experience of choosing to bear another's burden, and to allow one's own burden to be borne by another, is both intensely personal and strangely ordinary. In *Descent into Hell*, Paulina is almost shocked by how easy it is to allow Stanhope to take her burden of fear. Especially given Lewis's English reticence, it is entirely possible that he could have been practicing this form of practical prayer for years, and yet never said a word about it.

However, we do not need to be entirely speculative, as there is evidence to suggest that Lewis did indeed practice, or attempt to practice, substitution in his own prayer life. When his wife, Joy Davidman, was suffering from severe pain from bone cancer, it seems likely that he prayed to take up the burden of her pain. Nevill Coghill recounted a conversation that he had with Lewis about Lewis's substitution of himself for Joy during her illness: "'You mean that her pain left her, and that you felt it for her in your own body?'"; Lewis replied, "'Yes, in my legs. It was crippling. But it relieved hers.'"⁵⁵

Lewis also alludes to this in his letters. In July of 1957, he wrote that Joy, though suffering from terminal cancer, had at that point "no pain" while he was now suffering from osteoporosis, "common in men of 75 but almost unknown at my age (58). After full investigation by a great Professor of Pathology the cause remains quite obscure."⁵⁶ A few months later, he wrote to Sheldon Vanauken of Joy's continued improved health, noting that "The intriguing thing is that while I (for no discoverable reason) was losing the chalcium [*sic*] from my bones, Joy, who needed it much more, was gaining it in hers. One dreams of a Charles Williams substitution! Well, never was a gift more gladly given: but one must not be fanciful."⁵⁷ Lewis's disclaimer here—the suggestion that he might be "fanciful"—might be more reticence than a genuine dismissal of the possibility. Was what Lewis experienced

---

[54] C. S. Lewis to Mary Van Deusen, June 10, 1952, *The Collected Letters of C. S. Lewis, Vol. III: Narnia, Cambridge, and Joy 1950–1963*, ed. Walter Hooper (New York: HarperCollins, 2007), 200.
[55] Nevill Coghill, "The Approach to English," in *Light on C. S. Lewis*, ed. Jocelyn Gibbs (New York: Harcourt, 1965), 63; qtd. in R. J. Reilly, *Romantic Religion: A Study of Owen Barfield, C. S. Lewis, Charles Williams, and J. R. R. Tolkien* (Great Barrington, MA: Lindisfarne, 2006), 150.
[56] C. S. Lewis to Mrs Johnson, July 9, 1957, *Collected Letters III*, 866–7.
[57] C. S. Lewis to Sheldon Vanauken, Nov. 27, 1957, ibid., 901.

a genuine instance of a "Charles Williams substitution"? If so, was this a good thing?

Lewis may very well have successfully borne the weight of Joy's mental suffering; the letters from this time are full of references to her good spirits and to the way that, to the very end, they were able to enjoy their time together. However, what Lewis experienced as he attempted to substitute for Joy in the matter of her physical illness—particularly the "crippling" nature of his pain—does not entirely line up with Williams' presentation of substitution, at least as shown in *Descent into Hell*, where it involves only emotional and mental suffering, is not lasting, and is characterized by being easier for the second person to "carry." Lewis's osteoporosis and the corresponding improvement in Joy's leg bones may have been simply a coincidence that he attributed to an act of willed substitution. It is also possible that he genuinely "took on" Joy's physical suffering, but unwisely; Payne suggests that he may have done so, out of a misguided sense of empathy, and shortened his own life in the process.[58] It is not possible to know for certain whether Lewis really did engage in a "Charles Williams substitution," whether this was harmful to him, or whether any harm was due to the substitutionary act itself or to a mis-application of it.

Even setting aside the possibility that Lewis practiced substitution in the specific instance of Joy's cancer, and the question of whether this was a prudent thing to do, there are other indications that Williams' theology of substitution and exchange had a powerful effect on Lewis's spiritual life. The idea of bearing another's burdens centers on Christ's suffering on the cross. Only because of his suffering for us, are we able to bear others' suffering for them—and as we are called to become like Christ, this seems to be precisely what we are to do. Lewis was particularly drawn to the suffering that Christ experienced on the cross—not just the theological importance of it, and not just the coming Resurrection, but the suffering itself. As Michael Ward notes:

> Of all Biblical passages, the one which occurs most frequently in Lewis's writings is Christ's cry from the cross: "My God, my God, why hast thou forsaken me?" (Matt. 27:46 and Mark 15:34, a quotation of Ps. 22:1a). Not only are its appearances in Lewis's work very numerous, they are also spread across the whole range of his corpus . . . No other scriptural verse comes close to receiving a treatment in so many and various of Lewis's works.[59]

---

[58] Payne, *Healing Presence*, 227.
[59] Michael Ward, *Planet Narnia* (New York: Oxford University Press, 2008), 204.

Already drawn intuitively to that moment of the Passion, Lewis was likely very aware that Williams' theology of substitution and exchange helped to bring out more depths of significance in that moment, and could help the ordinary Christian to more fully identify with Christ and appreciate Christ's saving work.

Finally, there is simply the fact that Lewis designated *Descent into Hell* as one of the ten books that were most influential in his life. Certainly, the book had an influence on his literary style, but surely not to the extent that it would justify such a high place. Given that the book has as a central theme this idea of the practice of "substituted love," it seems more likely that Williams' primary influence on Lewis was spiritual, showing him a deeper and richer way to pray, one that Lewis could adapt and in so doing purge of any potentially unorthodox or unscriptural elements. The extent of that influence on Lewis's work has yet to be fully assessed.

Lewis's debt to *Descent into Hell* ran deep: Williams' novel influenced the literary form of *That Hideous Strength*; provided material for Lewis's literary exploration of salvation and damnation in a number of his works, including *Till We Have Faces*, which Lewis considered his best novel; and also deepened his own prayer life. Lewis's life, as well as his work, was powerfully influenced for good by this novel written by his friend and fellow Inkling.

Bibliography

Eliot, T. S. Introduction to *All Hallows' Eve*, by Charles Williams, x–xviii. Vancouver, BC: Regent College Publishing, 2003.

Lang-Sims, Lois. *Letters to Lalage: The Letters of Charles Williams to Lois Lang-Sims*. Kent, OH: Kent State University Press, 1989.

Lewis, C. S. *The Abolition of Man*. First published in 1943 and available in many editions.

—. *The Collected Letters of C. S. Lewis, Vol. II: Books, Broadcasts, and the War 1931–1949*, edited by Walter Hooper. New York: HarperCollins, 2004.

—. *The Collected Letters of C. S. Lewis, Vol. III: Narnia, Cambridge, and Joy 1950–1963*, edited by Walter Hooper. New York: HarperCollins, 2007.

—. "Ex Libris." *The Christian Century* 79 (June 6, 1962): 719.

—. *The Great Divorce*. New York: Touchstone, 1996.

—. *That Hideous Strength*. New York: Scribner, 2003.

—. *Till We Have Faces*. Orlando, FL: Harcourt, 1956.

Newman, Barbara. "Charles Williams and the Companions of the Co-Inherence." In *Spiritus: A Journal of Christian Spirituality* 9, no. 1 (Spring 2009): 1–26.

Payne, Leanne. *The Healing Presence*. New York: Crossway, 1989.
Reilly, R. J. *Romantic Religion: A Study of Barfield, Lewis, Williams, and Tolkien*. Great Barrington, MA: Lindisfarne, 2006.
Schakel, Peter J. "Till We Have Faces." In *Cambridge Companion to C. S. Lewis*, edited by Robert MacSwain and Michael Ward, 281–93. Cambridge: Cambridge University Press, 2010.
Ward, Michael. *Planet Narnia*. New York: Oxford University Press, 2008.
Williams, Charles. *Descent into Hell*. Grand Rapids, MI: Eerdmans, 1966.
—. *He Came Down from Heaven*. Berkeley, CA: Apocryphile, 2005.
—. "The Way of Exchange." In *The Image of the City and Other Essays*, selected by and with a critical essay by Anne Ridler, ix–lxxii. Berkeley, CA: Apocryphile, 2007.

Suggestions for further reading

This chapter on *Descent into Hell* can be productively read alongside the chapter on George MacDonald's *Phantastes* and G. K. Chesterton's *The Everlasting Man*, as all of these authors used fantasy or elements of the fantastic in their exploration of Christian ideas.

Ashenden, Gavin. *Charles Williams: Alchemy and Integration*. Kent, OH: Kent State University Press, 2008.
  An in-depth, evenhanded examination of Williams as an "occult" writer.

Howard, Thomas. *The Novels of Charles Williams*. San Francisco: Ignatius, 1991.
  A solid, basic introduction to Williams' fiction.

Lewis, C. S. *The Abolition of Man*. First published in 1943 and available in many editions.
  This short book is the rational explication of the philosophical ideas expressed imaginatively in *That Hideous Strength*.

—. *The Great Divorce*. First published in book form in 1946 and available in many editions.
  Here Lewis explores the question of Hell and damnation.

—. *Till We Have Faces*. First published in 1956 and available in many editions.
  Lewis's last novel is a profound exploration of suffering and "substituted love," bringing to maturity some of the important ideas in Williams' *Descent into Hell*.

Williams, Charles. *He Came Down from Heaven*. Berkeley, CA: Apocryphile, 2005.
  Here we find Williams' fullest explanation of substitution and exchange.

10

Arthur James Balfour, *Theism and Humanism*

Charles Taliaferro

I begin by referencing a recent, highly significant book that brings to light the enduring relevance of the work of both C. S. Lewis and Arthur James Balfour, the author of *Theism and Humanism*. In *Religion Without God*, the great legal philosopher and public intellectual Ronald Dworkin writes with great candor as an atheist about dreading what he sees as the inevitable, eventual, *total obliteration* of ourselves and the cosmos. In Dworkin's judgment, modern science has virtually proven that our cosmos will come to an end, and with no God, there is no hope for any values to last forever. Still, Dworkin offers us a vision of what he refers to as "the only kind of immortality we can imagine" and "the only kind we have any business wanting."[1]

> When you do something smaller well—play a tune or a part or a hand, and throw a curve or a compliment, make a chair or a sonnet or love— your satisfaction is complete in itself. Those are achievements within life. Why can't life also be an achievement complete in itself, with its own value in the art in living it displays?[2]

No one, I assume, would fault anyone for valuing the "achievements" Dworkin treasures within life. But in the framework of atheistic naturalism, it is hard to see how focusing on such goods would give us any consolation the moment we took our eyes off them and looked at reality more extensively; sadly, the cold comfort of Dworkin's "immortality" is made especially poignant in his dedicating his book to his wife ("to Reni—forever") when

---

[1] Ronald Dworkin, *Religion Without God* (Cambridge: Harvard University Press, 2013), 159.
[2] Ibid., 158.

we learn that Dworkin died before the book could be published (it was published posthumously the same year he died, 2013).

C. S. Lewis, like J. R. R. Tolkien and his other Christian friends, relished small things in life: taking great satisfaction in friendship, literature, married and romantic love, family, food and drink, walking and sharing stories, and more. But this gave Lewis reason to see how believing in ultimate, absolute oblivion cannot be sequestered; the ultimate end of oblivion in a godless cosmos (if true and reasonable to believe) should haunt all our lives when we take into account "the whole story."

> The whole story is going to end in NOTHING. The astronomers hold out no hope that this planet is going to be permanently inhabitable. The physicists hold out no hope that organic life is going to be a permanent possibility in any part of the material universe . . . Nature does not, in the long run, favour life. If Nature is all that exits—in other words, if there is no God and no life of some quite different sort outside Nature—then all stories will end in the same way; in a universe from which all life is banished without possibility of return.[3]

Using Dworkin's terminology, Lewis proposes that positive achievements *within life* are overshadowed if the achievement *of life* is subject to an irreversible and absolute death. On this point, C. S. Lewis and A. J. Balfour completely agree. Neither of them appeals to wish fulfillment, urging us to reject atheistic naturalism because it is simply too depressing! Instead, they argue that the values we have, the existence and continuation of our contingent cosmos, the emergence of conscious beings with the powers to reason with each other, provide us with reasons for thinking that there is *more to reality* than the cosmos as envisioned by atheistic naturalism.

In this chapter, it will not be possible to formulate an exact picture of how much Balfour's *Theism and Humanism* influenced Lewis because Lewis does not make explicit when he is drawing from Balfour's work. Based on his correspondence, there is evidence that Lewis knew of Balfour at least as of 1915, but we have no record of when Lewis first read *Theism and Humanism*. After offering an overview of Balfour, the man and his book, I point out where Balfour's influence may be found, but this will be a matter of speculative detective work except, in my view, in Lewis's book *Miracles* and in other contexts when Lewis develops what may be called "the theistic argument from reason." So, the fact that Lewis and Balfour shared a similar

---

[3] C. S. Lewis, *Present Concerns*, ed. Walter Hooper (San Diego: Harcourt Brace Jovanovich, 1986), 74.

view on how atheistic naturalism leaves us with a devastatingly tragic view of life, may be a matter of two perceptive, critical thinkers independently reaching the same conclusion without the older author influencing the younger.

Theism and Humanism is the only book, among C. S. Lewis's ten books that he rated among the most influential, that was written by a major political leader. Arthur James Balfour, the first Earl of Balfour, was prime minister of Great Britain from 1902 to 1905. He is probably best known for the Balfour Declaration of 1917, a declaration that supported the establishment of a Jewish homeland in Palestine. He was a conservative, well connected with the great leaders of his age (the Duke of Wellington was his godfather), and very active politically in various capacities. He was appointed First Lord of the Admiralty after Winston Churchill, and served as Foreign Secretary under Prime Minister Lloyd George during World War I. He was born in Scotland and was a life-long bachelor, educated at Eaton and the University of Cambridge, a member of the Anglican Communion, (although his remains were buried beside family members at Whittingeham in a Church of Scotland service).

In this chapter, I focus on his book, rather than his personal life and political profile, though it should be noted that it was not unusual in his day for philosophers to be active in public life and not primarily based in a university environment. Like Balfour, the utilitarian John Stuart Mill and the idealist R. B. Haldane were principally active in politics professionally, and, from the standpoint of academia, would be considered "amateurs" when it came to practicing philosophy. Václav Havel today would be in the same category. While the term "amateur" today may seem denigrating, in the early twentieth century being an amateur in certain fields, such as sports, was a sign that one was from the upper class, and this was considered superior to being a professional. (Think of the 1981 film *Chariots of Fire* about the 1924 Olympics when Harold Abrahams is questioned about the propriety of hiring a professional trainer.) Balfour was as well connected philosophically as he was politically: the famous philosopher, Henry Sidgwick was his brother-in-law, for example, and Balfour had the advantage of being able to get Sidgwick's comments on his work, and thereby improve his manuscript through revisions.

In terms of personal matters, however, I cite an amusing, and perhaps revealing remark that Balfour made: "I am more or less happy when being praised, not very comfortable when being abused, but I have moments of uneasiness when being explained."[4] I shall not risk making Balfour uneasy,

---

[4] See E. T. Raymond, *A Life of Arthur James Balfour* (Boston: Little, Brown, 1920).

but will focus instead on explaining his key thesis, rather than the key to his personality.

The book, *Theism and Humanism,* is Balfour's Gifford lectures, delivered at the University of Glasgow in 1914, published in 1915, and now available online. It is probably Balfour's most important philosophical work, the culmination of the promise he showed as a philosopher in his 1879 publication *Defense of Philosophical Doubt,* a book I highly recommend, and his fine book *The Foundations of Belief,* published in 1894.

Theism and Humanism consists of ten lectures. Rather than review these systematically, I will focus on some of the salient positions that may well account for why Lewis identified this as among his top ten books, and highlight the lines of reasoning that I believe to be of enduring and contemporary importance. Indeed, much of the material in this book bears on many arguments of contemporary interest that have captured the attention of Thomas Nagel, Derek Parfit, Alvin Plantinga, and many others.[5] I first highlight Balfour's central argument for theism, a position that very much informs Lewis's work *Miracles,* and, I believe, has considerable merit. I will then turn to engage Balfour's observations on aesthetics, art, and beauty, and conclude with remarks on the importance of Balfour's insights for today's intellectual climate.

Let me begin by clarifying some observations Balfour makes at the outset that may strike some readers as curious. He claims not to base his main line of reasoning on the foundation of a theory of knowledge. Nor is he arguing from common sense. He simply begins, with the fact that many of us share beliefs about reality based on (what we take to be) good reasons.

Why would Balfour take such a position? One reason is that there is considerably more debate about the theory of knowledge (or what counts as knowledge) than about whether we all share many of the same beliefs, and that we hold these without committing any blameworthy, epistemological mistakes. Today, there is considerable disagreement over what counts as having sufficient evidence to justify our beliefs or enable them to count as cases of knowledge—*internalists,* for example, contend that the evidence for a justified belief or claim to know X must be accessible to the believer subjectively calling to mind the evidence, whereas *externalists* stress the reliability of belief-formation without requiring subjective awareness. Balfour's starting point need not involve a commitment to a controversial theory of justification; his stance is similar to a position that

---

[5] See for example, Thomas Nagel, *Mind and Cosmos* (Oxford: Oxford University Press, 2012). This list could be expanded to include Robert Nozick, Stewart Goetz, William Hasker, Richard Tayler, Victor Reppert, and more.

is not uncommon in the field of ethics when a philosopher is confident that no argument for skepticism exists (or can exist) that would provide reasons for thinking that there are no clear cases of wrongdoing (child molestation). Balfour also need not address the charge that the theory of knowledge faces a regress problem. Let's say you have a theory of knowledge that uses methodology M: knowledge consists of those beliefs that satisfy M. But how do you know M is the right method? If you claim to know M is true, because M satisfies M it seems you are begging the question—or at least you would appear to be doing so to a skeptic. So you might propose there is another method M2 that shows that M is reliable. But then you seem to face the same problem of either begging the question if you claim M2 satisfies M2 or you are compelled to come up with M3, and so on, *ad infinitum*.[6] (As an aside, I can't resist noting the Victorian nursery rhyme that was popular in Balfour's day that goes: Big fleas have little fleas upon their backs to bite them, and little fleas have lesser fleas, and so on, *ad infinitum*.)

I think Balfour is on safer ground simply starting with the idea that we, his readers, trust that many of our ordinary beliefs are true and have good reason for doing so.[7] Without making some such assumption, it would be hard for someone to successfully read Balfour's book or trust that her skepticism was itself reasonable. It would not have impacted Balfour's main argument if he had declared that his reasoning is neutral with respect to any theory of knowledge, so long as that theory allows for the normativity of reason. By the "normativity of reason" I mean that "reason" consists of evident entailments, whether this be a matter of deduction (If A, then B. A. Then B.), or discovery through induction (identifying the properties of copper and conductivity), or abduction (given that the most plausible alternative explanations for X are T and N, and T makes X more likely or probable than N, then it is more reasonable to accept (believe, assume) T rather than N).

Next, Balfour asserts that the two most plausible accounts of the cosmos are naturalism and theism. By *naturalism* he has in mind a worldview that is based on modern science (especially physics, chemistry, and biology) and is, for the most part, a form of what might be called *materialism* or *physicalism*. His definition matches well with contemporary usage. For example, here is

---

[6] See Roderick Chisholm, *Theory of Knowledge*, 3rd ed. (Englewood Cliffs: Prentice-Hall, 1989).
[7] See Roderick Chisholm, *The Foundations of Knowing* (Minneapolis: University of Minnesota Press, 1982).

Daniel Dennett's account of the prevailing intellectual climate, which is a form of naturalism:

> There is only one sort of stuff, namely *matter*—and the mind is somehow nothing but a physical phenomenon. In short, the mind is the brain ... we can (in principle!) account for every mental phenomenon using the same physical principles, laws, and raw materials that suffice to explain radioactivity, continental drift, photosynthesis, reproduction, nutrition, and growth.[8]

One can be a card-carrying naturalist and not accept determinism, but Dennett is both a determinist and a naturalist, as are many of Balfour's contemporary naturalists. This form of naturalism—shared by Paul and Patricia Churchland and others—tends to be antiemergent. That is, they begin with a nonteleological or nonpurposive view of the cosmos, and then submit that the *apparent* emergence of new states and things (consciousness, selves, relations, and so on) are reconfigurations or more complex relations of the physical. As Paul Churchland puts it:

> Most scientists and philosophers would cite the presumed fact that humans have their origins in 4.5 billion years of purely chemical and biological evolution as a weighty consideration in favor of expecting mental phenomena to be nothing but a particularly exquisite articulation of the basic properties of matter and energy.[9]

This brings about at least two problems. The first is that we seem well acquainted with consciousness which appears to be a radically new reality, vis-à-vis nonconscious being. Balfour writes:

> The very essence of the physical order of things is that it creates nothing new. Change is never more than redistribution of that which never changes. But sensibility belongs to the world of consciousness, not to the world of matter. It is a new creation, of which physical equations can give no account. Nay, rather, which falsifies such equations; which requires us to say that, before a certain date in the history of the universe, energy in one shape was converted into precisely the same amount of energy in another shape, and into nothing more; that is matter in one position

---

[8] Daniel Dennett, *Consciousness Explained* (Boston: Little, Brown, 1991), 71.
[9] Paul Churchland, *The Engine of Reason, the Seat of the Soul* (Cambridge: MIT Press, 1995), 211.

was transferred to another position without increase or diminution; but that, after this date, the transformations of energy and the movements of matter were sometimes accompanied by psychical "epiphenomena" which differ from them in kind, which are incommensurable with them in amount, and which no equations can represent.[10]

The reference to "epiphenomenal" here is the technical term used by those who acknowledge the apparent emergence of the mental, but see it as not playing any independent causal role in the world of physical processes. Colorful images of the epiphenomenal at the time were suds on top of beer that has just been poured, foam on a wave, and harmless sparks that fly off a machine. Making reason (and mind) epiphenomenal (or eliminating it altogether) is the problem C. S. Lewis advances against naturalism in his book *Miracles*. When we reason, we accept conclusions by virtue of grasping reasons. When asked which is the smallest perfect number (that number equal to the sum of its devisors including one but not including itself) we answer 6 because we reason that $6 = 3 + 2 + 1$ and we see that there is no smaller number that is perfect. But now let us assume that our answer 6 was brought about by mechanical, nonmental causes. Why should we trust them? If we see what appears to be a statement, "Madison is five miles ahead" but we know that this was caused without any purposive, intelligent force—imagine it was caused by a bizarre squirrel or lighting bolt—there would be no reason to trust it. And more importantly, the supposition that only nonmental causes are at work simply removes the very thing that leads us to come up with answers through reason. As Balfour writes:

> We must realize that, on any merely naturalistic hypothesis, the rational elements in the causal series lie always on the surface. Penetrate but a short way down, and they are found no more. You might as easily detect life in the minerals wherein plants are rooted, as reason in the physiological and physical changes to which the source of our most carefully reasoned beliefs must, in the last resort, be traced.[11]

Now, one might object: don't calculating machines do very well with respect to reasoning and yet they involve no thought? Writing in 1914, it should not surprise us that Balfour does not include a lengthy discussion of artificial intelligence. But he would undoubtedly claim that artificial intelligence is artificial; calculating machines do not literally reason or have memory (the

---

[10] Arthur J. Balfour, *Theism and Humanism* (New York: George H. Doran, 1915), 52–3.
[11] Ibid., 60.

mental capacity to recollect the past) but they are so devised as to simulate our mental, interpretive skills so that we may employ such devises in our own reasoning.

I believe that Balfour's reasoning about reasoning is sound and if our choices are teleological theism or eliminative naturalism, the former wins out. But some naturalists, such as John Searle, do insist on emergence, and while I think Searle's philosophy of mind is mistaken it would not, in my view, be subject to self-refutation. I see the state of play as follows: the more contracted naturalism becomes (the more it eliminates the mental, including our reasoning as a process of drawing conclusions in virtue of certain evidential relations), the less plausible it is, but the more expansive it becomes (it adds consciousness; ethical and aesthetic properties are welcomed as emergent, non-epiphenomenal realities), the more tempting it becomes to abandon naturalism and embrace theism.

Second, I also believe naturalism does have problems accounting for the emergence of moral values, as Balfour maintains. We can certainly see this in the later work of Charles Darwin who worried about the contingent nature of evolution. Famously, Darwin predicted that the more fit races would exterminate the weaker ones. If, from the standpoint of evolutionary biology, the elimination of the weak, the mentally ill, and the destitute, would lead to the evolution of a stronger, healthier, more productive and reproductive species, then Darwin's prediction in *The Descent of Man* seems to be not just a prediction of exterminations to come, but something Darwin welcomes:

> With savages, the weak in body or mind are soon eliminated; and those that survive commonly exhibit a vigorous state of health. We civilized men, on the other hand, do our utmost to check the process of elimination; we build asylums for the imbecile, the maimed, and the sick; we institute poor-laws; and our medical men exert their utmost skill to save the life of every one to the last moment. There is reason to believe that vaccination has preserved thousands, who from a weak constitution would formerly have succumbed to small-pox. Thus the weak members of civilized societies propagate their kind. No one who has attended to the breeding of domestic animals will doubt that this must be highly injurious to the race of man. It is surprising how soon a want of care, or care wrongly directed, leads to the degeneration of a domestic race; but excepting in the case of man himself, hardly any one is so ignorant as to allow his worst animals to breed.[12]

---

[12] Charles Darwin, *The Descent of Man, and Selection in Relation to Sex, Vol. I* (New York: D. Appleton, 1871). 161. http://books.google.com/books?id=ZvsHAAAAIAAJ&printsec+frontcover&source=gbs_ge_summary_r&cad=O#v=onepage&q&f=false

One needs some form of moral realism to block such a conclusion and an assimilation of human life to the same codes that govern the breeding of nonhuman animals. I do not think all forms of naturalism must deny moral realism, but once one holds that there are not just nonreductive norms of reason, but also nonreductive norms of value (the value of person, for example, consists of more than a purely scientific account of person), naturalism begins to look as though it lacks the resources to properly ground such values. Theism, in the Platonic tradition that Balfour, Lewis, and I share, does not explain values in terms of nonvalues; we, rather contend that the binding, authoritative values and duties we have stem from and are grounded in the supreme goodness of God's nature. This is not a form of voluntarism, according to which God could have made it an ethical duty of the strong to exterminate the weak. Our duty to be compassionate with the vulnerable and those who are poor is a response to the goodness of persons created by a supremely good Creator who made us and the entire cosmos for the sake of goodness.[13] Although not written from a theistic point of view, Derek Parfit's 2011 magisterial two-volume work, *On What Matters,*[14] lends support for theism insofar as Parfit argues forcefully and effectively that naturalism leads to nihilism. Parfit's argument is very similar to Balfour's and Lewis's argument(s), but he does not acknowledge either of them as foreshadowing his own case against naturalism.

Turning now to the matter of aesthetics, I part slightly from Balfour in that I believe aesthetic concerns can lead to action. Balfour writes:

> Aesthetic interests, once aroused, do not prompt to action; and it is, I conceive, of their essence that they should not. The most emotional spectator does not rush to save Desdemona from Othello; and, though tragedy may (or may not) purify by "pity and terror," the pity does not suggest a rescue, nor the terror urge to flight.[15]

In so far as he is referring to the classic state of disinterested attention before a work of art and not (in this case) of aesthetics in general, we may agree. But I also suggest that aesthetics can draw us into moral action, as is evident when persons appeal to the ugliness of fascism or the beauty of reconciliation and justice.

---

[13] For a fuller development of this position see Charles Taliaferro, *Consciousness and the Mind of God* (Cambridge: Cambridge University Press, 1994).
[14] Derek Parfit, *On What Matters,* ed. Samuel Scheffler, 2 vols. (Oxford: Oxford University Press, 2011).
[15] Balfour, *Theism and Humanism*, 42.

Balfour claims that our experience of objects as beautiful rests on the assumption of intentional production.

> If by some unimaginable process works of beauty could be produced by machinery, as a symmetrical color pattern is produced by a kaleidoscope, we might think them beautiful till we knew their origin, after which we should rather be disposed to describe them as, ingenious. And this is not, I think, because we are unable to estimate works of art as they are *in themselves,* not because a work of art requires an artist, not merely in the order of natural causation, but as a matter of aesthetic necessity. It conveys a message which is valueless to the recipient, unless it be understood by the sender. It must be expressive.[16]

I agree that works of art require an artist (art is artificial, even if it's a found object), and I think the aesthetic experience of the world may be enhanced by theism, granting that theism is (as I believe it to be) true.

In the experience of beauty we may encounter what Balfour calls "a higher wisdom."

> But there is a higher wisdom. Without ignoring what experience has to teach, they may still believe that through these emotions they have obtained an authentic glimpse of a world more resplendent and not less real than that in which they tramp their daily round. And, if so, they will attribute to them a value independent of their immediate cause—a value which cannot be maintained in a merely naturalistic setting.[17]

There is here some foretaste of C. S. Lewis's Platonic Christianity in which the true Logres or Narnia is more resplendent in its transcendent reality than our own world.

Balfour is convinced that naturalism leads to the view that life is vain.

> Observe that history, so conceived, must needs compare faculty with desire, achievement with expectation, fulfilment with design. And no moralist has ever found pleasure in the comparison. The vanity of human wishes and the brevity of human life are immemorial themes of lamentation; nor do they become less lamentable when we extend our view from the individual to the race. Indeed, it is much the other way. Men's wishes are not always vain, nor is every life too brief to satisfy

---

[16] Ibid., 46.
[17] Ibid., 49.

its possessor. Only when we attempt, from the point of view permitted by physics and biology, to sum up the possibilities of collective human endeavour, do we fully realize the "vanity of vanities" proclaimed by the Preacher.

I am not, of course, suggesting that history is uninteresting because men are unhappy: nor yet that naturalism carries pessimism in its train. It may well be that if mankind could draw up a hedonistic balance-sheet, the pleasures of mundane existence would turn out to be greater than its sufferings. But this is not the question. I am not (for the moment) concerned with the miseries of the race, but with its futility. Its miseries might be indefinitely diminished, yet leave its futility unchanged. We might live without care and die without pain; nature, tamed to our desires, might pour every luxury into our lap; and, with no material wish unsatisfied, we might contemplate at our ease the inevitable, if distant, extinction of all the life, feeling, thought, and effort whose reality is admitted by a naturalistic creed.[18]

Balfour's position is not shared by all naturalists, but it is shared by perhaps one of the greatest living philosophers, Thomas Nagel. Unable to accept theism, and resolutely adopting atheism, Nagel concludes that we must either find some kind of Platonic, nontheistic teleological account of the cosmos or conclude that the cosmos itself and our existence in it is absurd.[19] I'll cite Balfour rather than Nagel on this point:

And, from a scientific point of view, this [non-purposive naturalist account of the cosmos] is quite satisfactory. But it is not satisfactory when we are weighing the aesthetic values of universal history. Shakespeare, in the passionate indictment of life which he puts into the mouth of Macbeth, declares it to be "a tale told by an idiot, full of sound and fury," and (mark well the climax) *"signifying nothing."* That is the point with which in this lecture we are chiefly concerned. It most clearly emerges when, in moments of reflection, we enlarge the circuit of our thoughts beyond the needs of action, and, in a mood untouched by personal hopes or fears, endeavour to survey man's destiny as a whole. Till a period within the memory of men now living it was possible to credit terrestrial life with an infinite future, wherein there was room for an infinite approach towards some, as yet, unpictured perfection.

---

[18] Balfour, *Theism and Humanism*, 57–8.
[19] See Thomas Nagel, *Secular Philosophy and the Religious Temperament* (Oxford: Oxford University Press, 2005), chapter 1.

It could always be hoped that human efforts would leave behind them some enduring traces, which, however slowly, might accumulate without end. But hopes like these are possible no more. The wider is the sweep of our contemplative vision the more clearly do we see that the rôle of man, if limited to an earthly stage, is meaningless and futile;—that, however it be played, in the end it "signifies nothing." Will any one assert that universal history can maintain its interest undimmed if steeped in the atmosphere of a creed like this?[20]

Consider, in closing, three objections to various aspects of Balfour's project: 1) an objection about the content of theistic explanations; 2) a reply to the above reasoning concerning time and value; 3) an argument from the success of science.

The first objection comes from Thomas Nagel. While he would side with Balfour (and Alvin Plantinga) about the inadequacy of naturalism in terms of accounting for reason, he contends that theism lacks sufficient content to be a superior theory to naturalism. Nagel writes:

> But even if theism is filled out with the doctrines of a particular religion ... it offers a very partial explanation of our place in the world. It amounts to the hypothesis that the highest-order explanation of how things hang together is of a certain type, namely, intentional or purposive, without having anything more to say about how that intention operates except what is found in the results to be explained.[21]

Reply: Nagel may have a point if the hypothesis is bare theism (the kind of God-hypothesis that Dawkins describes in which essential goodness is missing), but theism in the Platonic traditions of Judaism, Christianity, and Islam (as well as some theistic traditions within Hinduism) sees the goodness of God as central. So theistic explanations are not bare intentional or purposive accounts, but an account of intentional and purposive goodness. It is because of the centrality of goodness, that theism offers such a plausible account of the existence and conservation of a good cosmos. Actually, I believe that C. S. Lewis would point out that the theistic account is continuous with what we know about the explanation of action per se, which is that all agents act under the guise of the good. So saying that God acts for the good makes perfect sense and is continuous with how

---

[20] Balfour, *Theism and Humanism*, 100–1.
[21] Thomas Nagel, *Mind and Cosmos*, 25.

we all act. We all act under the guise of the good. We couldn't act in any other way. And neither can God. This is consistent with Plato's stance on Euthyphro's Dilemma. Nothing is ultimately good because of what anyone says. It is just good. And Lewis embraced Plato's view here. So we all know what is good and act under the guise of that good. God is no different. Lewis, I think, would stress that this is what makes theism so intellectually appealing.

There is, of course, "the problem of evil" (if the cosmos is sustained by an all good God, why is there evil?), but it is worth noting that the problem of evil can also be used in support of theism. Given naturalism, especially in versions in which the world is deterministic and there is no libertarian freedom, evil has to be viewed as an inevitable feature of the cosmos. Each evil deed could not have been otherwise, given antecedent and contemporary conditions and the laws of nature. Platonic theism, on the other hand, can do better justice to the thesis that evil is an aberration, something that violates the goodness and purpose of a sacred creation and its Creator.[22] I suggest also that theism accords very well, not with a Darwinian portrait of nature with red tooth and claw, but with the more symbiotic view of nature found in contemporary ecology.

Second, why should the demise of the cosmos or the thesis that it came about through chance and necessity lead us to think of life as vain or absurd? As George Bernard Shaw once remarked: even if life is a joke, it might be a good joke. Might it not be the case that the brevity of life makes it all the more precious to us, quite regardless of whether the cosmos cares about us or not?

Reply: I am sympathetic to this objection, and believe that sometimes the finality of a life on earth or a relationship can and should make us value it all the more. Returning to Ronald Dworkin's position, noted at the outset of this chapter, there may be times when we need to focus only on the immediate good or achievement. But I also suggest that in our deepest aspirations in loving persons we do desire (if it were possible) their ultimate flourishing and the blessing of an inexhaustible life of love. Some atheist philosophers, like Simone de Beauvoir and Nagel, acknowledge this longing, as does Albert Camus. The impossibility of fulfilling this longing is part of what leads these thinkers to conclude that life is absurd. Insofar as theism better matches our natural, loving desires, such a concord may be seen as yet one more clue that if life is

---

[22] For a fuller account, see Charles Taliaferro, *Philosophy of Religion: A Beginner's Guide* (Oxford: Oneworld, 2009).

not absurd, Platonic theism offers a coherent framework in which to understand the meaning and value of life.

Third, some critics of the argument against naturalism based on the normativity of reason contend that the argument underestimates the power and promise of future scientific discoveries. Even if we cannot now account for the normativity of reason in nonnormative, scientifically viable terms, why think that we cannot do so in the future? Such an appeal to future science has also been employed by philosophers of mind who argue that we should question the existence of consciousness, beliefs, desires, values, and so on.

Reply: If Balfour (and the many who have come after him, such as C. S. Lewis) is right, then the success of science itself needs to be accounted for and insofar as naturalism undermines reasoning, science seems at odds with naturalism. Moreover, there is no scientific reason for doubting that consciousness, beliefs and desires, values, and reasoning exist. Indeed, it is hard to imagine how science could continue unless scientists have beliefs and desires, values, and are conscious reasoning subjects. As Alfred North Whitehead once remarked, a scientist who sets out to show there is no such thing as purposiveness makes a very interesting object of study. An appeal to possible future scientific discoveries should make us humble in terms of ruling out many possibilities, but some possibilities can be ruled out. For example, no matter how powerful a future computer might be, it would be impossible for it to discover (assuming we keep the axioms of mathematics stable) either a smaller perfect number than 6 or to discover the greatest possible number.[23]

Balfour's *Theism and Humanism* was published about 100 years before I wrote this chapter, and yet it still rewards careful attention and deserves credit for advancing a rich, convincing theistic understanding of reason, values, meaning, and this contingent, good cosmos.

So, with this overview of *Theism and Humanism,* how might reading this book enhance our reading of Lewis? It will reward those who engage the first four chapters of Lewis's *Miracles* where Lewis develops a case against naturalism on the grounds that it cannot account for reasoning. This argument may also be found elsewhere (as noted in "Suggestions for further reading" at the end of this chapter). I believe that, given the close resemblance between Lewis's version of the argument and Balfour's, this is probably an instance of real influence. One point of difference between

---

[23] For further development of this reply, see Charles Taliaferro, *The Golden Cord: A Short Book on the Secular and the Sacred* (Notre Dame, IN: University of Notre Dame Press, 2013).

Balfour's argument from reason and Lewis's is that Lewis begins with a more confident assertion that we know that we reason. He does not offer the more modest position that Balfour endorsed. However, Lewis shared Balfour's skepticism about whether naturalism can account for the nature and origin of conscious, subjective experience. Lewis writes:

> All sorts of things are, in fact, doing just what the actor does when he comes through the wings. Photons or waves (or whatever it is) come towards us from the sun through space. They are, in a scientific sense, "light." But as they enter the air they become "light" in a different sense: what ordinary people call *sunlight* or *day*, the bubble of blue or grey or greenish luminosity in which we walk about and see. Day is thus a kind of stage set.
>
> Other waves (this time, of air) reach my eardrum and travel up a nerve and tickle my brain. All this is behind the scenes; as soundless as the whitewashed passages are undramatic. Then somehow (I've never seen it explained) they step on to the stage (no one can tell me *where* this stage is) and become, say, a friend's voice or the *Ninth Symphony*. Or, of course, my neighbor's wireless—the actor may come on stage to play a drivelling part in a bad play. But there is always the transformation.
>
> Biological needs, producing, or stimulated by, temporary physiological states, climb into a young man's brain, pass on to the mysterious stage and appear as "Love."[24]

I share with Lewis, Balfour, and a range of contemporary philosophers a similar judgment that naturalism is unable to offer as satisfactory an account of consciousness as theism. It is possible that here, too, Balfour's work may have influenced or reinforced Lewis's original thinking.

In all, the writings of both Lewis and Balfour address with power and insight the position of non-Christians today who, like the late Ronald Dworkin, wrestle with the implications of secular naturalism.

---

[24] C. S. Lewis, *God in the Dock: Essays in Theology and Ethics*, ed. Walter Hooper (Grand Rapids, MI: Eerdmans, 1970), 247–8. In this passage and elsewhere Lewis brings to light what will become known as the "hard problem" in philosophy of mind: the challenge of accounting for consciousness in terms of physical events. See David Chalmers, *The Conscious Mind: In Search of a Fundamental Theory* (Oxford: Oxford University Press, 1996) and Joseph Levine, *Purple Haze: The Puzzle of Consciousness* (Oxford: Oxford University Press, 2001).

Bibliography

Balfour, Arthur J. *Theism and Humanism.* New York: George H. Doran, 1915.
Chalmers, David. *The Conscious Mind: In Search of a Fundamental Theory.* Oxford: Oxford University Press, 1996.
Chisholm, Roderick. *The Foundations of Knowing.* Minneapolis: University of Minnesota Press, 1982.
—. *Theory of Knowledge.* 3rd ed. Englewood Cliffs, NJ: Prentice-Hall, 1989.
Churchland, Paul. *The Engine of Reason, the Seat of the Soul.* Cambridge: MIT Press, 1995.
Darwin, Charles. *The Descent of Man, and Selection in Relation to Sex,* vol. I. New York: D. Appleton, 1871.
Dennett, Daniel. *Consciousness Explained.* Boston: Little, Brown, 1991.
Dworkin, Ronald. *Religion Without God.* Cambridge: Harvard University Press, 2013.
Levine, Joseph. *Purple Haze: The Puzzle of Consciousness.* Oxford: Oxford University Press, 2001.
Lewis, C. S. "Behind the Scenes." In *God in the Dock: Essays on Theology and Ethics,* edited by Walter Hooper, 245–9. Grand Rapids, MI: Eerdmans, 1994.
—. *God in the Dock: Essays in Theology and Ethics,* edited by Walter Hooper. Grand Rapids, MI: Eerdmans, 1994.
—. "On Living in an Atomic Age." In *Present Concerns,* edited by Walter Hooper, 73–80. San Diego: Harcourt Brace Jovanovich, 1986.
Nagel, Thomas. *Mind and Cosmos.* Oxford: Oxford University Press, 2012.
—. *Secular Philosophy and the Religious Temperament.* Oxford: Oxford University Press, 2005.
Parfit, Derek. *On What Matters,* edited and introduced by Samuel Scheffler. Oxford: Oxford University Press, 2011.
Raymond, E. T. *A Life of Arthur James Balfour.* Boston: Little, Brown, 1920.
Taliaferro, Charles. *Consciousness and the Mind of God.* Cambridge: Cambridge University Press, 1994.
—. *The Golden Cord; A Short Book on the Secular and the Sacred.* Notre Dame, IN: University of Notre Dame Press, 2013.
—. *Philosophy of Religion: A Beginner's Guide.* Oxford: Oneworld, 2009.

Suggestions for further reading

Goetz, Stewart. *A Philosophical Walking Tour with C. S. Lewis.* London and New York: Bloomsbury, 2014.
  This book is likely to be the best book by a professional philosopher who brings readers into a philosophical engagement with Lewis's work. Goetz offers an engaging, clearheaded analysis of Lewis's best thinking as this

bears on the existence of the soul, and theism versus naturalism, and it offers readers a close look at an area of Lewis's life that is often neglected or misunderstood. Since his death in 1963, scholars, biographers, theologians, and general readers have wondered why Lewis was an Anglican since his conversion, and did not become a Roman Catholic (as some of his commentators, such as Thomas Howard, have vigorously suggested he should). Goetz offers a brilliant case for taking Lewis seriously on theism, the soul, and why he practiced his mere Christianity as an Anglican, and not a Roman Catholic.

Lewis, C. S. *God in the Dock: Essays on Theology and Ethics,* edited by Walter Hooper. Grand Rapids, MI: Eerdmans, 1994.
Several essays have themes that may echo the work of Balfour; see especially "Answers to Questions on Christianity" ("[no advance] in intelligence," p. 57), "Religion without Dogma," "Is Theism Important?" "Two Lectures," "Meditation in a Toolshed," "God in the Dock," and "Is Progress Possible?"

—. *Miracles.* First published in 1947, revised in 1960, and available in many editions.
The early chapters present an argument against naturalism and in favor of theism based on the reality and reliability of reason. This is probably the writing that is most shaped by Lewis's study of Balfour.

Index

Note: The authors and titles of the ten books from Lewis's List are in bold, along with the page numbers of the chapters.

Abraham 52, 60, 128
Abrams, Harold 203
Account of Corsica 158
Adam 9, 108
Addison's Walk 34, 36, 59
Aeneas 3, 14, 50–4, 58, 61–3
The Aeneid 3, **49–65**, 94
Aeschylus 59
aesthetics 130, 204, 209
"Affliction (IV)" 83
Agape 56
agnosticism 63, 82
Alanus 148
Alec Forbes of Howglen 24, 27
Alfred the Great, King 137, 150
All My Road Before Me: The Diary of C. S. Lewis 10n. 8, 12n. 16, 94n. 4, 107n. 52, 119n. 31
allegorical 17, 54, 126, 137, 154, 156
allegory 2, 72, 126–7, 135, 145, 148
The Allegory of Love 4, 137–8, 181
Anatomy of Melancholy 162
animals
    and the afterlife 23–4
    breeding of 208–9
    and humans, gap between 38–9
    and suffering 24
Anglican 146, 166, 203, 217
The Antiquary 163
Antony, Marc 53
apologist 2, 60, 62, 184
"The Apologist's Evening Prayer" 89
Apuleius 194
Aquinas, St Thomas 117, 137–8
Areopagus 56
Ariosto 122

Aristotle 59–60, 113, 135, 144–5, 148, 150
Armstrong, Chris vii, 6
artificial intelligence 207
Aslan 23, 44, 56, 60, 125n. 52, 129
atheism 33, 59, 63, 70–2, 73n. 24, 82, 211
atheistic naturalism 6, 201–3
Augustine, St 13, 135, 138, 148
Austen, Jane 142, 174
autobiography 3, 14, 33–4, 41, 54, 70, 95, 101, 106, 119, 162, 166–7
Autumn, the Idea of 98
Awe/awe 82, 100, 119, 123n. 49, 129–31

Bacchus 59–60
Bailey, John 158, 166n. 31
Baker, Leo 165
Balfour, Arthur J. 5–6, **201–17**
Balfour Declaration (of 1917) 203
Baretti, Guiseppi 172
Barfield, Owen 43, 55, 72, 74n. 25, 97, 111, 127, 144
Barkman, Adam viii, xiv, 4
Bate, Walter Jackson 174
BBC (broadcast talks/radio addresses) 37, 55, 138
Beatrice see *The Figure of Beatrice*
Beauty/beauty 16, 55, 57, 77–9, 105, 116–19, 123, 130–1, 150, 204, 209–10
Bennett, Jack 165
Beowulf 50, 60, 141
Bevan, Edwyn 32
"the Blue Flower" 119

Bodle, Rhona 37, 79–82, 195n. 53
Boethius 4, 6, 60, 62n. 7, 64, 117, **135–56**
Boiardo 122
Borhek, Mary 82
Boswell, James 4, **157–80**
Bradshaw-Knight Foundation xiv, 2
Brewer, Derek 165
Broadcast Talks see BBC (broadcast talks/radio addresses)
"The Bunch of Grapes" 78
Bunyan, John 6, 69, 106, 137
burden 49, 99, 182, 189–90, 192–7
Burke, Edmund 109, 130n. 81, 157

C. S. Lewis: Life, Works, and Legacy 2
C. S. Lewis Society of Madison, Wisconsin xiv, 2
Caesar Augustus 4, 51, 53–5, 57, 62
calling xi, xiii, 2, 6–7, 102, 104, 169
Calvin, John 124–5
Calvinist 81
Cambridge, University of 54, 68, 139, 203
Camus, Albert 213
cardinal virtues see virtues (theological, cardinal, Christian)
caritas (charity) 57
Carnell, Corbin Scott 123
Carolingians 137
Carpenter, Humphrey 32
Carritt, E. F. 144
Catholic(ism) 55, 58, 141, 217
catholicity 38
Celtic religion 141
Chair of Medieval and Renaissance Literature 64, 139
Chariots of Fire 203
Chaucer 49, 136–7
Chesterfield, Lord 172
Chesterton, G. K. 3, 5, **31–48**, 127, 142, 181, 199

choice(s) xi-xii, 5, 20, 41, 58, 60, 125, 183, 185–8, 208
Christ 7, 21, 23–4, 33, 35–9, 41, 44–5, 51–2, 54, 56–62, 65, 72–3, 77–81, 89, 103, 113, 125, 143, 151, 184–5, 189–93, 197–8
The Christian Century xi, 1–2, 7, 31, 50, 136, 138
Christian Gospel/gospel 52, 56, 59, 62, 140, 143
Christianity, Platonic 110
"Christianity and Culture" 119
Christopher, Joe 123
The Chronicles of Narnia 44, 50, 72, 141, 156
Churchill, Winston 203
Churchland, Paul and Patricia 206
Cicero 59–60
Cleopatra 53
The Cloud of Unknowing 136
Coghill, Nevill 165, 167, 196
coinherence 193, 195
Coleridge, Samuel Taylor 7, 94, 103, 105, 108, 118, 122, 148
"The Collar" 75–7
"the common reader" 5, 169
Como, James 114, 132
"Companions of the Co-inherence" 194
The Confessions 13
Confucius 148
conscience 70–1, 77, 80, 112
consciousness 95, 97–8, 105, 189, 206, 214–15
The Consolation of Philosophy 4, 60, 62n. 7, 64, 117, **135–56**
conversation 25, 34–5, 50, 71, 158–66, 173, 176, 196
conversion 103, 125, 142, 184
  Lewis's 12, 18, 33–4, 36, 43, 59, 62, 72–3, 75, 80n. 43, 94–5, 97–8, 102–3, 110–13, 123n. 49, 143, 145–6, 148, 217
  Lewis's philosophical 113, 145

copies (of Platonic Forms) 117, 123
Corn God/King 59–60
cosmic story 141
cosmos 156, 183, 201–2, 205–6, 209, 211–14
Cupid 194

damnation 5, 184–5, 186–9
Dante 49, 58, 136, 138, 141, 144, 146, 150, 160, 182
Dark Ages 139
Dark Ages, new 140
Darwin, Charles 208, 213
Davidman, Joy vii, 5, 54
  death of 82–8, 196–7
Davies, Tom 159
de Beauvoir, Simone 213
De Fide 146
death
  of Christ 59, 77, 125n. 52
  of city or culture 53
  of Joy Davidman 54, 82–8
  irreversible and absolute 202
  leading to happiness 120–1
  physical 6, 11, 21, 49, 51, 56, 84, 185–6, 188, 193–4
  in poetry 84, 116n. 12
  in prose 128n. 71, 188
  and resurrection 51, 56, 59, 73, 197
  second (of ancient learning) 139
Defense of Philosophical Doubt 204
deity of Christ 37, 41–2
demon 42, 129, 176
Dennett, Daniel 206
Descent into Hell 5–6, **181–99**
The Descent of Man 208
The Descent of the Dove 182, 195
Desdemona 209
desire
  argument from 143, 148
  eudaemonism 151, 154
  as "false Florimels" 102
  for God 14–15, 44, 55, 79, 97, 98, 100, 102, 105, 116–17, 121–3, 128, 131–2, 134, 146, 148, 150–1
  ordinary human 15, 76n. 31, 77, 210–11, 214
  as Platonic *eros* 116–17, 119–37, 123, 128, 131, 146
  in poetry 78, 87, 97
  in prose 106
  as "spot in time" 96
  for true home 117
  without hope 106
determined (actions not) 135–6
determinist/determinism 206, 213
Devil 41
Diary of an Old Soul 24
Dickens, Charles 174
A Dictionary of the English Language 160, 172
didactic writing 161, 169, 171, 174, 189
didacticism 176
The Discarded Image 50, 60, 136–7, 152
Dish of Orts 17
Divine, the 6, 21, 25, 39, 106, 109, 124, 127–8, 131
Divine Comedy 49–50
divine popularizer 4, 138
Divinity/divinity 14, 21, 37, 79, 89, 103, 108
Donne, John 67–8
doppelgänger 182, 184, 190, 192
Downing, David C. 114
Duriez, Colin 123
duties
  to an audience 167
  pastoral 68
duty 49, 53, 55, 62, 134, 168, 194, 209
Dworkin, Ronald 6, 201–2, 213, 215
Dymer 4, 72, 116
Dyson, Hugo 34–6, 45, 59

Eaton 203
eclogues 57

Eddison, E. R. 122
Edwards, Bruce L. xiv, 2
Elia 162
Elijah 52
Elizabeth I, Queen 137
emotion(s) 69, 108, 129, 130n. 81, 210
enchantment 16, 147, 149
English Literature in the Sixteenth Century 67
epic 49–50, 53–5, 60, 65, 95
Epicureans 56
epiphenomenal 207–8
eros 56, 146 *cf.* Platonic *eros*
eschatology 50–1, 58
eucatastrophe 55–6
eudaemonism 146–7, 149–51, 154
Euthryphro's Dilemma 213
Eve 108
The Everlasting Man 3, **31–48**, 55, 64, 199
evil 11, 16–17, 20, 23, 25, 39, 54, 117n. 11, 147, 151–2, 155, 175, 185, 213
evolution 33, 35, 38–9, 147, 206, 208
evolutionism 52
exchange *see* substitution and exchange
"Ex Libris" 1
An Experiment in Criticism 129
externalists 204

Faerie Queene 50, 115n. 7
fairy/fairie/faery (Lewis's spelling) 14n. 24, 16–17, 22, 34–5, 122, 130
faith 51–2, 193
  Christian 9, 11, 17, 36–7, 45, 55, 60, 69–72, 77, 80–1, 107–8, 114n. 4, 143, 151
  Lewis's 59, 69–70, 89, 145
  struggles with 55, 71–2, 82, 145, 147
faith/hope/love *see* virtues (theological, cardinal, Christian)

"false Florimels" 102
fantasy xii, 3, 9, 16–18, 20, 54, 60, 63, 96, 118, 183
Farrer, Nicholas 68
fatalist 135
Father (God) 23, 71, 76, 79, 81, 103
The Figure of Beatrice 182
"fine nets and stratagems" 3, 70
felix culpa 3, 51, 55–6, 108
first and second things 7, 104–5
The Forgiveness of Sins 182
Forms 117
  see also copies (of Platonic Forms)
fortune 4, 6, 135, 143, 151–2, 154
The Foundations of Belief 204
The Four Loves 105, 194
Francis, St 6, 69
Frazer, Sir James 59
freedom 55, 68, 75, 171, 175
freedom, libertarian 213
friendship 159, 165, 182, 202
Fussell, Paul 162

Gentleman's Magazine 160
Gifford Lectures 204
God 4, 6–7, 9, 13, 20–3, 36, 55, 59–63, 68–89, 102–5, 109, 117, 124–6, 128, 130, 135–6, 140, 142, 147–51, 184–5, 188–91, 197, 209, 212–13
  Dying 124
  Son of God (incarnate) 15, 38, 41, 57, 59, 121n. 36
  Triune 56–7
God-hypothesis 212
"God in the dock" 84
God-Man 14
Gods/gods/god 33, 35, 52–3, 58–60, 62, 95, 115n. 9, 116, 121–2, 130, 140
Goethe, Johann Wolfgang von 17, 118
The Golden Age 57
The Golden Bough 59

Goodness/goodness 3–4, 11, 16, 23, 25, 33–4, 55, 84–5, 116–17, 191, 209, 212–13
grace 56–7, 72, 74, 82, 89, 103, 125, 132, 186
  apostle of (Paul) 61
  irresistible 81
  in poetry 70, 83, 87
The Great Divorce 20, 22, 31, 50, 56, 59
"The Great Knock" *see* Kirkpatrick, William T.
"Great War" (between Lewis and Barfield) 127
Greek(s)
  gods 59, 122
  language 50, 55, 59, 172
  nationality 52, 56, 58, 61, 138
  poet(s) 41, 56–7
Green, Roger Lancelyn 10
Greene, Donald 160n. 9, 180
Greeves, Arthur 5n. 7, 10, 12, 15, 17, 27, 35, 36n. 30, 43, 55, 69, 80n. 42, 93, 118n. 20, 121n. 39, 161–2n. 12, 163n. 17, 164n. 21, 168n. 35, 170
grief 54, 73, 82–3
  in poetry 85
"Grief" 85
A Grief Observed 4, 54, 67, 82–8, 131
Griffiths, (Dom) Bede 111, 141, 165
Gulliver's Travels 175

Haldane, R. B. 203
Hamilton, Clive 72
happiness 4, 49, 116–17, 119–21, 135, 143, 146, 164
Happiness (true, perfect, otherworldly, infinite) 117, 121, 131, 147–51, 154
  pursuit of *see* eudaemonism
Havel, Václav 203
He Came Down From Heaven 182, 189, 192–3, 195
"He to Whom I Bow" 73–4

Hearn, Michael Patrick 17
Heath-Stubbs, John 167
Heaven/heaven 24, 73, 85, 109, 129, 132n. 89, 142
  child from 57
  hound of 62
  king of 88
  poetry 58, 75, 77
  as state of mind 104
heavens 14, 25, 131
"The Hegemony of Moral Values" 103
Hein, Roland 15–16, 26
Heinrich von Ofterdingen 119
Hell/hell 21–2, 24, 41, 73, 150
  as state of mind 104
Herbert, George 3–4, 6, 67–92
Herodotus 162
Hewlett, Maurice 122
hierarchy 4, 55
Hill, G. B. 172
Hilton, Walter 136
Hinduism 212
History of English Literature 162
"The Holdfast" 80
Holiness/holiness 3, 5–6, 9, 11–12, 15–16, 33, 69, 168
the Holy 89, 114, 124, 127, 131n. 87, 146
Holywell Cemetery, Oxford 182
Home/home 3, 43–5, 49, 63–4, 73n. 24, 81, 97–8, 109, 116–17, 119n. 31, 120–1, 131, 146
Homer 49, 59, 122
Hooker, Richard 137
Hooper, Walter 10
hope 49, 57, 64, 151, 202, 211
  Lewis's 49, 64, 85, 132, 136, 163
  in poetry 70, 97, 116n. 12, 122
  as a virtue
Horace 175
The House of the Octopus 195
Hume, David 63
Humility 3, 9, 15, 68, 73n. 24, 88, 126n. 59

The Idea of the Holy 4, 13n. 19, 113–34
Idealism 2, 102, 141
The Idler 160
idolatry 108
Iliad 49–50
images *see* Forms
Imagination/imagination 11, 14–15, 17, 94, 96–8, 101, 105, 107–9, 126–7, 142, 158, 164, 167
imago Dei 35
immortality 20, 116
Incarnation/incarnation 51, 73, 80, 141
Inferno 49, 58
inkling
  having an, Plato 145
The Inklings 82n. 48, 165–7, 179, 182, 198
The Inklings: C. S. Lewis, J. R. R. Tolkien, Charles Williams, and their Friends 32n. 13
"The Inner Ring" 169
internalists 204
Into the Region of Awe: Mysticism in C. S. Lewis 114
"Is Theology Poetry?" 16n. 31, 141n. 23
Islam 212
Israel(ites) 56, 59, 78

James, William 118
Jesus 21, 24, 39, 41–2, 59, 63, 68, 72, 88–9, 117, 124, 190–1
Jew(s) 42, 56–7, 59, 141
Jewish
  heritage 61
  homeland 203
  Messiah 56
  Scriptures 60
Job's answer from God 136, 149, 152
Joekel, Samuel 138
John the Baptist 52
Johnson, Mrs (Samuel) 171

Johnson, Samuel 4, 69, **158–80**
Journal of a Tour to the Hebrides 160, 179
Journey to the Western Islands 160, 179
Joy/joy 4, 14, 17, 41, 54–5, 61, 63, 73, 77n. 31, 78, 95–6, 98–102, 104–6, 108, 110, 112, 115n. 8–9, 116n. 11, 119–24, 130–2, 148–51, 185–6, 188, 193
Joy (Lewis's wife) *see* Davidman, Joy
"Joy" (poem by Lewis) 114, 119
Judaism 226
Julian of Norwich 49, 136
justice 55, 57, 59, 174, 209
  Divine 125
  see also virtues (theological, cardinal, Christian)
Juvenal 174–5

Kant, Immanuel 128, 130, 151
Keats, John 171
à Kempis, Thomas 37
Kidd, Noelene 82
Kilby, Clyde S. 34n. 21
kindred spirit 10, 32, 43, 113
King, Don viii, 4, 6
Kingdom of God 62
The Kingdom of God and the Son of Man 126
Kirkpatrick, William T. 63, 118, 140, 144

Ladborough, Richard 165
Lady Philosophy 143–7, 149–52
Lang, Andrew 162
Längtans Blåa Blomma 119
The Last Battle 24, 122n. 45
Latin 57, 138, 172
Law 61, 78
law 15, 35, 70, 190, 196, 206
  moral 148
  natural 123n. 49, 141, 145, 148, 213
  new 192

"Learning in War Time" 142
Letters to Malcolm Chiefly on Prayer 22, 23n. 57, 71n. 20, 92, 129n. 74
Lewis, Joy *see* Davidman, Joy
Lewis, Warren (Warnie) 36, 164n. 20 & 22, 170n. 40
Leyerle, John 173
Lichfield 159–60, 165, 171
"Life of Rowe" 172
The Life of Samuel Johnson 4, **155–80**
The Light Princess and Other Fairy Tales 14n. 24
The Lion, the Witch, and the Wardrobe 56, 125n. 52, 129
the (Literary) Club 160
Literary Magazine 160
The Lives of the Most Eminent English Poets 160
Lloyd George, David 203
London 158, 160, 165, 182
London 174
longing *see* spiritual longing
"Longing" 84
Lord 42, 70, 76–7, 81, 83–4, 86, 89, 128, 151
Lord/liar/lunatic 41 cf. trilemma
The Lord of the Rings 55, 60
Love, God's 72, 75, 77, 124
love 9, 15, 73, 102–3, 115n. 8, 116
 and fear 77, 131
 of Gomorrah 185
 mother 56
 of nature 7, 105
 in poetry 77, 81, 87
 of strangeness 11, 17
 substituted 5, 181–99
"Love (III)" 81
Love is Enough 12
loves, Lewis's
 Aeneid 65
 Johnson, Samuel 168, 176
 Medieval Cosmological Model 55

of old Narnia 44, 122n. 45
 Orthodoxy 43
 wife, Joy 82
Luther, Martin 1, 113, 124–5

Macaulay, Thomas 157
McClinch, Christopher 108
MacDonald, George 3, 6, **9–30**, 31, 34, 45, 55–6, 69, 118, 125n. 52, 150, 181, 189
MacDonald, Greville 29
MacKinnon, Donald 167
Magdalen College, Oxford 59, 73n. 24
The Magician's Nephew 23, 63
Magnanimity 148
Mahomet (Mohammed) 42
Malory, Sir Thomas 122, 163
Manlove, Colin 30
Markos, Louis ix, 3
Martlets (Oxford literary society) 163
martyr(ed) 139, 182, 184, 190, 193
Martyr, Justin 145n. 36
materialism 12, 40, 142, 206
melancholy 149, 164
membership 20, 22
"Membership" 2
memory 13, 96, 101, 105, 146, 207, 211
 Boswell's 164
 Johnson's 158, 171–2
 Lewis's 20, 72, 98–9, 135, 144n. 30, 155, 163, 171, 173n. 53
Mere Christianity 22–4, 37, 39, 41, 45, 59, 63, 79, 131, 141
Mere Humanity 38n. 42
metaphor(s) 3, 43, 62, 74–5, 84, 86, 95, 107
Middle Ages 51, 64–5, 137–8
Mill, John Stuart 203
Milton, John 49, 60, 108
Miracles 5, 19, 40, 63, 73n. 23, 139, 202, 204, 207, 214
Modernism 126

Moloch 76
monergism 149
moral
  literature, writing 169, 171
  philosopher 135, 155
  realism 209
  values 5, 208–9
moralist 4, 135, 169, 210
Morris, William 12, 32, 122, 181
Moses 42, 78, 107
Mozart, Wolfgang Amadeus 118
Muhammad see Mahomet (Mohammed)
"My Heart is Empty" 76–7
mysterium tremendum 128–31
mysticism 107–8
myth(s)
  as allegory 35–6, 126–7
  inciting the *numinous* 130
  Osiris and Balder 59
  pagan 145
  in Plato 116
mythmaker 2
mythology 10, 16, 45, 59, 62, 71, 141
mythopoeic 17

Nagel, Thomas 204, 211–13
Narnia 60, 122n. 45, 152, 183, 210
Narrative Poems 111
natural law 123n. 49, 141, 145, 148
naturalism 6, 201–3, 205–15, 217
Nature/nature 7, 57, 78, 86, 94, 100–9, 118, 122, 127, 148, 202, 211, 213
Neoplatonism 117, 154
Neuhouser, David L. ix, 3, 6
Neylan, Mary 6, 36, 69, 152
N.I.C.E. 40, 155, 184, 187
Nichols, John 172
Nihilism 209
"No Exit" 22
nonrational 113, 124, 130n. 81
nostalgia 76, 119
Novalis 118, 119

Numen/numen 124, 127, 131n. 87
Numinous/numinous 4, 61, 99, 100, 114, 123, 126–32

occult 107, 199
Odyssey 49–50
"The Old Lady and Curdie" 24n. 72, 150
Oldbuck, Jonathan 163
"the Omnipotence" 182, 191–3
omniscience, God's 135
"On Fairie Stories" 34, 47
"On Forgiveness" 20, 21n. 47
On What Matters 209
Ordway, Holly ix, 5–6
orthodox(y) 34, 108, 113, 135, 140, 168
Orthodoxy 43
"Othello" 209
Otto, Rudolf 4, 32, 111, **113–34**
Out of the Silent Planet 183–4
outline of history 34, 36
The Outline of History 3, 38
Ovid 137
Oxford don 114, 118, 123, 125n. 52, 138, 144
Oxford, University of 54, 59, 141–2, 144, 163, 166–7, 182
Oxford University Press 181–2

pagan(s) 52, 56–60, 75, 140–1, 144–5, 152
  myth that became fact 59–60, 63, 65
  myths 60, 141, 145
  philosophers 135, 144
  planetary mythology 141
  poet/poetry 57–8, 60, 75
  wisdom of 140
paganism 55, 63, 140–1, 147
Pandarus 137
pantheism 2, 102–3, 110, 141
Paradise Lost 50, 65, 94, 108
Parfit, Derek 204, 209

pathos 49, 67, 82–5
Paul, St 52–3, 56, 58, 61–2, 125
Payne, Leanne 191–2, 197
Pearce, Joseph 108
Pembroke College, Oxford 160
Perelandra 56, 183–4
personalities, dramatic 167
Personalities in God 7
Peter, St 58, 61
Phaedrus 115–16
Phantastes 3, **9–30**, 55, 107, 199
philosopher-poet 136, 138
philosophical conversion 114, 145
Philosophical Idealism 2, 102
philosophy
  Boethius's 136
  and faith 147
  of life 1–2, 5, 32, 67, 94, 136, 143–7
  materialist 186
  of mind (Searle's) 208
  religious 146
  of stories (Chesterton) 35, 45
  and theology 111
  Wordsworth's 103–4
physicalism 205
pietas 57
pilgrimage 43, 72, 80
  Lewis's 94
  in poetry 74
The Pilgrim's Progress 106
The Pilgrim's Regress 2, 4, 44, 47, 54, 59, 64, 72–6, 95, 98–9, 102–12, 122–3n. 46, 127n. 61, 143, 146n. 37, 147
The Place of the Lion 32, 181, 183
Plantinga, Alvin 204, 212
Plato 2, 59–60, 113, 115–17, 119, 135, 144–6, 148, 150, 213
Platonic Christianity, Lewis's 210
Platonic *eros* 4, 114–24, 128, 130–4, 149–50
"The Platonic Image of George MacDonald in C. S. Lewis" 29
Platonic tradition(s) 209, 212

Plotinus 117, 151n. 8
plundering the Egyptians 141
The Poems of George Herbert 90
Poetic Diction 140
popularizer 4, 135, 138
Porter, Mrs Lucy 171
post-Christian 140
praeparatio evangelica 16, 103
Praeparatio evangelii 146
prayer(s) 23, 73, 105, 136
  Boethius and 136, 140
  intercessory 195
  Lewis's prayer life 196, 198
  in poetry 74, 77, 89
  substitutionary, in *Descent into Hell* 190–1, 193
predestination 135
"pre-evangelistic" realization 143
The Prelude 4, 64, **93–112**
Prince Caspian 60
The Princess and the Goblin 24, 32
"Private Papers" 158
The Problem of Pain 6, 24–5, 63, 79, 82, 112, 123n. 49, 128–9, 150
Prodigal Son 42, 73n. 24
prophecy 53, 57
Providence 33
Psyche 24, 56, 112, 121, 128n. 71, 194–5
"The Psychology of the Self in MacDonald's *Phantastes*" 30
public intellectual 2, 4–5, 135, 138, 143, 154, 169, 201
punishment 152
  "homeopathic" 150
Purgatory 58, 65

The Quest of Bleheris 116, 130

Radcliffe, Mrs (Ann) 122
radio addresses *see* BBC (broadcast talks/radio addresses)
The Rambler 160, 170, 176
Ransom Space Trilogy 72, 183–4

Raphael 57
Rasselas 160
rationality 113, 124
reading
  "recovery of serious" 7
  and rereading 63, 162–3
Real World/real world 14, 117
Reason/reason 207
  argument from 5–6, 40, 202, 215
  versus emotion 108
  epiphenomenal 207
  and Imagination 94, 97, 107–9
  inadequacy of naturalism's account of 212
  Lewis's training by Kirkpatrick 63
  limits of 5, 126, 212
  normativity of 205, 209, 214
  in poetry 70
  scientific 38
  theistic understanding of 214
  unity of romance and 113
rebirth 56, 77, 141
reconciliation 209
Reflections from Plato's Cave: Essays in Evangelical Philosophy 39n. 46
Reilly, R. J. 191
Religion Without God 201
Religious Essays 113
Renaissance 49, 56, 64, 137, 139
Reppert, Victor 41n. 53, 204n. 5
The Restitution of Man: C. S. Lewis and the Case Against Scientism 38n. 42
Resurrection
  of Aslan 56
  of Christ 51, 59, 73, 197
Reynolds, Sir Joshua 160, 166
Riga, Frank 10
Ritter, Mary ix, xiv, 4, 7
Robert Falconer 13–14
Roman Catholic(ism) *see* Catholic(ism)
romance 113, 185
romantic movement 164

Romanticism/romanticism 4, 11–12, 103–4, 114, 121–4, 130–2
Romantics 94, 96, 103, 107, 109, 111, 118–19, 134
A Rough Shaking 13n. 19

sacrifice 3, 7, 104, 131
  actual (of Christ) 52
  Aslan's 125n. 52
  idea of 35
  near of Isaac 52, 59
  necessary
The Saga of King Olaf 98
salvation 5, 104, 108, 183–4, 188–9, 198
Samson Agonistes 60
Sartre, (Jean Paul) 22
Satan 103
satire 5, 174–6
Satires 175
satirist 174–5
"satirist *manqué*" 174
Sayer, George 46
Sayers, Dorothy L. xii, 32
Schakel, Peter J. 175, 194
Schiller 118
Schubert 118
Scotland 159–60, 179, 203
Scott, Sir Walter 142, 163
The Screwtape Letters 5, 63, 79, 175
Searle, John 208
Sehnsucht 4, 13, 18, 100, 114, 117–20, 122–4, 129–32, 147–8
Selig, Richard 173
Sentiment/sentiment 33, 115n. 8, 148
Shakespeare 2, 160, 163, 174, 211
Shaw, George Bernard 213
Shelley, (Percy Bysshe) 122
Sidgwick, Henry 203
The Silver Chair 143
"Sinne(I)" 3n. 5, 70
"A Sketch of Individual Development" 15n. 29
Socratic Club 82n. 48, 141

Son, Prodigal *see* Prodigal Son
Son of God 15, 36, 38, 41, 59, 121n. 36
Son of Man 114n. 4
sonnet 4, 68n. 4, 70, 73–4, 80, 163, 201
Sonnets, Shakespeare's 163
Sophocles 2, 59, 122
soul 13n. 21, 14, 21, 68, 71–2, 75n. 28, 89, 116, 131, 143, 217
   compared with spirit 142
   created by God 142
   disbelief in 41
   each "a curious shape" 6
   ecstasy of 128–9
   education of 106
   "having an inkling" 145
   illusion of being 186
   inexpressible 127
   led to, or seeking Home 122, 146
   and personal responsibility 187
   and Platonic *eros* 115–17, 119, 131
   in poetry 74, 81, 83–4, 97, 101
   preexistent state 119
   thirst of 115, 117
   vastness and smallness 69
Space Trilogy *see* Ransom Space Trilogy
Spenser, Edmund 49, 92, 115n. 7–8, 122
Spirits in Bondage 4, 72–3, 75, 91
spiritual longing 4, 13, 71, 77, 100, 114–15, 117–19, 121–4, 131–4
"spots of time" 95, 98, 100–1, 106
Sprightly Running xiv, 167–8
Squirrel Nutkin 98
Stephens, James 122
Stoicism 126n. 57, 136
Stoics 56, 151
sublime 100, 119, 128, 130, 133–4, 157
substituted love 5, 182, 189, 192–5, 198–9

substitution and exchange 189, 191–3, 195, 197–9
sui generis 127
supernatural 4–5, 55, 100, 119, 132, 182–4
supra-rational 124–5, 127
Surprised by Joy 3–4, 11–12, 14, 26, 34n. 22–3, 54, 62, 70–1, 73n. 24, 95–6, 98, 101–2, 104, 106, 115n. 10, 119, 121, 122n. 43, 143–4, 146, 162n. 15
"Surprised by Joy" 41, 101, 119
Suton, Max Keith 30
Swift, Jonathan 2, 175
symbol(s) 51–3, 126, 139
The Symposium 116, 134
syncretist 141

Taliaferro, Charles ix, 5–6
"Taliessin through Logres" 182
Tankard, Paul ix, 4
Tao 61
Tasso, (Torquato) 122
Taylor, (Jeremy) 137
teacher 2, 39, 41–2, 82, 107, 141
telos 50–2, 149
The Temple 4, **67–92**
Tennyson, Alfred Lord 121
That Hideous Strength 5, 40, 60, 63, 155, 183–4, 186–9, 198–9
Theism/theism 2, 5, 33, 36, 59, 73n. 24, 102, 123n. 49, 204–5, 208–15, 217
Theism and Humanism 5, **201–17**
Theocritus 57
Theodoric 139, 149
theologian(s) 1, 51, 70, 113, 124, 125n. 52, 167, 217
theological virtues *see* virtues (theological, cardinal, Christian)
theory of knowledge 204–5
There and Back 24

Till We Have Faces 5, 24, 56, 60, 112, 121, 126n. 57, 128n. 71, 131, 141, 155, 189, 194–5, 198
Tixier, Elaine 30
Tolkien, J. R. R. 30, 34–7, 45, 48, 55–6, 59–60, 121, 127, 155, 202
The Tolkien and Fantasy Society at the University of Wisconsin-Madison 3
Traherne, Thomas 68–9, 96, 102, 137, 148
transcendence 103, 184
transposition 127
"Transposition" (sermon) 5
trilemma 5, 39, 41, 42n. 61, 45
Trinity 104
Trinity College, Cambridge 68
Trinity Term (1929) Lewis's conversion to Theism 73n. 24
Tristram Shandy 162–3
Troilus and Cressida 137
Troy 3, 50–4, 56, 61
truth(s) 7, 73, 97–8, 113–14, 125, 145, 166
 awe, fear, strangeness 130, 142
 and beauty 57, 116–17, 131
 Paganism and Idealism 141
 in poetry 81, 98, 101
 ultimate, Christian 4, 14, 35–6, 47, 55, 57, 59, 61, 63, 79, 94, 116, 143, 147
typology 50, 53

unbelief 33, 71
Unitarianism 69
Unspoken Sermons 12, 20, 21n. 51, 125n. 52

van Beethoven, Ludwig 118
Van Deusen, Mary 37, 70, 119n. 29, 196n. 54
Vanauken, Sheldon 6n. 9, 37, 196
The Vanity of Human Wishes 174
Varieties of Religious Experience 118, 134

Vaughan, Henry 68
The Victorian Fairy Tale Book 17n. 35
Virgil 3–4, **49–65**, 137
virtue ethics 141
virtues, Roman 55
virtues (theological, cardinal, Christian) 57, 61, 150
virtus 57
vocation(s) 4, 6, 50, 88, 110, 136–9
vocational attitude 1, 2, 32, 67, 94, 136
voluntarism, (divine) 209
The Voyage of the "Dawn Treader" 1, 19, 151

Wain, John 166–8, 179
Walls, Jerry L. 39n. 46
Walton, Isaak 68
Ward, Michael 82, 141, 145, 151, 155, 191n. 35, 197
Warnie *see* Lewis, Warren (Warnie)
The Weight of Glory 4, 5n. 8, 6n. 12, 16n. 34, 20–22n. 52, 105n. 46, 119n. 30, 141n. 23, 147, 150–2n. 51
"The Weight of Glory" 4, 20–1, 147, 150
Wells, H. G. 38
Western Front 161, 164
Wheel of Fortune/wheel of fortune 152, 154
Whipsnade Zoo 36
Whitehead, Alfred North 214
Wholly Other/wholly other 25, 98, 102, 129
Wilfred Cumbermede 25
Williams, Charles 5, 10, 32, 155, 167, **181–99**
Williams, Donald T. x, 3, 48
Wilson, A. N. 175
The Wind in the Willows 129n. 77
wisdom 7, 58, 80, 95, 116, 135, 138, 140, 142, 144, 147, 161, 176, 210

Wisdom (in *Pilgrim's Regress*) 103, 105, 106, 109
The Wise Woman 22
Wolff, Robert Lee 30
Wordsworth, William 4, **92–112**, 118–20
World War I 3, 33, 54, 203
World War II 55, 142, 164, 166n. 31

worldview 3, 5–6, 205
worship(s) 25, 56, 74, 76, 140
Wu, Duncan 100n. 23

Yahweh 76
Yale University 172
"You Rest Upon Me All My Days" 75–6

www.ingramcontent.com/pod-product-compliance
Ingram Content Group UK Ltd.
Pitfield, Milton Keynes, MK11 3LW, UK
UKHW021900220326
469204UK00008B/98